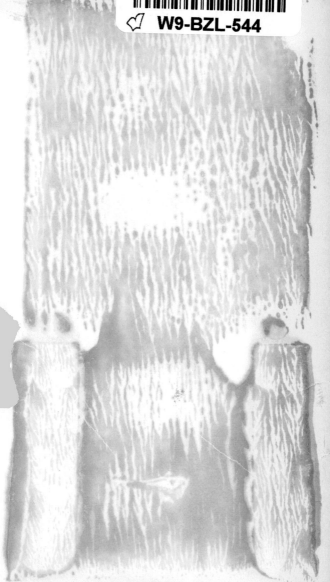

ANTHROPOLOGY
A Human Science

SELECTED PAPERS, 1939-1960

by

MARGARET MEAD

The American Museum of Natural History
New York

AN INSIGHT BOOK

D. VAN NOSTRAND COMPANY, INC.

PRINCETON, NEW JERSEY

TORONTO · LONDON

NEW YORK

D. VAN NOSTRAND COMPANY, INC.
120 Alexander St., Princeton, New Jersey
(*Principal Office*)
24 West 40 Street, New York 18, New York

D. VAN NOSTRAND COMPANY, LTD.
358, Kensington High Street, London, W.14, England

D. VAN NOSTRAND COMPANY (Canada), LTD.
25 Hollinger Road, Toronto 16, Canada

Published simultaneously in Canada by
D. VAN NOSTRAND COMPANY (Canada), LTD.

Preface

A selection such as this is designed to be useful to a younger generation of readers as well as to those of one's contemporaries who have recently become interested in the subject and to the great number of students who have little access to libraries, especially libraries containing older issues of journals. In thinking about this selection, I have had the advice of two very much younger anthropologists, Theodore Schwartz and Sally Snyder. The actual design was worked out with the help of my colleague, Rhoda Métraux. Given the need for rigorous choice, it seemed to us that the period during and immediately after World War II, a period which reflected work done in the 1930's, is least known among younger scientists today. The outbreak of World War II resulted in a tremendous loss of publication or diffusion of much of the research done in the 1930's; rejection of the postwar years completed this partial interment. And there is today a widespread tendency to act as if, in fact, the world of the behavioral sciences began in 1950.

For this volume I have chosen a set of papers the earliest of which was published in 1939, but which stem actually from the mid-1930's, when I was introduced to interdisciplinary work by Lawrence K. Frank. As a student I had been interested in economics, English literature, and psychology, as well as in anthropology, and I had been able to draw on parts of these disciplines in my first field work. I had also always tried to relate my field findings to contemporary problems of American life. But when, in the summer of 1934, Lawrence K. Frank invited me to join the Hanover Seminar of Human Relations, the idea of working with a group of fellow human scientists, specialists in different fields, was a new one. We worked together for a month to develop an outline for the presentation of our knowledge of human development to adolescents. Out of Hanover grew a second project, a multidisciplinary study of cooperative and competitive habits. Then I went to the field again for three years. When I returned in 1939, World War II was upon us.

Partly as an outgrowth of the work done in the mid-1930's and partly in response to the urgent need to apply our anthropological skills to ensure the survival of a threatened way of life, I began to relate anthropological materials to a great variety of problems, usually by invitation. As a result, the papers were widely scattered in publication, and through the years they have become steadily more inaccessible.

This selection is arranged in three parts. In Part I are papers written for anthropologists, which may also be useful to members of other disciplines interested in the methods of anthropology. Part II is concerned with major themes which were brought to the forefront of our scientific consciousness in World War II and have been kept there by the increasing gravity of man's situation in the contemporary world. Although the major situations to which we must address ourselves today have changed, both the underlying themes and the methods employed— the analysis of whole cultures so organized that the insights could be used to solve particular problems—are as relevant now as they were then. For Part III we have chosen a series of papers which show how anthropological thinking relates to the central concerns of other disciplines. We have reached a period in history in which every discipline is needed—needed as one voice in an orchestration of disciplines, where the lack of any single discipline is a loss in our attempts to deal responsibly with an endangered world.

In many ways the early 1960's remind me of the 1920's, for there is experiment and excitement in the air; and they remind me of the 1940's, for there is a renewed sense of danger and a call to us once more to use our science responsibly and constructively to make a safe transition from a world threatened by nuclear catastrophe to a warless world, many of whose characteristics are completely unknown to anyone as yet. Anthropologists first dealt with the past—with early men and the remnants of their lives—and with our primitive contemporaries whose simple technologies represented the conditions under

which our primitive ancestors once lived. Then we began
to include the present, and anthropology became, in part,
an applied science directed toward working on problems
of government, war and peace, transition and change. Now
anthropology has come to include the future, too, as we
use our knowledge about cultures in the past and the
present to help us project what they may become. This
book records some of our efforts to build the bridge from
a study of the past and the present to responsible thinking
about the future.

All my thinking life and all my field work are reflected
in these papers, but for the contemporary stimulation of
the years when these papers were written I have to thank
especially Gregory Bateson, Jane Belo, Ruth Benedict,
Margaret Brennan, Nicolas and Elena Calas, Eliot D.
Chapple, Carl Deutsch, John Dollard, Milton Erickson,
Erik H. Erikson, Lawrence and Mary Frank, Geoffrey
Gorer, Frances L. Ilg, Robert K. Lamb, Nathan Leites,
Margaret Lowenfeld, Robert and Helen Lynd, Frances
C. Macgregor, Rhoda Métraux, Philip E. Mosely, Gard-
ner and Lois Murphy, John Pilly, David Rapaport,
Frank Tannenbaum, Martha Wolfenstein, my daughter,
Catherine Bateson Kassarjian, and my parents, Edward
Sherwood and Emily Fogg Mead.

MARGARET MEAD

The American Museum of Natural History
New York
February 24, 1964

Contents

ACKNOWLEDGMENTS

The author acknowledges with thanks permission to reprint from
the following publications.

Chapter   1: *American Anthropologist*, 41:189-205 (1939).
Chapter   2: *American Anthropologist*, 49:69-77 (1947).
Chapter   3: *Transactions of the New York Academy of Sci-
             ences*, Ser. 2, 2:24-31 (1939).
Chapter   4: Hoch, *Psychosexual Development in Health and
             Disease*, Grune & Stratton, 1949.
Chapter   5: *American Anthropologist*, 49:69-77 (1947).
Chapter   6: *Social Structure: Essays Presented to A. R. Rad-
             cliffe-Brown*, The Clarendon Press, 1949.
Chapter   7: Lowrey and Sloane, *Orthopsychiatry, 1923-1948*,
             American Orthopsychiatric Association, 1948, pp.
             367-373.
Chapter   8: *Science, Philosophy and Religion, Second Sym-
             posium*, 1942.
Chapter   9: *Transactions of the New York Academy of Sci-
             ences*, Ser. 2, 9:133-152 (1947).
Chapter 10: *Asia*, 40:402-405 (1940).
Chapter 11: Quincy Wright, ed., *The World Community*,
             University of Chicago Press, 1948, pp. 47-55.
Chapter 12: *American Quarterly*, 3:3-13 (1951).
Chapter 13: *American Journal of Sociology* (The University of
             Chicago Press), 48:633-639 (1943).
Chapter 14: *Centennial*, 1950. Reprinted by permission from
             the American Association for the Advancement of
             Science.
Chapter 15: *Psychosomatic Medicine* (Harper & Row), 4:396-
             397, 1942.
Chapter 16: From *Feelings and Emotions* by Reymert, pp.
             362-373. Copyright (1950) McGraw-Hill Book
             Company, Inc. Used by permission.
Chapter 17: *PMLA*, 68:13-23.
Chapter 18: *Science*, Vol. 126 (1957). Reprinted by permission
             from the American Association for the Advance-
             ment of Science.

Part I

I

Anthropology Among the Sciences*

I count myself fortunate to be able to speak in 1960, at the beginning of a period when, hopefully, anthropology will be livelier, theoretically, and more useful to the country and the world than has been the case in the last decade.

The loss this year of Alfred Kroeber and Clyde Kluckhohn has brought acutely to my consciousness, and I believe to the consciousness of many anthropologists, the special need that we have for those who never let their active allegiance to their own discipline swallow them up and isolate them from the community of scientists and scholars. Anthropologists are better fitted than members of many other disciplines to contribute actively to the growth of ordered knowledge, but we are also subject to special forms of occupational temptations which isolate us. It seems appropriate in this year, in which we have lost the last of those who must always appear as giants because they embodied—by growing up within it—more of anthropology than those younger than they, for us to reconsider these special conditions which bind us in and sometimes isolate us from the wider intellectual community.

In 1932 I sat on a hilltop in New Guinea, in a village which I did not leave for seven long months, reading a letter which described the possibility that a great foundation might give $2,000,000 as a grant for a five-year field project to investigate the surviving, unstudied primitive cultures of the world. Here, from one standpoint, was a

* Delivered as the Presidential address at the Annual Meeting of the American Anthropological Association, in Minneapolis, November 1960.

dream coming true; Franz Boas and Radcliffe-Brown had
each made plan after plan for institutes which would
undertake to explore whole regions systematically, each
field worker's research dovetailed into each other's. The
central responsibility of anthropologists to rescue and
record and publish the information on these vanishing
cultures and peoples would be discharged. But, as I sat
there, the tiny village hemmed in by the mists which
would not rise for another hour so that only an occasional
papaya leaf stood out against the walls of impenetrable
white, I realized sharply and acutely that there were not
enough of us. There were not enough trained anthropologists in the world to spend that money quickly, wisely,
and well. Either we would have to send young, untrained
students into the field with commissions enormously
heavy for such young shoulders—as Radcliffe-Brown sent
Hogbin to Rennel Island because the chance came and
there was no one else to go—or the few of us there were
would have to set to work with a frantic disregard of
when and how anything would ever be published, filling
up our notebooks with undecipherable notes for other
workers to pore over unprofitably years after we had died.
There were field deaths that were very close in those days
—Deacon died in the New Hebrides (and Camilla Wedg-
wood was just then giving years trying to piece together
his uncompleted work); Sullivan died in 1925 of tuber-
culosis; Haeberlin died of diabetes before his work was
well begun.

We were "not enough, not enough," I kept repeating;
and, under the sharp sting of worry, I wondered what
other ways there were. Would it be possible to ask each
of the disciplines (that word "discipline" had not then
been invented in its present usage) dealing with human
behavior—sociology, economics, psychology, political science, law—to choose one or two of their best-trained
and most promising students, give them extra, special
training in anthropology, and then send them out, each
free to follow his own special research interest but obli-
gated also to bring back a respectable account of the
whole culture. Their accounts would have been somewhat
incommensurable and one-sided, of course; but we would
have recorded a great number of vanishing cultures and

we would have had in every discipline someone who understood what a culture is and who would have been able to use the findings of anthropology from first-hand experience.

As you know, that dream was never realized. Intra-professional disagreements ended in our being judged an unsuitable scientific repository for such great resources. But today, almost thirty years later, as we are again approaching a chance of adequate financing for the same task, it has to be said as truly as it could be said then: there are not enough of us. Our numbers have tripled, but the growth of new methods and the possibilities for field work today have far outstripped our growth. So, again, it seems appropriate to consider our place among the sciences, the special vanishing materials which are our responsibility, and those special conditions which may hinder or facilitate our ability to use this new opportunity. It is important also to realize that funds available for research—especially research in any particular field—do not continue to increase exponentially. In our rapidly changing world, the next few years may well be a high point in the availability of funds for the human sciences.

I think it is still fair to treat anthropology as a field science, whose members work with fresh field material, studying living speakers of living languages, excavating the earth where archeological remains are still in situ, observing the behavior of real mothers' brothers to real sisters' sons, taking down folklore from the lips of those who heard the tale from other men's lips, measuring the bodies and sampling the blood of men who live in their own lands—lands to which we have to travel in order to study the people. We still have no way to make an anthropologist except by sending him into the field; this contact with living material is our distinguishing mark. Where the sociologist deals, characteristically, with marks on paper made by the census taker or the respondent to a questionnaire, and the psychologist deals with artificially contrived laboratory situations, we make our own marks on the paper as we listen and accept the situations provided by history rather than those created in the laboratory.

This approach has certain consequences. It involves a

willingness to suspend judgment—not until a hypothesis is verified, but before we make any hypothesis at all. It involves a willingness to expect that which cannot even be formulated, to wait upon the material and to surrender to what it tells us as we encounter it. Rigid cross-cultural frames of reference, tight taxonomic systems, and incipient analogues of periodic tables all cramp and distort the necessary uncommittedness of our approach. Furthermore, the uniqueness of our materials lies not in some single clear set of measurements or a set of markings on the feather of a bird newly observed, but in the whole system of second- and third-order relationships within the phenomena with which we work. Because the nature of our method also involves months and years of concentrated work away from other scientists, while we work—involved twenty-four hours a day in details of an excavation, a language, the ongoing life of a village—the uniqueness of each system is brought home to us, not only at the conceptual level but in our every muscle and nerve. So it is perhaps not surprising that anthropology is suffering from a lack of the orderly cumulative growth of liberating hypotheses, tests, verifications, consolidations, and breakthroughs which characterize the physical and biological sciences. In the 1920's, American anthropology could be seen as a science among the sciences, with its own set of concepts, its own domain, its own taxonomic system, and an orderly relationship to the related sciences of physiology, psychology, botany, geology, paleontology, biology, etc. When anthropology was grouped with the biological sciences within the newly founded National Research Council, the work that was needed seemed to be placed in a clear scientific context. When the Social Science Research Council was founded, our inclusion only attested to the width of our interest in man, as our membership in the American Council of Learned Societies gave evidence of the depth of a humanism which did not yet feel science as alien to man's deeper values. I can remember Boas' delight when Kroeber was elected to the National Academy of Sciences.

We are in no such clear position today. There are many more of us and anthropologists are offered many more kinds of jobs. But, again, there are not enough qualified people to play the role that is peculiarly our own in technical assistance, international relations, the processes of racial integration and educational change, planning and the economic transformations that accompany the new technologies. These are practitioner activities; they multiply in demand if not in fulfillment. But the central body of theory within which we can communicate with other sciences, and so in an orderly way with each other, is—although far richer—far more poorly articulated than it was in the 1920's. The fear of the 1920's that, with the death of the senior generation, anthropology would fall apart into separate, isolated specialties was not realized. The 1952 Wenner Gren International Seminar of Anthropology assured that anthropology would not disintegrate, at least here in the United States, and extended a possibility of closer articulation in other countries. But, in spite of the activities of some individual anthropologists, the great body of men and women called anthropologists communicate with the other sciences very poorly. As a consequence, eschewing our part in the general development of science, our own communications are becoming trivial and idiosyncratic. The need to handle our materials in an orderly and codified way has been expressed symbolically by an obsession with kinship. The break in the old acceptance of a central value placed on man has become an atomistic study of values. The field is filled with burgeoning systems of terminology which are used by no one but the originators, each system treated as the unique product of the particular anthropologist's field experience.

As we have become better known and better established, more students have chosen anthropology while they were undergraduates. Where their predecessors entered the field from marine biology, or optics, or English literature, they have entered with only a high school level of knowledge and experience of natural science and the humanities. Within anthropology itself, they find, in many, many instances, an unwillingness to cross disciplinary lines, and later—like young Christian Scientists discovering the glories of medicine—they are attracted away from the center of the field. I understand that some 13 per cent of anthropologists are now working in the field of mental health—which often means that not only are they seeking contact with other sciences but, in doing so, they are leaving their own field to those who feel no such need.

We have also shown another sign of isolation from the main body of science in the development of schools, sects which depend upon an esoteric language, hostility to other schools, shibboleths, and idiosyncratic vocabulary and controversy, which effectively prevent contact with members of other sects within anthropology and with members of other sciences. I need only point to such activities as the continuous "rediscovery" of old ideas, on the one hand, and the reproaches against anyone who dares to climb on the evolutionary "bandwagon"—an approach which, if it is scientific, is not a bandwagon but part of what is probably the most significant ongoing activity of our time. It would sometimes seem, at present, as if the first step in writing an article is to list those inside and outside the discipline who might have had something to say about one's subject, to exclude them from one's sources, and then to proceed. Science does not grow in this way. One of the by-products of such an approach has been the development of three parallel disciplines— anthropology, sociology, and psychology—each hampered in its own peculiar way in its relation to the other sciences and each claiming as its subject matter much of the same material as the others. The originality and jurisdictional claims of each are, of course, mightily advanced by their persistent and intentional mutual ignorance of each other's work and by the failure of all three to preserve articulate communication with the other life sciences and the conceptual schemes and instrumentation which those sciences use.

I should like to select for brief mention five areas where our failure to make appropriate cross-disciplinary relationships has reacted unfavorably upon our own central communication among ourselves and upon our capacity for orderly growth.

The first area is that of models, which permit rapid

communication among sciences with very different contents, different-sized units, and needs for different mathematics. Cybernetics represents one such model, within which it is possible to discuss details of the central nervous system, or the behavior of a variety of life forms within an ecological setting, or a mother weaning her child. Anthropologists participated in the initial formulations and a few anthropologists have used the family of models that come from information and communication theory; but the use of such models has not penetrated the central core of the discipline.

Second, there is the area of content. There is an adjacent science which has developed enormously during the last three decades and now can provide us with highly variegated and well-established information about the behavior of living creatures that could be of the greatest fruitfulness for our own studies. This is the discipline called ethology in Europe and the comparative study of animal behavior in the United States. Here, the anthropologist and the ethologist, each with his wealth of detail, can communicate in the concrete terms so dear to both and no conceptual model is needed beyond some basic familiarity with biology—though the anthropologist often lacks this, so that the recitation of identifying zoological names turns into a form of seductive or forbidding ritual, preventing instead of encouraging communication.

Third is the area of instrumentation. It may be most plausibly argued that the growth of science has been a function of the growth of instruments—the telescope, the microscope, the computer and, for the study of living creatures, cinema film and sound recording. Yet, even when the use of film and tape is relevant to our historical responsibility for the preservation of vanishing cultures, anthropologists have taken little or no interest in them. We still send most of our students out into the field equipped with notebooks, pencils, and a still camera, with the expectation of bringing back perhaps two or three hundred illustrative photographs. This is unforgivable when we now have the technical equipment adequate to collect bodies of material—on film and tape—which can be analyzed with finer and finer tools, both technically and conceptually, as in Birdwhistell's analyses of film with the perceptoscope,[1] or Chapple's development of the Interaction Chronograph.[2] Large collections of stills make it possible to have a permanent record of complexes which cannot be described in words or diagrams and which can furthermore be juxtaposed in presentation.[3] This makes it possible for us to handle series of complex diachronic events simultaneously—a recurrent necessity in science. Together, these fine-detail records provide us with a new kind of experimental material; the events we record are too complex for repetition or replication, but the analytical situation, with new analytic tools, can be repeated as often as we wish, decade after decade, as our conceptual systems grow. If we stop to think where astronomy and biology would be if they had treated the telescope and microscope in as casual, unaware, and irresponsible a fashion as anthropologists have treated the camera and the tape recorder, the strange archaic palsy that has come over parts of our science is only too clear. Boas, at the age of seventy and then President of the American Association for the Advancement of Science, went into the field to use the new tools on old problems and took with him also that precious and irreplaceable eager humility— the fear that this time the task would prove to be too difficult. But even as computers have become ever more perfected in the direction of being able to work with complex data, we, in our field work, have neglected to use the new instruments to collect material that will be capable of such treatment. A science that does not welcome new instruments which raise its capabilities by a factor of ten has somehow got out of step.

Fourth, there is the use that we do make of other systems of thought without the fullest exploration of what these systems really are. Genetics is one science which is enormously relevant to problems absolutely central to our discipline, but we have—again with a few conspicuous exceptions—relegated it to the outer periphery as the special concern of physical anthropologists. And now, rather suddenly, we are faced with the terrible problems raised by the identification of *kuru* in the New Guinea Highlands[4] and the plans for the quarantine of a whole population—a population of the sort for which we have traditionally assumed not only scientific but ethical responsibility.

Where we have dealt with genetics mainly by ignoring it, our handling of the whole field of dynamic psychology initiated by Freud has been of another order. Psychoanalysis, more than most of the human sciences, has involved a system which has cloistered itself in order to survive—and that rather poorly—the distortions and vulgarizations that accompany the rapid diffusion of half-understood ideas about human behavior. Psychoanalysis is an intricately interrelated system, based upon the most minute observation of single individuals that has ever been made, within a framework which has taken the operation of only one aspect of the human mind as both the instrument and the object of research. It cannot be used in a half-understood, analogical, or shorthand sense in which the super ego is equated with culture, aggression is seen as explanatory of human behavior, and projective tests—the basis of which is not understood—are substituted for observation in the field. Instead of making the laborious and often painful effort to understand psychoanalysis, we have been content to use some of the products, particularly projective tests. Ironically, these tests—which, for the most part, are only useful in a context of full cultural and full psychodynamic sophistication[5]—are treated as "instruments," in the way psychologists use the phrase, and are presented as a kind of scientific front. So we fail to use the instruments that are appropriate for our own problems and misuse half-understood instruments from a half-understood field. Recently, LaBarre published the results of a questionnaire sent to those who were teaching personality and culture, a field in which a good knowledge of psychoanalysis is necessary, which showed how few of the anthropologists, who presumed to give a course for which there is great popular demand, had ever read Freud properly.[6]

Here I am making no plea for the incorporation of psychoanalytic theory; but if we intend to draw upon it we must know what we are doing. A related plea can be made for use of the Human Relations Area Files. Here a resource was fashioned by anthropologists, for anthropologists, which, within the limits set by the method within which it was constructed, is genuinely useful. Overuse of the Human Relations Area Files or an uninformed use of projective tests leads to revulsion, disproportionate overreaction, and a tendency to throw the baby out with the bath water.

Finally, there is the opportunity provided by the new upsurge of interest in the whole field of evolution, in which human evolution is just one part and cultural evolution a smaller one. The willingness of biologists like Waddington and Huxley, an ethologist like Lorenz, an ecologist like G. E. Hutchinson, a geneticist like Dobzhansky, a paleontologist like George Simpson to learn enough about anthropology to communicate with anthropologists has been only sketchily matched so far among ourselves.

Recently a conference was called to discuss how we might apply the knowledge of the participating sciences to the problems of human survival. Anthropology was given the lion's share of the seats and eight of those invited came. But we proved to be unable really to grapple with the problem or to deal simultaneously with our confreres from other fields, our own provincial sect-like battles, and the tremendous danger that confronts mankind. Although there were responsible contributions by individuals, these were overbalanced by suggestions that the topic of survival was outside our field, belonged to other sciences, was beyond our grasp.[7]

Yet it is precisely here that anthropology, as the science of man, has a responsibility which I believe we cannot evade. We have been bold and forthright enough when our scientific knowledge has been called upon to deal with problems of racism and genocide. During the difficult postwar years, no anthropologist of whom I have heard yielded to the temptation to incorporate Communist practice into American practice and became an informer on his fellows. But our ethical responsibility is widening. As specialists in the study of cultural inventions made by biological creatures called men, in an age in which we are beginning to control the direction of invention itself and are able to make almost any invention with appropriate specification, we have a peculiar task ahead of us. We must understand and command the direction in which the human sciences and the human race are moving well enough to be able to contribute what we know. We have not been sure enough of what we could do to parry the attacks that are made upon the human sciences on the ground that we are unable to make predictions. It is important to stress that in the real world of events no science can predict with certainty; but responsible, scientifically based endeavor can outline possible alternatives, narrow the choice within each set of alternatives, and develop new and totally unforeseen alternatives. The history of mankind has been the history of the extension and complication of boundaries which can be crossed, to a limited degree, safely. Our subject matter stretches from the days when there were perhaps many species of earlier man on earth through the emergence of *Homo sapiens*, through the shifting histories of special civilizations, carriers of the cumulating inventions which have brought us to the present day. A knowledge of this process is what we, as a discipline, can bring to the conference tables of the world. It is not for us to say that there should be conferences of "the people who know about these things"—either the political scientists or the biologists alone. Our whole claim that we are a science rests upon the completeness with which we have taken the whole of man—earlier species and present species, primitive cultures and modern cultures—into our conceptual scheme. Our subject is mankind as it must have been, as it is, and as it may be—if man survives. Undoubtedly, it will be the political scientists, the statesmen, the international lawyers, and the strategists who must now spend their time planning for and against destruction and who will work out many of the details. But unless we can think right down the reaches of mankind's long past and into a future in which the earth is only one part of a known and explored solar system, and in which mankind's problems will become extraordinarily different, we shall not be what we want to be: anthropologists, whatever our area, whatever our specialty, whatever our subdivisions.

American Anthropologist, Vol. 63, No. 3, 1961.

REFERENCES

1. Birdwhistell, R. L., 1963.
2. Chapple, E. D., 1949; Chapple, E. D., and C. M. Arensberg, 1940; Chapple, E. D., and L. R. Sayles, 1961, see especially pp. 114-41; Matarazzo, J. D., G. Saslow, and R. G. Matarazzo, 1956.
3. Bateson, G., and M. Mead, 1942.
4. Gajdusek, D. C., 1962, see also for further references.
5. Gladwin, T., 1961; Hallowell, A. I., 1955; Henry, J., and M. E. Spiro, 1953.
6. LaBarre, W., 1948.
7. Hoagland, H., and R. W. Burhoe (eds.), 1961.

2

Native Languages as Field-Work Tools

The use of native languages as part of the routine of investigating living primitive cultures was given its first strong impetus as a basic methodological tool by American and British field workers in the 1920's. The change in method from the use of dictated texts and interpreters to the use of the native language in direct contact with large numbers of natives, and living as a partially participating member of an intimately known community, marked perhaps as significant an advance in ethnological field techniques as did the late 19th century expeditions which eliminated the distinction between the theorist at home and the amateur collector of native customs upon whose accounts the theorist had previously relied.

In England, it was mainly due to Bronislaw Malinowski's work in the Trobriands and his enthusiastic discovery, so brilliantly described in *The Argonauts of the Western Pacific*,[1] of the superiority of using a native language over using a pidginized lingua franca.* The fact that the use of the native language in the Trobriands was associated with so many other alterations in field methods and in methods of presentation undoubtedly served to intensify the importance which followers of the Functional school attached to the use of the language and assured a widespread recognition of the method. Since the publication of the *Argonauts*, not only Malinowski's own students, but students from other British universities have assumed when they went into the field that they would work as far as possible in the native language.

---

* Although Malinowski's work in the Trobriands was completed in 1917, its effective impact on English ethnological methods dates from the first publication of the *Argonauts* in 1922.

In England, however, ethnological source materials had often been collected even in earlier years either in native languages or in a lingua franca such as Hindustani, Swahili or Malay, and the works of missionaries and colonial residents drew extensively upon the kind of knowledge of native life which comes from close contact and use of the native tongue. To the English ethnologist the idea that Europeans could use native languages when working with native peoples was neither new nor strange; the significant step was to insist that the theoretical ethnologist must use them as part of his field technique. In America, however, the case was very different. The distance between the amateur recorder of native custom and the professional ethnologist trained to a delicate phonetic recording of the exceedingly difficult American Indian languages was much wider than in the British possessions. The emphasis which had been laid upon the collection of accurate verbatim texts put a premium on linguistic accuracy and work at a table with one efficient interpreter. English-speaking interpreters were available, and the majority of Indian cultures were no longer functioning sufficiently to tempt the investigator into studying them by participatory methods. Tremendous efforts had been made to rescue as much as possible of the dying cultures, and to rescue them in a form which, because recorded in text, would be authentic despite the decayed condition of the culture and the deculturization of the informants. Functional studies, using the term in its least parochial sense to mean the study of the way in which a living culture functions, were, except in the case of a few tribes, impracticable. Given the type of problem being studied and the type of broken cultures within which they were being studied, there was no reason then why an ethnologist should have made any attempt to learn to use a native language. He merely learned to record it, learned enough technical terms to direct the course of his inquiries, and analyzed the form of the language or the literary form of songs or myths from his collection of texts.

The beginning of the use of the native language as a necessary field method came in America with a shift in the type of problem. When Professor Boas selected such problems as the relationship of the individual to a highly formalized religious structure, or the relationship between cultural forms and the social and psychological manifestations of physiological adolescence, he told the students who undertook this new type of problem that learning to use the language must be part of the field technique.

True to this difference in origins, native languages, with certain notable exceptions, have been used in England by students predominantly interested in studying social functioning, in America by students interested in problems of personality and culture.

The acceptance of this new technique of field study met however with considerable opposition, especially from seasoned field workers in the American Indian field who found it difficult to visualize conditions in a living culture, and from linguists whose respect for the fine subtleties of primitive linguistic forms made them feel that the field worker's claim to "speak" a native language must inevitably be false. Parallel with the tendency to discredit workers who claimed to have used the native language, another tendency became apparent: apologies and explanations by field workers who did not use the native language. That this apology sometimes took the form of attacks on "the myth that it is impossible to work except in a native language," still leaves clear the fact that the field worker who used the time-honored methods of interpreters and lingua francas felt that he must defend himself. These attitudes generated an atmosphere in which important considerations were lost sight of.

The time has passed when wholesale doubt can be cast upon investigators who use the native language. Today, in the face of the substantial body of work now in existence as a result of such use, it should be possible to discuss seriously just what is meant by the use of a native language in field work and what situations and what problems justify and even enjoy such use and which do not.[2]

The alternative to using the native language is in the case of native people among whom there are many people who speak some language other than their own, which the investigator, either because it is his own language (and this is the type situation of which Americans think) or because it is a simplified lingua franca, such as Hindustani, Malay, pidgin, or Swahili (and this is the type situation of which British anthropologists are more likely to think), can handle with less difficulty than he could the native language itself. I shall exclude from consideration work done exclusively through interpreters—all work, that is, where the interpreter acts merely as a linguistic mediator and all information is in the hands of persons linguistically inaccessible to the investigator. The type of problem which can be approached by this highly suspect method need not concern us here.*

Where another European language than the one which the investigator speaks readily, or where an exceedingly difficult lingua franca, also new to the investigator, is the *contact language*, the problem of communication bristles with so much difficulty that only exceptional circumstances can justify scientifically an attempt to undertake the task. Obviously all the objections which are raised against a field worker's being able to handle a native culture in the native language which he must learn for the purpose hold true in even greater degree, when he attempts to handle a native culture in a language strange to that culture, which its people speak indifferently, which he must also learn for the purpose. When the natives speak the language of the investigator, there is some chance of understanding; when both use a simple lingua franca strange to each, there is again some possibility of its becoming a good means of communication; when the language is European and therefore alien to the native in feeling, and not wholly familiar to the investigator, the chances of mutual misunderstanding are so great that there seems every argument in favor of abandoning the contact language as soon as possible in favor of the native language.

There are two major aspects involved in the use of

* I do not mean that interpreters should not be used by investigators who have not learned the language, in order to get at special information from persons who do not speak the contact language, but that such information can only properly be controlled if the investigator has informants, and enough of them to check against each other, who do speak the contact language.

contact languages which deserve special consideration:
(1) the practical question, in relation to the problems
which are to be studied, of the number, sex, age, caste,
class, geographical distribution, and literacy of the available
informants speaking the contact language, and (2)
the question of the affective tones of the contact language
and the extent to which these may prejudice or
distort the results of working through that language.

Whether the type and number of informants available
are adequate can only be estimated in terms of the particular
problem studied and the age and sex of the investigator.
In general women and children, old men and the
members of the society who are most thoroughly imbued
with the culture and least influenced by culture contact,
will not speak the contact language. This will of course
vary as between cultures which broke down a long time
ago and cultures which are only now breaking, and also
between peoples who have been formally educated by
mission or government in the contact language and peoples
who have learned the contact language through work
situations. But if the student who is considering working
without the native language, asks, not: "Can I get interpreters?"
but "What types of informants will be available
and what doors will be absolutely closed to me if I use
the contact language?" these practical considerations are
immediately thrown into relief.

Of another order, but equally significant, is the question
of the affective tone of the language in which investigator
and informant communicate with each other. In
most cases of culture contact, the contact language has
very different connotations for the two sides in the contact
situation. It may be that the language is regarded
as chiefly appropriate to the master-servant situation
(pidgin English), or as a language which represents a step
up for the native and a step down for the investigator
(Creole languages); as a language which is definitely
associated with missionization and carries with it the
highly affective values of religious loyalty (the Blanche
Bay dialects which have been specialized as a written
lingua franca by the Mission in New Britain); as a fostered
language which lacks the fine adjustment to caste
of the native language and so permits two people of

unequal caste or status to speak as equals (Malay in Bali), or as a language which involves national issues and previous changes in sovereignty. In all these or other similar situations, the fine adjustment to affective values will be distorted, whether the language be used for interpreting as in old methods, or, in communities where many natives speak it, for field work of the new method in cases where the student does not learn the native language. All such distortions as these should be allowed for, and the investigator should form an estimate of the way in which his materials are skewed by this situation. These contact languages often have a complete ethos associated with them, and as they are regarded by one or both of the cultures in contact as instruments of hypocrisy, wheedling, ingratiating, or bullying, a great many values besides those specifically linguistic may be jeopardized. It is reasonable that the field worker, when he uses only a contact language, should be asked to give an account of his contact language conditions in terms of its affect and implications.

Turning now to the use of native languages in the field, it is first necessary to define what is meant here by use of the native language as a field tool. I do not mean, of course, recording dictated texts which can only be elucidated by analysis, recording native words for kinship terms, religious idea, or parts of a house, nor do I mean a minimal knowledge of the form of the grammar, of dialectical variations of distribution, etc. Such linguistic records as these are essential to any account of a culture, however formal, however directed toward the solution of problems external to that culture, e.g. distribution of material culture objects, etc. But while such treatment of the language adds to the field worker's mass of material and often facilitates his effective use of the contact language, it is not of such use as this that I am speaking here, but of the practice of using the native language to obtain ethnological information.

Some problems hardly require such use. The types of study for which the investigator needs to use the native language least may be classified as:

1. The rescue of the remains of dying cultures.
2. The study of survivals of the primitive culture in a

hybridized cultural situation in which everyone speaks a contact language.

3. Studies where the emphasis of the research is upon some formal element, e.g. survey studies of Australian kinship systems.

4. Surveys in which the orientation is *outside* the various cultures studied, as inquiries into the distribution of themes or incidents—in folk lore, or design motifs in art, when the investigator has no interest in the significance of these widely distributed elements within specific cultures.

5. Formal studies of primitive languages in which the linguist is uninterested in the psychological problems of language, in feeling tone, in correspondence between linguistic form and other forms of symbolism in the culture, in nuances of usage which can seldom be adequately handled merely through dictated texts.

On the other hand, the types of study for which maximal use of the native language is essential and which cannot be done without it, are conspicuously:

1. Studies of social functioning, that is, studies of the actual way in which a society works, which must be done mainly by following up a series of actual events during the course of field work. As it is impossible to arrange that the significant events will take place in the households of selected informants, the ethnologist has to get his material from the individuals involved in the events in question. If there is a case of incest, he must study the reactions to the situation of the individuals concerned; if there is a theft he must be able to talk to the man who stole and the man who was stolen from, to their fathers and brothers and wives, and to uninvolved persons not immediately affected by the event. Very occasionally, communities may be found in which a lingua franca is sufficiently widespread so that a male investigator may follow the operation of social forces in a series of specific situations without a knowledge of the language. There are exceedingly few places in the world where a woman investigator, using women as important informants, finds the knowledge of a lingua franca sufficiently widespread so as to use it for this sort of research, e.g. certain parts of New Ireland, where, however, the culture is correspondingly broken and typical social functioning badly impaired.

2. Studies of the relationship between culture and per-

sonality. In such studies the unit of research is the identified individual, within a known cultural setting and within a reasonably closed social group. Whether it be the mechanics of character formation, the way in which the culture, as represented by a series of individuals who act as cultural surrogates, moulds the developing child, or a study of the personality of religious leaders, or a study of the artist personality as compared with the personality of his fellows, or the delineation of the ethos of sex, age, caste, or class groups, the native language must be used. It is very difficult in primitive societies to find enough representatives of any age, sex, occupational, or temperamental group, to arrive at any results at all, even when every available individual is drawn upon to provide material. If one is limited to those babies whose fathers speak pidgin English, one will find out very little about babies.

3. The native language as something that is used as well as collected is necessary also in linguistic researches in which the linguist wishes to go beyond the formal analysis of the language and to study the correspondence between linguistic symbolisms and other forms of symbolism in the culture, the cultural background of idiom, the way in which the language is learned, the variations in the use of the language by different personalities, the degree and type of verbalization which accompanies overt activities, the relationship between the language and the thought habits of those who speak it.

There is another possible attack on cultural problems which has risen to the attention of research planners in field anthropology, after having lain almost dormant since the Torres Straits Expedition in 1899, and that is work by a team, in which the members of the team represent different disciplines, notably social anthropology, psychology, psychiatry, child development, linguistics with special emphasis upon problems of symbolism and the delineation of thought problems, endocrinology directed toward the relationship between physical type and functioning and cultural standardization of personality. One of the principal obstacles to the functioning of such a team is the matter of learning the language; the most suitable persons from other disciplines may have had no experience with non-European languages at all; the time which they can give to work so far from home is limited. In some of these fields, notably, experimental psychology and work on physical type, it may be possible to devise ways in which literate native assistants, capable of being trained, and close cooperation with an anthropologist thoroughly conversant with the language and culture may be substituted for a knowledge of the native language. This might also be done in studies of infancy, of motor development, of dancing, of the bodily manifestations of trance, of special types of abnormality, such as Arctic hysteria, always provided that the relevant material which can only be obtained by using the language had been or was being obtained and made available to the researcher using non-verbal material for his subject matter.

There is much misunderstanding of what is meant by *using the native language,* a phrasing which I prefer to *speaking the native language.* The latter form of expression arouses the suspicion of linguistic purists, terrifies students who have not yet tried field work, and puts an undue premium on virtuosity at the expense of emphasizing that a language is a tool, not a feather in one's cap. We may consider the use of the native language in relation to the problems which confront the field worker and divide them into the need to speak and the need to understand, always bearing in mind that the field worker is not in the field to talk but to listen, not there to express complicated ideas of his own which will muddle and distort the natives' accounts. The demands upon him for active linguistic participation are lower than they are in any normal period of his life. It is probable that those persons who are in agony when they cannot express the exact and exquisite nuance of their own thought in a foreign language and can take no pleasure in the fact that they understand what is said *to them* in that language would show serious personality disabilities as modern field workers.

Needs to speak may be classified as follows:

1. *The need to ask questions correctly and idiomatically.* Circumlocutions and non-idiomatic questions will not do, because questions may have to be asked of anyone, an old woman, a deaf man, a frightened child, in the midst of an excited scene, at a birth or a death bed or while the attention of the group is fixed upon the hunt or upon the wild antics of someone in trance. The questions *must* be

intelligible. But twenty or thirty locutions at the most, with allowance for inflection, of course, is usually enough to permit the investigator to ask who, how, when, where, for what reason, what relationship, by virtue of what status, as a result of what previous event, etc., something is happening or has happened.

A little careful planning of questions will simplify question asking. Where the local idiom gives age in terms of illustrative persons, the investigator can select a set of conspicuous persons of different ages, and present a likely pair or series from which the respondent may choose. Social status is usually indicated by clichés and the investigator has merely to have critical ones—hair cut? house with 12 posts built yet? etc.—at his fingers' ends. A few key genealogies memorized will short-cut the preliminary questions about relationship if one is forced to ask a badly informed person in order to get any answer on the spot. It is also necessary to organize one's expectation, as for instance in cultures where if you ask a man "whose house is that?" you will receive a male owner's name, but if you ask a woman, you will receive the name of the owner's *wife*, in answer. Similarly, among the Iatmul, a male cannot give the kinship term which a woman calls a man if the term is at all obscure. One must ask for the reciprocal. A great deal of hesitancy and doubt about whether or not one understands a language and whether or not one dares to work without an interpreter may be overcome by making a serious study of the optimum forms in which questions may be cast and the standardized peculiarities which are likely to characterize the answers. Needless to say, it saves time to learn early which classes of persons will refuse to answer certain types of questions and merely shrug one off with an "Unfortunately I am too young to know," or "You will have to ask the women the name of that offering. I (qua male) know nothing about it," or "I do not live in that division of the village and unfortunately cannot speak of their affairs," as well as the simpler dilemmas which involve calling a name which the person questioned must avoid or even using a word which occurs in some one of the names which he avoids. Questions which involve ways of thought alien to the people being studied also should be categorized and eliminated from one's current repertoire, such as, in Samoa, asking why A left a party, or refused to go fishing. The first answer will be that A was *musu*, unwilling, and if the question is pressed one will be told some irrelevant and already known point such as that A is deaf, or right handed, or lame. Similarly in Bali, it is fruitless to ask: "Why did your wife take an offering to the temple," because in 9 cases out of 10 no one, not even the wife herself, will know the answer. Instead one may substitute the question, addressed not to one person, but to a group of twenty, "Did anyone here bring an offering which had been promised?" and get a significant answer. The number of questions which may have the aura of black magic or of esoteric information about them, also may be plotted out with profit, if one is not to waste time asking A, while there are other people present, how he got the sore on his leg, or B why he gave his child such and such a name. Learning to ask questions which will get an answer, which will get an answer with the smallest amount of dickering back and forth, which will get an answer from a person of given sex and status when asked by a person of the investigator's sex and status, and which will get an answer which when given is significant—this is part of the problem of learning to use the language to ask questions. It will be immediately apparent how little of the problem lies in memorizing thirty or forty linguistic locutions, how much of it lies in adaptive planning and attention to cultural usages as a whole.

2. *The need to establish rapport.* This is one of the ways in which language may be used almost at once; if one knows enough to exclaim "how beautiful!" of an offering, "how fat!" of a baby, "how big!" of a just shot pig; if one can say "my foot's asleep," or "my back itches" when one sits in a closely packed native group with whom one is as yet unable to hold a sustained conversation; if one can ask the simple questions: "Is that your child?" "Is your father living?" "Are the mosquitos biting you?" or even utter the culturally appropriate squeals and monosyllables which accompany fright at a scorpion or startle at a loud noise, it is easy to establish rapport with a people who depend upon affective contact for reassurance. Similarly among a more formal people, such as the Balinese, who are not trained to appreciate warmth of feeling in strangers, an ability to say things like "This is Boedah Wageh Pang," thus commenting on the date in terms of the 7 day week, the 5 day week and the 3 day week, is reassuring. It makes no difference whether one can name the days in all the 10 systems of weeks correctly or not. For rapport purposes, one piece of scrupulously accurate habitual formal comment is sufficient. To be able to say

to visitors in Samoan "Alas for your coming, the tide is
out," and thus to apologize for whatever one will offer
them, sets them immediately at ease. There may be fifty
other similar phrases which one might have used, and
which one must recognize when they are used; but to use
one correctly is adequate for purposes of establishing
rapport. Beginning field workers, imbued with the maxim
that they *must* establish rapport usually devote a disproportionate amount of time to doing so, when much
less time more carefully spent would have done as well.
To be able to name every common object in the house
will accomplish very little as compared to being able to
name one rare and unusual object, or being able to produce the verb for "to sleep in another person's house," or
"to beat your child when you are angry with your wife,"
or "to eat food which comes from another person's
kitchen." Especially in the houses of strangers, where one
wishes the maximum non-interference with one's note-
taking and photography, and for which the establishment
of rapport is an absolute essential, half a dozen accurate
touches which will serve to reassure and please the people
of the house are all that are necessary—unless of course
there are fixed routines of eating, smoking, or drinking
which are prescribed by etiquette. But in most cases, there
are also culturally approved ways of circumventing these
time-consuming attentions, in which the correctness of the
refusal more than compensates for the refusal itself. A
little time, taken early in field work, to select the affect-
loaded, laughter-loaded etiquette phrases, is well spent.
And here again, it is apparent that the investigator must
draw on the cultural usages more than upon linguistic
virtuosity.

3. *The need to give instructions.* Here again linguistic accuracy is essential. All the phrases for time and space
orientation, for expressing a sequence of activities, for a
conditional statement ("if the box for the cameras is open,
shut it") have to be available for use. If the ethnologist
cannot give quick and accurate instructions to his native
servants, informants, and assistants, cannot tell them to
find the short lens for the Leica, its position accurately
described, to put the tripod down-sun from the place
where the ceremony is to take place, to get a fresh razor
blade and the potassium permanganate crystals and bring
them quickly in case of snake bite, to boil and filter the
water which is to be used for mixing developer—he will
waste an enormous amount of time and energy doing

mechanical tasks which he could have delegated if his tongue had been just a little better schooled. When it is realized that under genuine primitive conditions, probably a third of the ethnologist's waking time goes into various mechanical activities, directing hunting and fishing for food for himself and his servants and creditors, trading for native foods, directing house building, arranging for transport of supplies, preserving specimens and photographs from the inroads of insects and mould, developing films, dressing wounds and treating skin diseases, devising new routines by which new emergencies may be met with native materials so that the top of a pillow becomes a crutch or a bamboo mat painted white becomes a reflector, it is obvious that the more of this work he can delegate the better for his field work. And the delegation is primarily a matter of being able to give directions that are comprehensible.

Here again, preliminary exploration is worthwhile. In a language which has, for example, no word for cut, but ten words for cut transversely, longitudinally, diagonally, in small regular pieces, in small irregular pieces, etc., it is worth considering whether any given set of verbs will probably crop up in situations where it is not possible to pantomime the instruction. It is probably not without significance that in Balinese, which is a language of this sort, the natives themselves tend to abandon verbal instructions in favor of "learning with the eyes," as the Balinese say. To get the best results in some languages, it is necessary to verbalize and pantomime simultaneously— a procedure which would only confuse a Balinese. It is also essential to know whether the natives can digest complex instructions or whether the instructions must be given them piecemeal, sometimes permitting them to answer and repeat between each item in a series. The New Guinea native will in most cases make a stab at following out a half-understood request, often with disastrous consequences; the Balinese will stand paralyzed if there is a single detail which he is not absolutely sure he has heard correctly.

If the field worker can learn to handle these three situations—the need for questions, rapport and instructions—he will be able to use the native language in so far as speaking is concerned. If he has learned to ask questions accurately, he will find little difficulty in answering the smaller and more standardized questions which will be put to him. Exclamations and the formalities of etiquette combined soon develop into sufficient stock in trade for conversation of which naturally the field worker wishes to limit himself to the minimum, so that he will be free to observe what is going on around him. If it is necessary to tell a myth oneself before one can get myth telling started, one can memorize a carefully worked out translation, or more conveniently, privately prime an informant to start the ball rolling. Giving accurate instructions means that one will be able to respond rapidly to instructions to duck, watch one's step, lean to the other side of the canoe, look out for the centipede, pray three times, or bend low because that strange man is a chief.

I do not wish to minimize the pleasure which derives from virtuosity. Especially when one is working alone, the more amusements one has which bring one directly in contact with native life the better. Many field workers derive part of the energy which keeps them grinding along in solitude for months at a time from acts of virtuosity, from learning to paddle a canoe, or play a musical instrument, or dance a native dance, or perform stunts in the native language, such as making speeches, giving improvised dramatic performances, playing verbal games, guessing native riddles, or telling our folk tales in the native idiom. Such procedures undoubtedly make for rapport; in the course of perfecting himself in them the ethnologist learns more than he does by mending the natives' Ford cars or sewing machines, or playing the phonograph to them, or showing them chemical tricks. At the same time the chief value of the virtuosity is in the way it feeds the field worker's drive. It is *not* a necessary part of using a native language, and the field worker with no leanings toward theatricals need not feel apologetic in not using them.

For speaking purposes discriminating attention should be given to vocabulary. One wishes to speak fluently and to avoid the impression of fumbling for a word. For this, a maximum of general words, set in *one* of a series of alternative syntactical forms—when alternatives exist—is useful. All the words for "what you call them," for "object which supports another," "object which surmounts another," "something that is part of something else," ways of expressing similarity or customary togetherness of objects, a good set of attributive adjectives, and the syntax necessary to form relative clauses serve to give fluency on a small vocabulary. Also all the native devices for giving the speaker time to pause, phrases like "what is it that it's called," "what's his name," repetitive verbal constructions, such as "he went, having gone, he sat; having sat, he ate," should be mastered as early as possible. They impart an idiomatic flavor, give one time to think, cover blunders, and help to inhibit one's attempt to use a more exact word, which one has forgotten, in favor of a general word. With the exception of the special vocabularies necessary for interrogations, instructions, and rapport situations, the learning of technical vocabularies for purposes of use in speaking is a heavy waste of time, especially technical vocabularies which will be used only once, as details of house building terminology which are often never used again once one has recorded house construction. Instead a technical vocabulary may be prepared in advance in the form of a compact word list, giving one maximum speed in recording and questioning. The words can be learned well enough for recognition, and the memory is not burdened with them for purposes of recall. This is one respect in which the field worker who depends principally upon the native language in gathering his material will reverse the procedure of the field worker who uses a lingua franca. Rivers pointed out that in using a lingua franca effectively, one should memorize from the native language as many as possible of the most technical terms one will need, and interlard the lingua franca with them. In speaking a native language, one avoids burdening one's memory with technical terms and specific words, and relies instead upon the most general words, except when very special words are needed to establish rapport.

Speaking skills such as I have outlined must under present conditions be acquired by the investigator on his own initiative. The traditional method of teaching students linguistics in America is aimed toward giving them maximum skill in accurate phonetic recording and in linguistic analysis, with an assumption that the task of analysis is to achieve a final understanding of the form of the language from a mass of phonetically accurate and absolutely unintelligible material, plus a literal translation furnished by an interpreter. The student is taught an enormous respect for native categories and made to feel that to impose any of our categories upon the native language is to violate it. While such a method is excellent in training students to handle non-Indo-European categories, the laborious collection of a large number of texts in the field and careful translation of the texts does not teach the field worker to *use* the language. In text taking, he may wait weeks for the simplest interrogatives, the most ordinary imperatives to turn up. So while taking enough texts to get the feel of the language and preserve one's sense of its categories, it is necessary to supplement this with preparing systematic vocabularies and getting the linguistic informant to respond to the interpreting language as stimulus, so that the field worker rapidly acquires, for instance, a complete set of interrogatives, a full set of pronouns, the complement of tenses, a reasonably complete set of noun classes, etc. Vocabularies must be built up, not merely on language slips as they come up in texts, but systematically, and oriented toward *use*. Such an approach is so directly in contravention of the implications of much linguistic training in America, that it seems worthwhile mentioning it. It would quite obviously take months, perhaps years, to learn to use a native language if one relied upon the repertoire gained from translating texts. And in recording new words, a distinction should be made between words which are needed for use in speaking and so must be recalled, words which need to be looked at several times for purposes of recognition, and words which should be filed for reference only.

The need to understand. Individuals vary greatly in the ratio of ability to recall, ability to recognize, and it may roughly be said that the larger the proportion of words which one can recognize without needing to know them well enough to recall them, the greater is one's fitness for using language as a research tool. The ability to recognize is a responsive behavior, and field work is in great part a responsive situation, a matter of listening with full emotional and intellectual appreciation to what is said. Where the emphasis is laid upon recall and performance, the student of a foreign language is more likely to become unresponsive—easy to listen to and hard to talk to. Field workers must aim at the exact reverse. From the very start the field worker may begin to recognize without making any effort to memorize further, to make a point of trying to get the gist of the conversation, working down later toward precise details. He uses in fact the exact opposite of the techniques he uses when learning to speak, for then he must aim toward meticulous accuracy and idiomatic expression.

There are, however, various devices for expediting the understanding of masses of spoken material without fully analyzing it. A feel for categories may be developed early, however the categories are defined—by the form the word takes, the position in the sentence, the tone of voice in which spoken, etc. The listener learns to say: *that* is a name, *that* was a ritual word, *that* is a place word, although the word itself is still vague. In the same way the syntax emerges at first blurred, so that one merely knows, *that* was the object, *that* was an attributive statement, and the heard sentences assume form, although the exact meanings may remain obscure. Meanwhile the field worker can save himself a lot of trouble by learning, for instance, all the personal names in the community, if names are frequently used, and also all the commonest place names. In the type of conversation to which he wishes to listen, names form a considerable percentage of the vocabulary, especially where names are words in common use or are compounds of common words, and the listener is at a loss if they are not immediately identified. An early knowledge of the interrelationships of as many persons as possible, of existing marriages, of clan allegiances, of habitual associations, will also serve to make ordinary heard conversation more intelligible. Very often when the field worker thinks despairingly that although he knows the words used and he knows the syntax involved, he cannot understand a word that is said, it is not ignorance of the language but ignorance of names and relations, ignorance of what is meant in their context by "and then A went north" or "those who had hunted with him said," or "all those of the other half." One quickly reaches the position where one says "I can follow a conversation if I know what the subject is," not realizing that seizing the subject matter is only in part a linguistic job. If one comes into a group just as someone says, "and he hadn't even paid for the pig, his mother's brother had just given it to his wife to feed," and one knows that there is a quarrel going on about a woman for whom a pig was paid, and the ownership of the pig was subsequently questioned, one has some chance of following the conversation. If one doesn't, one goes away discouraged and decides according to one's temperament that one will never get the hang of those reversed subordinate clauses and what an unintelligible language it is, or what a dolt one is.

Half-learning is also a time saving device which can be applied to vocabularies which are to be used only for recognition purposes. One learns to learn the English for the native word but not the opposite, and this type of learning saves a great many situations. Temporary learning or cramming, as of the names of strangers who will be involved in a ceremony, or of articles of trade in a barter which one will witness once only, or of the names of offerings to be used within the next half day, can also be used to facilitate understanding. It pays to have a large number of classified vocabularies which can be "brushed up" just before a ceremony.

Most cultures also afford a large number of nonlinguistic clues as to types of conversation, in the tone of voice, expressions on the face, type of laughter or type of constraint, cliché phrases which show that a serious matter is being discussed or that enjoined jesting is taking place. If the culture forbids obscenity in the presence of a man's sister, when a remark is made which has two possible meanings, one of which is obscene, a glance around the group to see whether there are any sisters present may provide the clue. Similarly, in Manus, a knowledge of the kinship positions of the speakers may reveal whether a harsh remark was a jest or the prelude to recriminations; a knowledge of the caste of two speakers in Bali will clarify the overheard use of the familiar second person pronoun which a man of higher caste habitually uses when addressing a man of low caste, but which two low caste men who are not intimate will only use to each other when they are angry. It is I think a safe statement that of two individuals, one with an intimate knowledge of the local scene, the formal and casual interrelationships between individuals, the recent events of interest, and but an indifferent knowledge of the language, the other with a fine analytical knowledge of the language and a much larger general vocabulary, but with a slighter knowledge of the local scene, the former will understand much more of a general conversation. Understanding the language so that the results of that understanding become usable data involves a great deal more than linguistic virtuosity, and this may be achieved with a lower degree of linguistic virtuosity than the professional linguist dealing with written records of narrative texts would believe possible.

An old style interpreter may well be used to advantage in many situations after the investigator has a fair command of the language. If questions are asked through an interpreter the field worker has a chance to listen to the question and to the answer, and he has time to record both his question and the answer given during the progress of interpreting. Many difficulties of frankness or constraint which might occur in a direct answer given to the field worker's direct question will vanish as the informant explains discursively and intimately to the interpreter, oblivious as he usually is that his reply is understood by the investigator. If one is handling an informant single-handed, there is usually not time to record the question asked and thus the stimulus, which is as important as the response, is missing from the record; there is seldom even time to record the answer in full. The record tends to falsify the whole procedure by including the question in the recorded answer so as to make the note intelligible. So a conversation which actually went:

Query? Why didn't you go to the front of the house.
Answer. My wife's mother.

will be necessarily reduced in note taking to something like:

"A said that he didn't go to the front of the house

because his wife's mother was there," giving little or no clue as to how much of this was volunteered information. Although devices such as:

? A said, etc.

can be used, the record can never be verbatim, as it can with the time given by interpreting. Furthermore, in using an interpreter when he is not needed for actual interpreting, both interpreter and informant become subjects for recording. The interpreter embellishes the bald question with illustrations and opinions, expresses amazement, admiration, contempt for the behavior referred to in the informant's answers, re-questions for further elucidation, revealing his own confusion and ignorance—these are specially significant in cross-sex, cross-age, and cross-class interpreting—and all this is grist to the ethnologist's mill. A combination of such recorded conversations and a careful verbatim record of the illustrations which spring spontaneously to the interpreter's lips when he is helping to translate a text provide valuable material on the personality of the interpreter, or as he may more accurately be called, linguistic informant.

In conclusion it will be well to state some of the things which are not implied by the phrase "using the native language." (In making this list I wish to cast no aspersions upon any field worker who has stated that he is able to do any of these things, but merely to stress the fact that a field worker who cannot do them may still be said to use the native language.) Using the native language does not mean:

1. That the investigator expects to speak it so well that he will substitute it for the lingua franca or European language, which is his contact language, even if he and his informant of the moment both speak the contact language fluently.

2. That he will not need continual help in translating most types of texts with the exclusion of simple narrative. Texts of magical charms, songs, speeches, snatches of dialogue from dramatics, descriptions of ritual, verbatim records of conversations, will all contain many words which will have to be elucidated either in the contact language or by specially trained informants who have learned to paraphrase their own language in a way which is intelligible to the field worker.

3. That he will not need help in the composition of significant sets of directions whether these be, for example, to direct a native patient in the use of a medicine, give directions for any sort of test, give directions as for taking up a position for body-build photographs. But such directions, once properly constructed, can be memorized.

4. That he may not need help from natives who are familiar with his errors of pronunciation and syntax in making initial contacts with strangers.

5. That if he can train an intelligent and literate native to record verbatim texts, particularly during group conversations, that such records will not be superior to his own, except under circumstances where he wishes to record idiosyncrasies which even the best trained native, deeply familiar with the standard forms, will tend to iron out in the course of the recording.

American Anthropologist, Vol. 41, No. 2, 1939.

NOTES AND REFERENCES

1. Malinowski, B., 1922.
2. Where the chief sources are one's own field experiences, it seems most appropriate to cite these. The experience which lies back of this article is as follows:

1. Use of a native language after preliminary lectures on another dialect by an ethnologist who spoke it, followed by intensive work with a literate English-speaking linguistic informant, and use of a Dictionary; ethnological work on an island where two natives spoke fluent English and three others some English. Samoa.

2. Use of a native language on which there was a brief published grammar, and a series of published texts, followed by work with a linguistic informant who understood some English and spoke fluent pidgin; ethnological work in a community where about 25 per cent of the men spoke pidgin, and a few small boys spoke some pidgin. Manus.

3. Complete non-use of the native language, and no use of interpreters, working entirely with English speaking informants, most of whom were women. Omaha Indians.

4. Use of a native language of which a very brief preliminary investigation of the grammar was available, followed by work with a linguistic informant who spoke plantation pidgin, and work in a community in which five adult men spoke pidgin. Arapesh.

5. Partial use of a native language on the basis of work

with a linguistic informant who spoke good Rabaul pidgin; work in a community in which about 15 per cent of the men spoke some pidgin—all of them very young. Mundugumor.

6. Partial use of the native language on the basis of work with a linguistic informant who spoke Rabaul pidgin; work in a community where some two dozen of the very young men spoke pidgin English. Tchambuli.

7. Use of the native language, on the basis of intensive linguistic work with a well-educated, English-speaking informant, followed by work with natives who spoke no English. Bali.

(Supervision of work of collaborators who used Malay instead of English, both in working on Balinese texts and with many of their informants, as well as speaking some Balinese.)

8. Use of the native language on the basis of a completely worked out grammar and sample texts, combined with individual teaching in the field, in a community where half the men under middle age spoke good pidgin, most of the men and small boys understood some pidgin, and one woman spoke pidgin. Iatmul.

I have had no experience of using, as a contact language, a European language not my own, or of using English as the contact language where none of the informants was literate.

3

On the Concept of Plot in Culture

Anthropology is such a young science and its materials are so rich and varied that the study of almost every culture suggests to the investigator new approaches to the material, approaches which are often not immediately applicable to other cultures. Although eventually every approach, every method of analysis which has proved fruitful in the study of a particular culture, must be systematized so that it has cross-cultural significance, and the absence of a special type of relationship between cultural phenomena must be integrated with the presence of this relationship elsewhere, the fact that this systematization is not yet possible need not discourage us from using as completely as possible the special leads which given cultures provide. Bali is an extremely rich culture, rich in symbolic forms which may be studied in relation to the type of personality which they express on the one hand, and help to create on the other.

Certain forms of trance in Bali illustrate particularly well one of these special approaches to the analysis of cultural forms, the idea of "plot," originally sketched out in almost allegorical terms by Freud,[1] and later reduced to terms more consistent with cultural diversity by Róheim.[2] This approach suggests a close and patterned relationship between a type of experience in early childhood, which is standardized for a given culture, and the ritual or other symbolic forms found in the same culture. This conception proves exceptionally fruitful in some cases; we do not yet know whether it is applicable to all cultures and caution must be observed even in its application to the analysis of a given culture.

Bali shares with many other regions of the world an emphasis upon trance states, as a way in which the will of extra-natural beings, the dead and the Gods, communicate through possessed persons with human beings. In many of its forms Balinese trance does not differ in any conspicuous way from trance in other parts of Oceania and even in other parts of the world. It is possible to distinguish various types of Balinese trance, from the simple spontaneous trance in which a private, unsanctified, and uninstitutionalized person falls down in a faint and makes associated comments, which may or may not be accepted as having supernatural import, through institutionalized seers and oracles who play an important role in providing the slight impetus toward change, toward the adoption of new forms of rituals, building new temples, consecrating new religious officials, etc., which is permitted within the rigid and static structure of Balinese society. There is another important variety of trance, in which the performers, called *sangijangs*, go into states preceded and followed by short deep trances, during which, in a condition which seems to parallel somnambulistic states induced by hypnosis, they perform a variety of stereotyped dances and dramatic representations. Although the details of the *sangijang* forms reflect important aspects of Balinese culture, they apparently do not necessarily depend upon any particular traumatic childhood experience, and they would presumably be possible to any child who had been exposed to the general impact of Balinese culture. I mean exposure in the sense that Chinese and Europeans living in Malay regions sometimes manifest the peculiar form of madness known as *amok* which is characteristic of that region of the world.[3] The proportion of individuals able to attain these special states, although heavily dependent upon local styles (e.g., in the ward of one large city almost every girl had been in trance at sometime during her childhood or young girlhood; in another village trials over two months failed to find a single suitable girl who would go into trance when presented with the customary stimuli), does not seem to differ radically from such distribution in other regions where trance has been institutionalized.

There is, however, one form of Balinese trance, which appears to bear a close relationship to a definite type of childhood experience in the child-mother relationship which is characteristic of Balinese culture—this is the so-called "kris dance," which is typically brought on by a whole or partial re-enactment of the *Tjalonarang* story. Careful records, in still photographs, cinema, and verbal accounts, have been collected to show this basic mother-child situation in which the mother overstimulates the young child by setting up jealousy and coquetry situations, borrowing younger babies and suckling them to arouse jealousy, placing younger babies on her own child's head, stimulating her child sexually, and offering no emotional rapport in return. The mother teases and flirts with the child until she produces either a state of hysterical delight or of violent weeping, and then, refusing to become involved herself, she turns casually to something else. By the time the Balinese child is three to four years old, it learns not to respond to this one-sided situation; instead, it withdraws more and more into itself, and the basis is formed for the insulated type of personality which is typically Balinese and which fails to enter into close emotional relationship with anyone, relying instead upon ritual and art as a means of emotional expression.

In this particular form of trance, which re-enacts this childhood experience, the preface to the trance is a theatrical performance based on the story of the witch who sends pestilence upon the land. She is unsuccessfully attacked by an emissary of the king of the country, who then is transformed into the dragon (*barong*)—a double mask representing a guardian supernatural potent against disease—who, accompanied by a series of human subjects armed with krises, attacks the witch in her supernatural masked form. The witch does not fight against her attackers. She merely looks at them and they fall to the ground to rise and attack again when she takes her eye off them. They attack her in hand-to-hand combat, and, indifferent, relaxed, casual—even as the mother who has teased her child into a temper tantrum—she reels back and forth, unhurt by their blows, and they fall down into deep trance, to be revived into a somnambulistic state by the dragon. Then, in a frenzy, they turn their krises, which were powerless against the witch, against their own breasts, pressing the kris points against areas of skin felt to be itching intolerably. Finally they fall to the ground and go again into either a limp or a rigid deep trance state from which they must be ceremonially roused with holy water and incense.

The "plot" correspondence here between the childhood experience and the special form of trance is very close and is supported by a variety of materials. But in assessing the theoretical importance of the concept of such plot correspondences it is necessary to bear in mind the probability that (1) standard traumatic experiences may occur in a culture without any such accurate ritual or artistic expression; and (2) ritual forms, originally developed or secondarily altered to correspond with the special culturally standardized childhood experience, may be borrowed and used by peoples whose cultures do not provide for any such childhood experiences. In order to establish, not the origin of the ritual in the childhood experience, but the mere fact of contemporary correspondence between childhood experience and ritual form, it is necessary to have full material on both aspects—the typical experiences of childhood and the ritual in question. There is at present no evidence to show that one can be inferred from the other. Our material suggests strongly that such correspondences as do exist can be most effectively studied by methods which record posture and gesture—i.e., photographic and ciné records and also native art products.

Transactions of The New York Academy of Sciences, Ser. 2, Vol. 2, No. 1, 1939.

REFERENCES

1. Freud, S., 1918.
2. Róheim, G., 1934; also Mead, M., 1935a.
3. Palthe, G. Van W., 1933.

4

Psychologic Weaning: Childhood and Adolescence

Cross-cultural comparisons suggest that it may be useful to describe, in a form suitable for scrutiny by students of psychodynamics, patterns of psychologic weaning in a number of contrasting cultures, and the behavior shown during childhood and adolescence, to explore the possibility that we may find systematic inter-relationships in these culturally determined sequences.

The study of homogeneous primitive societies presents us with examples of such sequences in a different form from the way in which they are experienced in the lives of individual patients within a heterogeneous rapidly changing society like that of the United States.[1] Where people live in small communities, closely bound together by ties of kinship and marriage, the individual version of family experience is subject to continuous reinterpretation; it is blurred, softened, or intensified in terms of the experience of other comparable members of the group. The distinction between sibling rivalry as experienced by children with siblings and by children without siblings does not present the same sort of contrast as it does in our culture; cousins, and even unrelated neighbors, provide sibling models toward whom a large amount of the culturally expected sibling behavior may be lived out. The position of just weaned child whose mother is expecting a baby and just weaned child whose mother is not expecting a baby are far closer together because there will be a style of behavior toward a child of that age manifested by the true parent and by all the parent surrogates in the group. In the same way, although only the occasional infant may have been subjected to some particularly drastic

41

form of weaning, such as the wreath of human hair on the nipple, used by some Iatmul mothers, the possibility of such weaning is implied in the way in which each mother handles her own and other mothers' overeager babies, in the teasing rebuke which is given to the child that still seeks the breast, in the tone of voice in which the word "wean" is spoken, and in attitudes toward hair which occur in other contexts. Thus every Iatmul experiences, to some degree, in some way, at some times in his life, the weaning with a wreath of hair, which is the actual concrete weaning experience of only some Iatmul babies. Where in a heterogeneous culture like ours, we find children who resent the historical fact that their mothers deviated from approved practice, or did not do something which was done for another child, in a homogeneous society, we are more likely to find the acceptance by the child that it has experienced behaviors which in actual fact it has not experienced. So that while a fantasy in a bottle-fed child of having been breast-fed, might have to be regarded as having special significance in the psychodynamic interpretation of a particular patient here, in primitive societies such as those of which I speak, such fantasies can be referred to the all-embracing and all-pervasive cultural context within which the occurrence or non-occurrence of each precise detail has to be given a different kind of meaning. (Even in our own heterogeneous society, we may argue that every child— even the few who are actually breast-fed and never took a bottle at all—experiences bottle feeding, as it later watches babies being bottle-fed, bottle feeds a doll, and reacts to figures of speech and nuances of voice based on the widespread practice of bottle feeding.)

So, in following the pattern of weaning for a series of South Sea societies,[2] it will be useful to focus attention upon the sequence of events disregarding such questions as "but what if the mother is not pregnant?" "but what happens if the child is the youngest?" as requiring a finer level of analysis than is called for by this preliminary discussion. If the sequence is regarded as central, it should be possible for students of psychopathology to invoke either individual cases, or clusters of cases, which show the same order of inter-relationship as that found in these patterned cultural behaviors.

The Samoan[3] infant was breast-fed by its mother; if her milk was inadequate, a specific wet nurse was sought, who was then rewarded for her services. Thus the infant was fed by only one woman, and slept with the woman—usually the mother—who fed it. From a few days after birth it was fed sugar cane juice, coconut milk, and premasticated papaya, fed it on the mother's finger, or on a piece of tapa. Substitute foods were available if the mother and baby were separated, but not a substitute human breast. The Samoans live in very large households, all of the women and girls hold and care for a baby. There is usually one small girl, an older sister or cousin, or affinal relative, aged five or six, who carries the child about most of the time, taking it back to its mother when it cries for food. The child sleeps with the mother as long as it is nursed, and is not weaned until it is two to three years old, unless the mother is pregnant again. Final weaning, which follows a long period in which more and more food has been substituted for the breast, and the child has seen less and less of its mother and more of its child nurse, is accomplished suddenly. The mother smears lemon juice on her breast, and the child goes to sleep with some other woman, usually an older woman, a grandmother or great aunt. At the actual weaning then a link which has been growing slighter through time, is severed suddenly, and the child nurse and the old grandmothers, already very important parts of the child's life, take over a more important role. The tie to the mother has been specific, concrete, and pleasurable, embedded in a variety of ties to women of all ages, all of whom have succored the child when it fell or was hurt, and none of whom have disciplined it, as the practice is simply to punish the child nurse if she lets the child in her charge cry and disturb the elders, defecate in an unsuitable place, or touch something that it should not touch. From the time of weaning on the child's relationship to its own mother is even slighter; it spends much of its time with the child nurse, often being carried long after it can walk because this saves the child nurse trouble.

Finally as a four or five year old, it tags along after the slightly older little girls, each of whom will have a baby on her hip or in tow. The child learns that the threat of crying can bring the small child nurse to heel, and during the end of early childhood becomes a petty tyrant. Then if the child is a boy, he will go through a period of some responsibility for a younger child, usually not as young an infant as that which would be entrusted to a girl, and in turn experiences the rebukes, cuffs, and reproaches which he brought down on his own child nurse's head. At the same time he will begin—together with other little boys—to hang about the fringes of older boys' activities. Here they are only tolerated as long as they are quiet and helpful, and they begin to cooperate in making themselves useful to the older boys. They form themselves into neighborhood gangs and when not helping with older boys' activities, engage in guerrilla warfare against the gangs of small girls.

A second weaning is meanwhile taking place between the little boy and his older "sisters" (all the girls classified as his sisters within the large household, as the brother and sister taboo comes into play), always at the instance of the younger child. The older girl speaks lovingly of her *tei*, younger sibling, but gradually the younger boy becomes "ashamed" and the taboo which means that brother and sister must avoid all contact with each other until old age—never talking together, except very formally on ceremonial occasions, never participating together in a group where there is laughter and joking—is put in force. Thus early childhood—as the period following the period at the breast—is finally inaugurated by the mother snapping the thread of breast feeding which has been growing thinner and thinner, and is ended by the child gradually breaking the tie with the elder sister, his child nurse, which replaced the mother's care. During the next few years until puberty, he will live as a member of the small boys' gang, having little contact with girls, fed and cared for and ordered about by all the elders of his household, cut off by the brother and sister taboo from all the girls of his own generation in the household.

At adolescence, his first sex experience will be—in almost every case—with an older girl, and will be patterned on the many love affairs which he has peeked at through childhood, when the children spend a good deal of time spying on lovers. Through a series of minor, unweighted sex episodes, he will gradually select, and be selected by, some particular girl with whom a more permanent liaison will be set up and ideally and usually, such a girl will come from a status acceptable to his own family, so that if pregnancy results, the marriage can be celebrated. Pregnancy so resulting is believed by the Samoans to be a sign that the pair are fitted for one another. After marriage, although divorce is easy, there is a high degree of fidelity, which reflects but slightly the apparent promiscuity of the adolescent period, as if the boy and girl found again the slender but specific gratifying relationship originally experienced at the mother's breast, so lightly and yet so definitely distinguished from the mass of other warm diffuse relationships which the little child experiences in the contacts with all the women of the household.

Crucial theoretical questions here would seem to be the relationship between the capacity for stable and happy marriage and the double weaning, first by the mother of the child, and then by the child of the child nurse, in which it may be that the weaning initiated by the child is, at least partially, a resolution of any rejection experienced in the weaning initiated by the mother, leaving the child free to form viable, stable sexual ties later, on the basis of wide adolescent experimentation.

Among the Mountain Arapesh,[4] the whole question of weaning is tied up with the requirements made on both parents for the protection of the growing child from any contact with its parents' sexuality. The father is not only expected to abstain from intercourse with the mother of the child, but if he has another wife, he is expected to abstain from intercourse with her also, and to sleep continently beside the mother and the newborn child. Only after menstruation has been re-established and the child itself is showing vigor, walking about, is this taboo relaxed. Proper keeping of the taboo means the postponement of another pregnancy until the child is at least about two years of age, and preferably older, and the weaning occurs gradually. During the suckling period, if the child is left by its mother, it is suckled by any other woman who has milk, but because of the very small size of Arapesh hamlets, there may not be such a woman. The child may be exposed to long hours without nursing, and occasionally without food, so that fear of food deprivation becomes interwoven with the feeding situation. The whole nursing and feeding is conducted with much pleasure and gentleness by the mother, and the deprivation is in spite of the mother's wish, due to some exigency of the very severe conditions of subsistence. When the child, whose parents have taken proper care of it by avoiding pregnancy, is between two and three, it is gradually verbally shooed away from the breast by the mother and other women, who tell it teasingly, and pleasantly: "Thou, child, hast had enough of milk. See, I am getting all worn out with feeding thee. And thou art far too heavy to carry about with me everywhere. Here, eat this taro and hush thy wailing." This very gradual weaning, in which more food is substituted for milk, the mother slipping small bits, gently, into the child's mouth, as its lips relinquish the breast for a moment, is the Arapesh ideal of weaning. If the mother becomes pregnant, so that the child has to be weaned on account of her pregnancy, the weaning pattern is very different. It is done harshly and abruptly by smearing mud on the nipples, which the mother pretends are feces, pantomiming disgust. These two methods are sufficiently different so that they are probably reflected in the behavior of individual children. I had only an opportunity to study two such children, and it was of course impossible to estimate how much weight to put on the weaning and how much on the general behavior of the parents who felt guilty about the whole situation. Whatever the actual behavior, the Arapesh agree that good parents favor the growth of the child above their own sexual activity, and that the result of active aggressive interest in sexuality is unpleasant and depriving. Children slip from babyhood into weaned childhood and from young childhood into adolescence very imperceptibly, tagging along after older relatives, all of whom are regarded as friendly and succoring. There is no patterning of relationship by kinship taboos, no gangs, no playful opposition between the sexes. Both sexes taboo

certain foods as they approach puberty to protect their
reproductive functions. Little boys learn from older boys
how to let blood from their penises to facilitate their
growth, and little girls at first menstruation learn how to
run stinging nettles in and out of their vulvas—also to
facilitate growth. Girls are betrothed in prepuberty and
go to live in the families of their future husbands, who
ideally are several years older. The new little wife is fed
by her future husband and his male relatives, until, after
she has matured and he has matured, the marriage is
consummated quietly, the actual time of consummation
unmarked. This gradualness of the weaning procedure is
mirrored in the gradualness of the absorption into the
marriage relationship, with food giving paralleling the slow
relinquishment of the breast and also the slow acceptance
of marital sexuality, which is valued directly as it is gentle,
unexciting, and domestic. A permanent fear of death by
sorcery as a result of sexual contacts with women from
other places, especially inland women, who are believed
to be more strongly, assertively sexed, remains. The type
of parent-child relationship, in which fostering and feeding regardless of sex of parent is emphasized during childhood, when the father takes almost as much care of the
child as the mother, is repeated in the marital pattern in
which the adolescent boy grows his wife and exercises
authority over her by virtue of having "made her body."
Then together they build up the body of the child by
repeated copulations which are regarded as "work"—as
opposed to copulation before conception occurs.

Among the Iatmul[5] of New Guinea, the child sleeps
with its mother, in a little bed of bark which is pushed
into the woven mosquito proof miniature room in which
the mother sleeps. The father dislikes the infant's excreta
and avoids the mother's sleeping basket as long as the
infant sleeps there. Thus a certain amount of rivalry is
set up between father and child. This is dramatized again
later when the father who takes an active interest in his
wife may try to get her to accompany him to the garden
—which includes an implication of sex activities in the
garden—and leave her walking, but still suckling child
behind. The child is treated by the mother as a willful
strong individual and is made to demand food vigorously

before she will feed it. Weaning has a repetitive, mock
quality in which the mother may wean her child by putting a wreath of hair around her breast, and then after
twenty-four hours relent, take it off, only to repeat this
later, perhaps once, perhaps more than once. Such weaning comes after the child has learned to walk about and
fend for itself, and to rely on food for actual nourishment.
The nearly weaned or just weaned child is quite independent, wanders about in the neighborhood of the
house, or is carried about by child nurses of either sex
as part of the children's playgroup. Then when a new
baby is born to the mother, or sometimes to some other
woman who stands as a mother—father's co-wife, father's
brother's wife, etc.—the child who has attained such
locomotor independence returns of his own accord to become part of the family constellation again, drawn by
interest in and rivalry for the baby. This rivalry with the
mother for the baby seems to be related to the way in
which the mother has always placed the child vis-à-vis
herself and has treated it as very strong and independent
since birth, and to the way in which the child has been
taught to demand food from the mother as from an
adversary of equal strength which she then gives warmly.
This return to the home will be repeated a second time
if another baby is born when the child is five or six, after
which both little boys and little girls become more independent, the boys playing, the girls working in groups.
Children's playgroups, in which adult life is acted out,
are formed by older girls and younger boys, in which the
girl remains the initiating and challenging person, and
the boy's first sex experience is as a very early adolescent
with an experienced girl of sixteen or seventeen. Her
teasing challenge becomes the pattern for initiating sex
experiences in later life, when a woman arouses a man's
desire by verbally questioning his masculinity. During this
entire period little boys see the adult men in limited
domestic contexts and on staged occasions involving elaborate theatrical display, in which women and children are
audience. At initiation, the boys are taken into the men's
group, allowed to enter the men's house, which is spoken
of as a womb, and ceremonially born into the men's
cult. When as young adolescents they attempt to rejoin

women's groups, still feeling more comfortable there, they are shooed back by the women, forced vis-à-vis the women to accept a masculine role which is harsh and exhibitionistic. This parallels childhood experience in which little boys hear constant mention of homosexuality, but are severely chastised by boys and men if they ever assume any semblance of a passive role. Thus weaning, acceptance of initiation and adult sexual activity, all have the same pattern in which the woman plays upon an assertiveness in the male which she has herself played a strong part in developing as a part of his initial close association with her.

Among the Manus⁶ of the Admiralty Islands, we find still another pattern. They are a prudish people; the wife may not tell her husband directly that she is pregnant, but instead will tell her own family. When the child is born her husband is excluded, and she is cared for by her brother's wife. During this first month after childbirth she has the new baby to herself. But then she is returned to her husband, and he begins to take a strong interest in the child. The child is kept in the house with the mother until it is about a year old, when the mother has to go back to heavy work, and the father, drowsy in the daytime from night fishing, takes over more care of the child. She is the disciplinarian, he the indulgent one who orders his wife to feed his child. The child is nursed at its demand or that of the father long after it is eating all kinds of food, and it may even have begun to smoke before it is weaned. Nursing itself is seen as giving food rather than giving the breast, so something material intervenes between mother and child. The final period of nursing is one in which the mother is wholly reluctant; she may already be far advanced in another pregnancy, and the child enforces its demands, assertively, as if from mastery rather than from desire. At the birth of the next child, the father takes much of the care of the knee baby,* and all through early childhood, both little boys and little girls are closer to their fathers than to their mothers, going with their fathers many places where their mothers cannot go because of the complicated taboos which exist

---

* Knee baby: penultimate child, the child that has been displaced by the birth of a younger sibling.

between women and their male affinal relatives. Little girls are withdrawn from this easy association with their fathers by increasing age and their own or their sisters' child betrothals which involve heavy avoidances of future husbands and male relatives-in-law. The little girl, denied the earlier association with her father, relapses into a woman's group where she does not re-establish relations with the mother, and the boy becomes more absorbed in an adolescent boys' gang, which later—in the days before government control—became the nucleus of a men's group which often carried off a neighboring woman as a prostitute. Any sex relations between the Manus adolescent boy and girl is heavily forbidden, under pain of supernatural penalties from jealous ancestral guardian ghosts. The boy's relationship with his future wife is further surrounded by shame because he will owe his right of access to her to a payment made by a relative, a debt which he will have to work out and for which he will have to feel ashamed until he has paid it off. In later life, his relationships to women will have three facets, affection and material help to his sisters, pornographic public joking with female cousins whom he cannot marry, and shame and disrespect toward his wife with whom he has sex relations, which is itself regarded as excretion, and with whose relatives he is continuously engaged in exacting exchanges of property.

In these four cases from the Southwest Pacific, it is possible to trace a correspondence between the way in which the child's physical relationship to the mother is patterned during nursing and weaning and the establishment of a physical sex relationship between man and woman later on. Thus the nursing and weaning situation may be seen as the prototype for heterosexual relationships. The paths taken by male and female to reach adulthood of course differ in the extent and time at which the male child and female child have to differentiate themselves from the mother. The acquisition of a sense of maleness and femaleness is complete enough in Samoa so that it is heavily reflected in childhood behavior and courtship is highly and specifically sexual. In Arapesh, the parental feeding role assumed by both sexes blurs the distinction between father and mother, and also overrides the specifically sexual aspect of the husband and wife relationship. In Iatmul, the stress on the willful demand-ingness of the child vis-à-vis the mother, is congruent with the later Iatmul high valuation of symmetrical, assertive relationships between men and women, com-bined with a high recognition of the complementary character of sex relations between men and women, which involve a reversal of role but not of pattern from the active mother thrusting her breast into an active infant's mouth to the active male relating himself to an active demanding female. Among the Manus, the separation of the parent-child relation and the marital relation, and the preference for father-child over mother-child relations is reflected in the later low value placed on specific sexuality, with parent-child ties regarded as both competing with and artificially holding together marriage relationships. The emphasis is upon reciprocal relationships, in which food, property, and semen pass from one person to another.

In describing these sets of regularities, I am making no claim for the adult pattern of behavior, characteristic of the society, having been developed as a projection of the child's experience. Rather, I am attempting to demon-strate the order of inter-relationship which can be found between learning patterns of children and adult patterns of sex behavior, in which the treatment of the child not only teaches the child, but reinforces in the adult, a style of human intercommunication which permeates the whole cultural pattern. The selection of weaning experience was made because it provides a point upon which it is easy to focus observation, not because weaning is given any crucial significance in a theory of cultural learning.

Psychosexual Development in Health and Disease, 1949.

REFERENCES

1. Mead, M., 1942b, 1942d, 1947b, 1947c.
2. For more intensive discussions of the learning patterns of these societies, see Mead, M., 1949a.

3. Mead, M., 1928a, 1928b, 1928c, 1930c, 1931, and 1937, Ch. IX.
4. Mead, M., 1935b, 1937, Ch. I, 1938, 1940c, 1947e, 1949c.
5. Bateson, G., 1936; Mead, M., 1940b 1941.
6. Fortune, R. F., 1935; Mead, M., 1930b, 1931, 1932, 1934, 1937, Ch. VII, and 1947a.

5

On the Implication for Anthropology of the Gesell-Ilg Approach to Maturation

One of the recurrent problems which face the anthropologist is the selection from current researches in our own culture of concepts which have cross-cultural promise, which are capable of a sufficient degree of heightened abstraction, or of extrapolation, so as to be useful in increasing our interpretation of other cultures.[1] Each time that a field of research is developed, by a scientist in our own society, there is a chance that a new tool will be provided to the field anthropologist. In remaining alert to such possibilities there are two cautions which are worth making. The anthropologist who goes into the field, well equipped with the most rewarding conceptual frame which he has found in some current psychological research, may confine himself to illustration of that theme, paying so much attention to the relationship between his data and the hypothesis in which he is interested that he will have no time or energy to spare for a fresh responsive approach to the *new* relationships among his data. When this is done, the results will be less rich, because while it may be useful to have some illustrations from primitive cultures of an hypothesis which was constructed to include, at least partially, the concept of culture, finding such illustrations is incomparably less important to the advance of science than is draining the last drop of new suggestive meaning from the culture being studied. If we arrange in a sequence work done among primitive peoples by individuals, either psychologists, psychiatrists, or anthropologists, with varying degrees of specificity in the hypotheses which they wished to test out, we find a

correlated difference among their results in the richness
and suggestiveness of the new hypotheses which are
brought back.[2]

But while there is real danger that some of the rewards
of months of painstaking field work, under difficult conditions, may be lost if the material is observed too rigorously from a predetermined point of view, there is also
the danger that without theoretical tools, the field anthropologist may not see enough and may not sense the significance of what he does see.

In selecting the developmental point of view, especially
some of the recent aspects of the Gesell-Ilg[3] approach to
the study of maturation, for discussion in an anthropological context, I have done so because I believe that
certain of the concepts emerging from this approach may
be of the very greatest importance to the field worker,
especially the field worker who is concerned with child
development as a major approach to the study of culture,
and also to the theoretical student who is looking for
convenient terms for expressing differences in the culturally determined character structure of members of
different cultures. But because I think it is so important,
I am going to discuss initially in some detail ways in
which it could be used which would lead not to greater
insight but rather to the opposite. Gesell has delineated
a sequence in maturation and, allowing for individual
differences—individual differences within which it may
ultimately be possible to discriminate types of maturation
—he has located nodal points in this sequence at definite
chronological-age points, with a plus or minus two
months, or six months or more, systematically implied if
not always explicitly stated. This sequence has been determined by the detailed study of middle-class children in
New Haven and its environs and is based on a very large
number of exceedingly detailed records. If the field worker
should take into the field the series of descriptive norms
which Gesell has established and simply attempt to verify
that the same norms did or did not obtain in a given
primitive culture, this would be of relatively little final
value for science. His conditions of observation would be
infinitely inferior to some of the highly controlled situations in which Gesell has worked; he would not be able

to extend his observations over anything like the number of years nor with the same large staff and battery of recording devices. The chance of his having enough cases to make his results in any way comparable would be minimal.

Nor approaching the matter from another angle is it possible to take the Gesell standards as a way of placing the age of infants whose age is not known. The field worker comes into the field to find some children whose age is already beyond the point at which accuracy of maternal reporting can be expected, although this point will vary from five or six days in some cultures to 210 days or larger calendrical units in others. It is then necessary to place the children which are being observed in some approximate age group, and the observer calls upon past clinical experience of infants, combined with such data as appearance of a first tooth, as a partial guide, supplemented whenever possible with other data, such as relative age of other children, puppies, ceremonial events with a known time-span or calendrical placing, etc.* But even though the Gesell descriptions of characteristic age behavior are so complete and contain statements of range, they would only provide an approximation, and because they are stated in relationship to a concrete American environment, might easily be misleading.

However, there is another level at which the Gesell-Ilg findings can be of the very greatest significance if we recognize that their observations provide us with a model, a basic way of thinking about the maturation of the individual, in terms of which any given culture's expectations and demands can be calibrated. They themselves use their description of maturation rates and rhythms, differential capabilities, and individual differences in development as a set of criteria which culture, at least a democratic culture, should meet. However, for research purposes we can use these descriptions which, properly abstracted from the cultural matrix, give us a picture of the pattern of human

* In Bali, normally ages are not given accurately beyond the second *oton* (210 day unit), but because the date of the earthquake in 1918 was known and because the Balinese had named children born during the earthquake, I Gedjer (I Earthquake), it was possible to identify 21-year olds in 1939.

growth, as a means of *studying* cultural developmental mechanisms without necessarily evaluating them. (Such study should lead in turn to further criteria for evaluation if we find, for instance, that the effect of asking a child to do a too difficult task, or keeping him at a too simple one, may contain sufficient rewards in general personality differentiation to justify it, in spite of its demonstrated discrepancy with an innate growth rhythm.)

Although the progressive application of this type of thinking will doubtless show a series of more complex problems, it will be sufficient here to point out a few major ways in which it can be used. Dr. Ilg uses the spiral as her mechanical model, which provides for the concept of continuous growth that nevertheless contains both upward and downward gradients, and allows for the systematic inclusion of repetitions of behavior characteristic of previous stages, as part of growth, rather than as regression. This is an exceedingly important distinction to bear in mind, because the quite different psychiatric concept of regression,[4] in which an individual fails to conquer his reality problems on one level of maturity and so regresses to an earlier technique of adjustment, is itself a useful concept and one with cross-cultural validity. (We may for instance study the extent to which different cultures institutionalize regression—lying in bed, being nursed and fed, etc., in the case of illness or in various life crises and *rites de passage*. We may also with adequate psychiatric equipment study the types of regression which are characteristic of different cultural character structures.) But there is an important difference between temporary or permanent failure to adjust and consequent regression, and the discontinuities of normal growth, by which the growing child concentrates now upon one segment of behavior, now upon another, learns a new skill only temporarily to relinquish mastery in another. The intermediate periods, when some former interest or skill seems to have vanished and when behavior characteristic of an earlier period of growth appears, are seen as the downsweep of the spiral, while the forerunners of a new period are seen as the upsweep.

In the maturation process, certain nodal points of consolidation may be recognized, stages in the sequence in which there are no extreme discontinuities apparent so that the child seems especially well balanced and able to confront life. Furthermore, this spiral model can be used to express another phenomenon which has been observed in the Yale clinic, the recurrence of certain types of adjusting, as to eating, or reading, etc., in definite sequences. So Dr. Ilg is able to place the periods at which a child's appetite is likely to alter, and say: "If it does not happen within the next two or three months, then it will not happen for another two years. At about age 'Y' you can expect another period of potential shift, etc." Or she can say: "If a child has not shown some interest in letters by Y age, it is probable that at the next period of paying attention he will not fully learn to read—that reading will not come until about such and such a time." As individual differences are discernible in the duration and intensity of different interrelated points on this growth spiral, it becomes possible to characterize different types of children as those who show different patterns of sequential repeat, stressing more the type of development which comes around 4, 6, and 8 years, for instance, or around 5, 7, and 9 years. (The exact and probably logarithmic relationships between these repetitive emphases in sequential development have yet to be determined.)

We can now take these three concepts, a rhythm of growth with a definite sequence which can be distorted or by-passed, but not hurried; a concept of growth as proceeding from periods of consolidation to periods of expansion to new consolidation, so that different points on the spiral will have a different quality (in ability to adjust, vulnerability to external pressures, accidents, etc.); and a concept of patterned individual differences expressed in differing emphases on different phases of the growth process. If we attempt to apply these concepts to studies of culture, we find that we may look at any culture as to whether the cultural expectations of growth anticipate, coincide with, lag behind or fail to recognize altogether, the innate growth pattern in the generalized form in which it may be attributed to all human infants. There are cultures like the Arapesh[5] in which crawling is discouraged before the appearance of teeth, or like the Balinese[6] in which a child cannot set foot on the ground

—and therefore has little freedom off the carrier's hip—until it is six and one-half months old. Cultures which strap or bind their infants interfere with the child's capacity for certain types of motor activity. While it has been reported that students found that Balkan infants who had been swaddled in a very few days attained the level of movement which other infants would have arrived at through a series of stages, we do not yet have any way of measuring the change in quality which is introduced when an activity is engaged in later than was organically possible. There seems every possibility that the pattern will be altered and that, while children in all cultures learn to walk, the way in which they learn to walk and the time at which they learn to walk, in relation to their actual innate maturational capacity, may be very significant as a factor in personality formation. For instance, the Balinese child is encouraged to walk earlier, as creeping is culturally abhorred, and the child has frequent experiences of overextension and loss of balance; and loss of balance is a preoccupation of Balinese throughout their lives, playing a role in their rejection of alcohol, disorientation after traveling in motor cars, etc. At each stage the degree of discrepancy or exact correspondence will be registered at a deutero level[7] and become a factor in later development. So throughout the maturation cycle, the cultural pattern is one factor in the development of the total personality. The innate rhythmic maturation potential is a second.

If one compares this hypothesis with the *tabula rasa* school of thought, it will be seen how much more complicated and how much more systematic it is. Each act of learning will have occurred in one of a series of definite relationships to the organism's degree of readiness for that act, and from these relationships deutero learnings will occur which may be finally stated in such terms as attitude toward effort, trust in physical environment or in own skill, etc. The differences among cultures in which readiness for a given piece of learning is looked for, and cultures in which the importance of a given item of learning is so emphasized that the child is prematurely hurried into it, and cultures in which it is felt that capacities for behavior are revealed at socially premature points and so need be retarded or interfered with are very striking. Once we seriously begin to explore cultures from this point of view, we may find, for instance, that the learnings which a culture most successfully transmits are those which are most closely attuned to the human growth rhythm, or we may find that hypertrophy of certain skills or arts may be due to such a coincidence of emphasis and timing. Throughout such inquiries it is necessary to recognize that such differences may be due, for instance, not to the age at which a child is taught to draw, but to the presence or absence of opportunities for certain sorts of free and certain sorts of precision movements at a stage before the child would be capable of drawing. The Gesell-Ilg method makes it possible to follow through the development of special bodily emphases or special emphases on segments of the body, as on arm movements, leg movements, or the importance of the head, as these reappear in different stages in the maturation sequence.

The most striking differences will be found between those cultures in which learning is regarded as an individual matter, where the appearance of walking, talking, heterosexual expression, etc., is waited for until the individual displays readiness, and those cultures in which by the use of a calendar, or through a ceremonial of initiating novices in groups, or because of the extreme fluctuations of seasonsal life, a new step of development is enforced, either upon an individual or upon a group with very slight recognition of degree of readiness. Initiation ceremonies for adolescents, which include the eight-year-old children of especially important men and the twenty-year-old who went away to work before he was initiated, are examples of this order. So are such pediatric dicta in our society as that a "baby should feed itself at fifteen months," and that an infant which weighs seven pounds and over should be fed at four-hour intervals—from birth on—while an infant which weighs one ounce less should be fed at three-hour intervals. Although measurements enormously enhance this tendency to substitute man-made patterns for innate patterns by the use of calendar, clock, scales, calipers, etc., essential contrasts of this sort may be found in cultures in which there is nothing but the rhythm of the seasons and the sun to go on, or in which through ceremonial calendars there is artificial structuring of behavior. A striking instance of numerical imposition is the frequent relationship between the sacred number of a group and the day on which the umbilical cord "falls off": in Bali, where the mother is in a special state for the first three days after birth, the cord falls off in three days; in Iatmul,[8] where five is the magic number, it falls off in five. Such usages reinforce the imputation to the organism of the cultural pattern, an imputation which is justified in detail in the case of hunger at meal-times or sleepiness at bedtime, where innate rhythms have been altered to suit a cultural time-scale. However, the difference between the sleep of those who went to sleep when they were tired as children, rather than by the clock, and those whose sleep has been patterned and decreed is probably something which will ultimately be measured and studied.

The second relevant concept is the concept of periods of varying degrees of consolidation and expansion, as the child learns, consolidates its learning, casts back toward older forms, and projects forward new forms. Some of these periods may be sufficiently well defined—for all children—so that it is possible to discuss the way in which some cultural demands coincide with periods of relative stability or vulnerability. According to Gesell and Ilg, our national custom of sending children to school for the first time at six is an example of such a significant lack of correspondence, five being a period when a higher state of consolidation is to be expected. (We do not of course yet have any way of knowing to what extent these periods are internally regulated and to what extent culture can alter them. The characteristic behavior of a six-year-old, especially in dependence upon parents, may be as related to an intensification in some earlier period of some items in our child care pattern, as it is to the current state of the growing organism.)

However, the systematic occurrence of such periods of varying consolidation presents a good case for the possibility of an innate pattern of growth which provides a ground plan. Adolescence is of course the most striking instance of this phenomenon. There are very few cultures in which the disruptive concomitants of adolescence are so successfully muted as in Samoa.[9] It is possible that one might use care of the sick as a model in thinking about this problem. An individual may have a disease which will run its course so that recovery will set in quickly under conditions of mild rest. In some cultures, however, under such circumstances, sweat baths, religious pilgrimages, bloodletting, or other measures will be decreed which will aggravate the condition, while in other cultures—of which our own has been a sample, in the upper economic levels—a degree of total rest may be imposed which is also inappropriate and which will also aggravate the patient's state. The more intense and complex the state of the patient becomes, however, the more chance there is that the treatment may lack certain necessary elements. When we are dealing not with a temporary illness but with a state of temporary out-of-phaseness peculiar to a stage of growth, the situation becomes all the more complicated because many of the cultural conditions necessary for an easy adolescence may be enhanced by patterns laid down in early childhood, in methods of feeding, in relationships to parents and siblings, etc. For example, if a child makes a successful separation away from his mother *before* the next child is born, so that the separation is seen not as due to the entrance of a rival but as part of the child's own natural exploratory tendencies, the break with the parents which comes with leaving home or with marriage may be of a very different character.

In spite of these necessary considerations, the extent to which in different cultures individuals are put under pressure at points of maximum or minimum ability to stand those pressures is exceedingly important. Where, for any reason, there is anxiety lest a child display behavior characteristic of an earlier age (as among some American Indians watching their male children for signs of manhood or in our cultural attitudes toward enuresis), or where there is anxiety about precocity (as in Samoa, in regard to the overt display of social initiative, or among us in regard to sex) either characteristic of the growth spiral—the downgrade with recurrence of earlier forms of behavior or the upgrade with its premonitory bits of future behavior—may selectively come in for cultural disapproval. A mother may fly into a tantrum when her knee baby begins to crawl or seeks her breast at the funeral of its younger sibling. A flirtatious glance from a girl who has not passed through her puberty ceremony may arouse harsh measures.

So there are useful implications in this delineation of periods of differential degrees of consolidation, whether we consider the degree to which in a given culture a given period, like adolescence, is made difficult or easy, whether we consider the extent to which precocity or slow development is culturally disapproved, or whether we consider the extent to which cultural devices protect the individual during periods of vulnerability, such as "weaning," "acquiring a new skill like walking or talking," "birth of a sibling," puberty, first parenthood, climacteric, etc. (It will be noted that I am assuming that the Gesell-Ilg approach should apply to the whole life cycle and not only to the rising curve from conception to maturity.) Even such cultural attitudes as the Samoan acceptance of a "state of unwillingness or disgruntlement," or the English acceptance of "mood" in children may provide a sheltering state within which the individual can develop more easily.

The third facet of the Gesell-Ilg approach, the possibility of discerning a series of patterns or types among the individual differences, still awaits more work and need only be mentioned here. If it becomes possible to discriminate types of maturation and to place them schematically on different sides of the spiral-of-growth model, we will then have an instrument which will make it possible to deal systematically with the hypothesis that in different cultures different constitutional types have been institutionalized. It has seemed clear for a long time that the best approach to this problem would be through differentiating types of maturation as opposed to working with types of adult constitutional difference. But the material has never been available to do this. If it were found—from the examination of Gesell's data and other similar types of data—that types of innate maturation style could be distinguished, these differences could be counterpoised against detailed records of cultural expectations, and we would be able to study those cultures which had come to specialize in exactly hitting a natural rhythm, peculiar to one constitutional type, and also those cultures where child-rearing practices tend toward smoothing out the differences by superimposing patterns specifically congenial to no type, or intermediate patterns which blur the distinctions between types. It should also provide a device by which such problems as class and sex typing and regional differences in larger cultures can be approached. Finally, by giving us a conceptual tool with which to handle the question of deviance, it will provide a method for studying social change, which may be seen as becoming effective to the extent that the customary patterning of maturation is altered for part or all of the population, thus embodying in their character formation the character changes appropriate to the changed cultural state.

American Anthropologist, Vol. 49, No. 1, 1947.

REFERENCES

1. Bateson, G., 1932, 1941b; Mead, M., 1930a, 1932, 1942b, 1942d, 1944c, 1945c.
2. Dennis, W., 1940; DuBois, C., 1944; Erikson, E. H., 1943; Gorer, G., 1938; Nadel, S. F., 1937a, 1937b; Whiting, J. W. M., 1941.
3. Gesell, A. L., and F. L. Ilg, 1943; McGraw, M. B., 1935.
4. Kris, E., 1944.
5. Mead, M., 1935b.
6. Bateson, G., and M. Mead, 1942.
7. Bateson, G., 1942b.
8. Bateson, G., and M. Mead, 1951.
9. Mead, M., 1928a.

6

Character Formation and Diachronic Theory

As anthropologists, we deal with two levels of analysis—on the one hand, the study of the structure and functioning of social groups, in which, although detailed observations may be made on individual behavior, the psychology of the individual is not examined; and, on the other, the study of the relationships between the psychology of the individual, the culture within which he lives, and the structure and functioning of the social groups of which he is a member. Radcliffe-Brown has repeatedly argued that it is possible to give a self-contained account of a society without recourse to any examination of the psychological structure of its individual members, and without invoking in any way the individual differences among them, except in so far as these differences are formally patterned. Thus the study of culture as an abstraction based on observed traditional behavior of the members of a given group at a given period of time has proved a workable approach to a synchronic statement about many primitive societies.*

---

* I say "many societies" advisedly, because in giving an account of Arapesh socio-economic life,[1] I found it impossible to give an adequate sociological statement which did not include the specification of each actor in terms both of his social position and of his personality. The specification in terms of social position alone could, of course, be made without invoking individual psychology, and I am not prepared to say that another investigator, with a more purely sociological frame of reference, might not have devised a way of presenting the peculiarities of Arapesh social organization without this extra degree of specification.

64

However, as soon as any diachronic questions are raised the whole position is altered. If we are to avoid statements of action at a temporal distance, such as "the slowness of the industrial revolution in Germany was a major cause of World War I," or "the open frontier was responsible for the fluidity of the American class system," and substitute for them scientifically valid descriptions of social process—descriptions of how, in fact, an antecedent condition of society is converted into some subsequent condition—it seems necessary to include in our investigations a study of the individuals who are concerned in the change. We need to consider such individuals both as representatives of cultural regularities which are themselves undergoing change, and as specified persons who have been able to act in given ways because of the peculiarities of their own life histories. Many of the changes which are recorded in the long time spans of conventional history (such as "the decay of the monarchy" or "the rise of popular government") occur sporadically in the behavior of individuals, and only gradually become consolidated into identifiable pattern changes. While such changes are going on, innumerable moments of choice occur, and the explanation of the choices taken may often lie in idiosyncratic factors in the lives of key individuals. It seems probable, therefore, that, as we approach a study of diachronics, making contemporary studies of social change as it occurs, rather than relying upon reconstructions from haphazardly preserved and fragmentary materials, it will be necessary to develop methods of dealing with the relevant aspects of the individual psychology of the participants.* Any systematic attempt to

* Recent mathematical studies[2] make it possible to examine these questions with somewhat more rigor. Von Neumann is concerned only with "static" (i.e. "synchronic") analysis, and demonstrates, as I understand it, that in those conceptual games in which the players rationally seek to form coalitions (i.e. allegiances, segments of social organizations, etc.) a self-contained description of the "solution" will include: (1) a statement of the number of players; (2) a list of the rules; (3) an externalistic description of the psychology of the players, each of whom, in the Von Neumannian games, is by hypothesis specifically described as completely rational, i.e. able to solve

include the psychological structure of individuals must rely, of course, not only upon an adequate psychological theory, but also upon adequate cultural theories regarding the process of cultural standardization of behavior, the nature of character formation, and the way in which idiosyncratic behavior is to be referred systematically to a cultural and societal base. Such an adequate theory will be dependent upon theoretical advances in a number of different fields (e.g. the fields of neural codification, perception, *Gestalt*, developmental psychology, motivation, learning, constitutional type, formal analysis of social interaction, etc.). This paper will attempt to introduce a preliminary degree of order into one aspect of this problem. It will deal with the sorts of regularities which

---

all problems of strategy presented by the game, and as motivated only in terms of a single linear value scale; (4) a statement of the "conventions and standards of behavior" specific to the given system of coalitions; and (5) a list describing the positions taken by the identified players in the system of coalitions.

From this we may judge that a purely empirical psychological description of the individuals will suffice for sociological purposes. We shall need to know their system of values, which may be complete, and their species of "rationality," i.e. a description of the formal relations between their courses of action and the contexts in which they occur; but we shall not require any understanding of the internal workings of their brains, though any such understanding may, of course, help us to write our externalistic description.

The step from the hypothetical Von Neumannian game played by definable "players" to a human society composed of human beings is fraught with difficulty, but it is profitable at least to examine the nature of the difficulties which we face. Human beings *learn*. This means that their degree and species of "rationality" and their motivational systems become a function of past sequences of events, and still more important, that the rules of the game and the "conventions" of the particular solution become in part incorporated into the psychology of the players. It is this last peculiarity of human systems which makes the psychology of learning crucial to diachronic study. When we are discussing changes in the rules or conventions it is vital to know how far these are incorporated in the psychology of the individuals and the general characteristics of change in such incorporations.[3]

can be discriminated in the character structures of individuals in societies which are changing at different rates and with different degrees of culture contact.

The problems of describing the correspondences between the structure of a homogeneous, slowly changing society and the character structure of the individuals who embody the culture of that society are beginning to be defined.[4] We have blocked out conceptually a large number of such areas as: the relationship between the representations of family structure and political structure in the psychology of the individual, or the relationship of both family and political structure to the conception of the supernatural; the pattern of sequences of initiative and response characteristic of parent-child or child-child relationships as they appear also in the interaction between master and servant, leader and follower; and the correspondences between the types of sanction used in a society and the types of conscience structure found in the individuals. We have already a considerable amount of observational work on, and analysis of, these problems, and, while the subject has in no sense been fully explored, some of the outlines at least may be said to have been sketched in.

In this preliminary attempt to introduce one degree of order into the data on cultural change, the unique features of each society and the special insights to be derived from a study of its particular institutions will no longer be emphasized. Instead, attention will be focused on those regularities of character formation which are functions of cultural homogeneity. Here we shall be dealing with well-described societies, about which formal statements can be made with considerable confidence. On the other hand, all statements of regularities postulated for changing culture contact societies will necessarily be tentative and, to a degree, suggestive rather than systematic.

The terms "homogeneous" and "slow-changing" will be used as synonyms, provided the rate of change of items of culture is less than the rate at which adults can assimilate the new items.* Cultures to which these terms apply

* This use of the word "homogeneous" does not exclude caste societies or societies with many different sub-groups, so long as

will be contrasted with those which are changing rapidly. No rapidly changing culture has real homogeneity, since rapid change results in differences between generations comparable to differences in culture, in that there are groups of individuals, belonging to different generations, who embody different discriminable attitudes.*

As relevant characteristics of personality development in homogeneous and slowly changing societies, we may identify: the *sequential consistency* between the experience of a growing child at one period and at another; the *summation* or total expression of the gamut of cultural experience in the behavior of the adult members of the society; the *prefiguring* of future experience as the child sees others go through sequences through which he will later go; the *consolidation* of past experience as the growing individual sees younger individuals go through se-

---

the relationships among such groups are part of the common shared culture and change slowly. Thus gypsies, foreign migratory workers, dissident religious sects, and the like, may come to be so included in the recognition of the other members of a culture as not actually to interfere with its homogeneity.

* For a discussion of the comparability of theories of contact between members of different cultures and members of different generations, see Bateson's "Culture Contact and Schismogenesis." [5] But, however systematically useful it may be to compare generation contact under rapid social change with contact between cultures suddenly juxtaposed, there is still the possibility that, as our psychosomatic conceptions develop, we may find that the biological nexus existing in one case but not in the other may have very significant implications for differences in the personality. Whether the new learning occurs in the family situation or outside it may also be very significant. Thus, the children of an oriental people who import western furniture and learn to sit on chairs by preference whereas their parents sit upon them only with difficulty on state occasions may have learned something radically different in kind (i.e. to do easily what their parents do with difficulty), from that which is learned by oriental children who learn in school a form of behavior which their parents continue to repudiate, and so have learned to do with difficulty something which their models, the European teachers, do with ease. Undoubtedly a higher level of abstraction would bring these two conditions within one conceptual scheme again, but at this early stage of formulation it seems unwise not to leave them differentiated.

quences culturally identical with those through which he has passed; and the increasing *automaticity* of behavior and the consequent increasing *sureness* which accompany maturation.[6]

These characteristics of growing up in a homogeneous society need little elaboration for anthropologists, who will recognize at once that an indulgent childhood and a harsh initiation—or an exacting childhood and indulged adolescence—may coexist within the learning pattern of a given culture, and that experience of such contrasts may have consistent implications for character structure. They will often have documented the extent to which a single act—the presentation of a gift, the avoidance of an affinal relative, the arrangement of an offering—contains within its ritual idiom the major presuppositions of a culture. Whether we describe the resulting personality types in words implying ethical judgment (e.g. attributing value to them as having dignity or denying them value because they lack the ideas of progress and the divine discontent bred of sharp cultural contact), or, in time, develop some neutral terms for the purpose is not relevant here. The products of homogeneity are a vanishing type at this period in history, but, as they constitute the group participating in the primary phase of culture contact, an accurate appraisal of the regularities in their character formation is essential.

By "primary culture contact" I shall mean those situations in which an individual reared in one cultural setting has to adjust, either as an immigrant or as a native into whose group others immigrate, to another set of cultural values, both sets of values coming from homogeneous, slowly changing cultures. Whenever one part of this contact relationship is no longer to be referred to a homogeneous culture, but rather to some later stage of culture contact, certain complexities are added to the picture. If, for example, a regiment of soldiers, all from the same remote rural region of the occident, come into face-to-face relations with a non-occidental people, the situation may have primary culture contact character. If, on the other hand, the regiment is composed of men drawn from the mixed population of a metropolitan city, the contact may contain secondary as well as primary culture contact features. A full "secondary culture contact" condition occurs when both sets of individuals under discussion have been reared in groups already affected by primary or secondary culture contact, and in which representatives of homogeneous cultures are relatively rare, even aberrant. Because there may be any number of varieties of such culture contact, no rigid distinction can be made between primary and secondary culture contact. Even a very loose distinction, however, seems to be useful, although, of course, actual situations will not, in most cases, be as clear-cut as any systematic discussion makes them seem.

In primary culture contact the impact on character formation will differ systematically as between the effects of the new environment on the personalities of the immigrants and the effects of such immigration of members of other cultures on the personalities of the native members of the community. Among the immigrants we find a variety of adjustments, all derived from the fact that the immigrant brings to the new environment a personality shaped in a previous and different environment. He may, while living and working in the new culture, continue to refer all of his behavior to the values of his original culture, adjusting only to the concrete realities of his new situation—learning proper names, bus routes, how to give change—but continuing to interpret these activities in the old terms. He may enter the new culture so determined to become a part of it that he actually succeeds in putting large sections of his former life and values out of his consciousness, and even his use of his mother tongue may become stumbling or disappear altogether. He may pattern his relationship to the new culture in terms of work alone, continuing to live in a cultural enclave in all other respects. He may work among immigrants from his original culture but marry a wife from the new culture and channel his culture contact relationships through a changing home pattern. He may continue to preserve only single items from the old culture—continue to take a newspaper from his former country, maintain membership in a national organization, or insist on the familiar old rituals at holiday time or for *rites de passage*, and so on.

We may next consider the native population into

whose society immigrants come. The content is of another order here, whether the immigrants enter in superordinate relationships as governors and teachers, in coordinate relationships as traders or travelers, or in subordinate relationships as slaves, unskilled workers, or performers of socially devalued tasks. The study of this sort of contact situation may increase our understanding of the differences between culture contact and generation break. The native remains among his own people, surrounded by an environment to each detail of which he has learned to respond in a culturally coherent manner. Into this environment intrude individuals who either take the place of familiar figures or introduce into his life new types of events toward which he has no traditional behavior. His habitual responses are interrupted and distorted, even as he himself attempts to pursue an even course in a familiar world. As he makes one ineffective attempt after another to evoke intelligible responses from the immigrant—who stands in a familiar place and is often clothed like the native himself, but whose posture and gestures are all keyed to a different emphasis—the result is not a feeling that he must review his own character, but a feeling that his world has been fragmented. "In the beginning God gave to every people a cup of clay from which they drank their lives—our cup is broken," said the California Indians; "We have lost our road," said the Plains Indians, as the figures and forms of an immigrant and alien culture crowded into their lives.[7]

The position of members of the older generation faced by drastic alteration in the behavior of their sons' generation is somewhat analogous to that of the native whose orientation is disturbed by the invasion of his familiar world by individuals with different sets of habits. The members of the older generation still see the cultural scene as theirs, and the behavior of the next generation as inappropriate and disruptive. In occasional instances, of course, the culture of the next generation may be accepted by the older generation as more valid than their own, and in that case they may invade it. Their disorientation is then more like that of the immigrant, while the younger generation is subjected to a disorientation more like that of the native.

Secondary culture contact, even in its very simplest forms—as in the case of children of a group of Sicilian immigrants to a rural American community, or American Indian children whose parents have just been placed on a reservation—is a great deal more complicated than primary culture contact. The growing child receives simultaneously impacts reflecting the original cultural values of his parents and impacts from the contemporary culture in which he is growing up. If his parents migrated from a rural economy to a large industrial center, he experiences a disciplinary pattern shaped on the farm combined with a wage-earning pattern fitted to the city. If his parents have come from another country, the language spoken at home may come to be a symbol of one part of life, that spoken at school of quite a different part. If his parents belong to a native group whose way of life has been disrupted by immigrants, he will experience no such sequence, but instead will be presented with both the native ways of his parents and the new ways of the immigrants as parts of one world in which he is being reared. Perhaps a useful analogy here is the matter-of-factness with which the child of parents who have seen the invention of the automobile or the airplane accepts automobiles, airplanes, and horses as all equally intelligible parts of transportation, without any realization of the sequence of invention. Events which have been sequential in the lives of his forebears become contemporaneous in his own life, and his responses will differ accordingly.

Individuals reared in a secondary culture contact situation which has become stabilized may show a considerable degree of regularity in their character structure. In the United States, certain expectations may reasonably be entertained of the children of immigrant parents. Parental values will decrease in importance, and children and adolescents will turn more to their contemporaries for approval and disapproval. Sanctions, such as shame and pride, appropriate to such a horizontal organization will appear. If such a second generation group forms either a very large majority or a very small minority in a given society, the process of stabilization will be easier than if the group which has experienced secondary culture contact and the group that has not are more evenly matched in size.

The patterns of behavior developed by the second generation are likely to be thin, but sufficiently reliable and internally consistent to permit of viable relationships both with other second generation persons* and with native members of the country in which they live. However sharp the contrast—whether it be between a nomadic North American Indian tribe and New England-bred farmers, between South American Indians and Italian immigrants, between Lapps and Russians, or Eskimos and Danes—the individual who is reared in the culture contact situation still learns that there are systematic patterns of behavior. There will be conflicts, especially in the relationship between parents and children, but, if no new changes take place, the second generation may be expected to develop a type of character structure upon which a different but integrated culture can be built.

If, however, the growing child experiences not one simple contrast in the behavior of those about him, but a great variety of degrees of contrast, we have a still more complicated situation. This condition is becoming increasingly characteristic of the modern world, in which individuals and groups migrate from one country to another, live, not in enclaves, but intermingled with members of groups in different culture contact phases, move easily from one type of industrial pursuit to another, oscillate between rural and urban economies, and make great shifts in class alignment in a very few years. Children grow up in homes in which each parent represents a different form

---

* The development of the boys' gang in large American cities is a typical example. Born of European parents who are no longer able to serve as models, and reared in a world which demands that parents accord applause to their children (which the European parents are unable to give) the adolescents segregate themselves into a world of their own, in which the values of the gang leader and of the gang members are paramount over the values of the larger society. The boarding-school, which, on a small scale, attempts to substitute a new standard culture for the diversities of the homes from which individuals come, also tends to develop the same sort of overriding emphasis upon the immediate judgment of the group of contemporaries.

of secondary culture contact; all four grandparents may have different backgrounds. Teacher, physician, nurse, social worker, policeman, grocer—each in turn represents some different form of culture conflict or generation conflict. The child who is reared in a homogeneous culture undergoes a large number of experiences which are all part of one whole, however great the apparent discontinuities among them. The child whose parents have undergone primary culture contact, experiences, in confused and often unsystematic fashion, two sets of internally coherent patterns. But for the modern child in a modern city, virtually all coherence disappears. Each act which the child encounters as he is fed, bathed, dressed, hushed to sleep, and wakened again may stem from some different background, and there may be no consistency between any two of them. Gentleness of touch and ferocity of corrective methods alternate without meaning, and rewards and punishments follow no recognizable sequence. Clothes are unadapted to activities, furniture unadapted to ways of sleeping and sitting, cutlery and crockery unsuited to the ways in which the child is taught to eat and drink. The arrangement of every room is unpredictable; the electric switch is seldom in the same place. A hand held out for help may meet instead a slap, a pinch, a lollipop.

Out of a social structure which permits modern man such mobility, both horizontal and vertical, which places hardly any restraint on the cultural gap he may attempt to bridge by marriage, which provides an economy no longer requiring high skill and long habituation, there has developed a learning situation which is producing a special type of character formation. This new type of character structure is bound to become more characteristic of ever wider areas of the world, unless the changes now in progress are arrested by totalitarian regimes of enforced homogeneity. We do not yet know whether it is a type of character structure which will be capable of building up new social forms after the "residue of an age of faith" is exhausted.

It is possible, however, to advance some preliminary hypotheses about the order of regularities which will be found in the character structures of those reared under continually shifting conditions of secondary culture contact, where rapid technological changes, sharp generation conflicts, and frequent new migrations prevent any stable second generation pattern from developing. The illustrations will be taken from the American scene, with an assumption that comparable features would be found elsewhere.

First, the growing child develops an approach to life which I, stressing the habit of taking each situation as a single unit and adapting rapidly and fully to it, have called *situational*,[8] and Erikson, stressing the type of commitment which occurs when every situation in life must be so regarded, has called *tentative*.[9] Thus we have the extreme surface openness of the American character, with its capacity for rapid intimacy and rapid acceptance of group membership, and also the lack of expectation of the coherence or permanency characteristic of homogeneous cultures.

Second, there is a tendency to reduce all values to simple scales of dollars, school grades, or some other simple quantitative measure, whereby the extreme incommensurables of many different sets of cultural values can be easily, though superficially, reconciled and placed in a hierarchical order. Such a reduction of incommensurable values appears to be a usual phenomenon in societies which have recently undergone marked changes involving culture contact. The fairly recent cultures of the American Plains Indians, in which groups with different traditions all adjusted to the buffalo-hunting horse culture which developed after the discovery of America, show a curious resemblance to the present American culture, where money income or the size of one's name in neon lights are analogous to "counting coup" as a measure of success. The rapidity of the spread of an institution like the Ghost Dance may also be referred to the way in which a new, simple value scale simplifies intolerable conflicts resulting from contrasts in culture.*

* In a comparative study of thirteen primitive societies,[10] we found that "in three competitive cultures" (as distinguished from the other ten) "there is no way of measuring success except by comparison with another's, and there are no fixed positions to which an individual can attain without fear of

It is in these latter phases of secondary culture contact, in which the child's learning experiences are among individuals representing a great variety of forms of primary and secondary culture contacts, generation change and intra-societal shift, that we find expressions of the immigrant's sense of personality distortion and the native's sense of a shattered outer world. The perception of the outer world becomes atomized, as the growing child is no longer presented with a coherent set of culturally interrelated experiences to guide his perception. Relationships disappear and experience is broken down into small, discrete bits which may be given temporary meaning in any one of a thousand patterns but lack coherent relationship to any one pattern. It is as if a child were taught to perceive a human skeleton not as a single system of functionally relevant, articulated, non-interchangeable units, but instead as composed of two hundred-odd irregular and comparably meaningless bits—as if, in fact, a picture of a skeleton had been reduced to a jig-saw puzzle, each bit of which might also fit into a hundred other designs.*

---

subsequent loss." Lawrence K. Frank has pointed out[11] that competition tends to reduce the complexity of values by forcing any given individual to compete on the same set of terms as other members of the society. It is important to recognize that the converse statement may also be true: that a reduction in complexity of values which occurs as a part of a culture contact situation may, by introducing some simple unit which will increase the comparability within the diversity, itself facilitate the development of competitive behavior.[12]

* Such an atomization of external reality is, of course, not in itself incompatible with an integrated culture, provided the character formation of the individuals is such that there is a genuine relationship between the series of temporary patterns imposed upon the aggregation of bits. Balinese culture is filled with instances in which some material or event sequence is first atomized and then rearranged in a new form, and of instances in which the violent disruption of some ceremonial event sequence by an irrelevant interruption is ignored because of the persistent pattern into which the Balinese themselves reassemble what appears to the Western observer to be shattered, discontinuous bits. Extreme atomization of alien cultural elements is a characteristic cultural phenomenon by which culture contact is rendered relatively ineffective in Bali. The conspicuously small

This atomization of the external world has a variety of manifestations. Instead of a wide modulation of affective tone, in which very different tones of voice and quality of attention are given to the disparate and incommensurable elements in a complex pattern, all orders of experience come to be treated in the same tone. The master of ceremonies in a radio program has no difficulty in maintaining an even-tenor voice as he deals *seriatim* with soft drinks, the batting average of a baseball player, a recent great president, and the atom bomb. Knowledge becomes a matter of facts as such, rather than of their organization and interpretation, and skill becomes a large number of small, precise aptitudes, rather than a way of life. In the schools science is taught in separate segments —chemistry one year, physics another—without cross-reference. Instead of a single international policy, or a co-ordinated domestic policy, there are many distinct programs advocated by groups or parties who show very little recognition of the inconsistencies among and within the

amount of routine fatigue and the capacity of the Balinese to shift easily from one activity to another are probably also systematically related to the way in which the individual responds only partially to external stimuli or imposed tasks. When Balinese ceremonial is analysed regionally, the jig-saw puzzle figure becomes more meaningful, because many details in a *rite de passage* are unintelligible unless referred to some equally meaningless detail in the *same rite de passage* in another village or district. Without a historical record it is impossible to interpret this curious distribution further. There may be a premium upon reducing the meaningfulness so as to reduce its coercive effect upon the attention of the individual. Such a reduction would, in fact, be made possible by a random dissection of ritual wholes into disconnected items which could no longer reinstate the whole. Another possible—and undemonstrable— explanation would attribute the random distribution of various apparently related bits to some process of assimilation of alien elements, in which one community had selected one set of bits, another community another. It has been suggested by Dr. Theodora Abel, after an analysis of the responses of Balinese subjects to her "limited free design test" [13] that this reduction in the meaningfulness of external detail is related to a very great rigidity of personality at a deeper level—a rigidity which may be partly preserved by this cultivated lack of attention to the external world.

programs they advocate. Human beings are perceived within a set of categories which permit ready interchangeability.[14] Courtship and marriage come to be almost as impersonal as the choice involved in marrying one of three cross-cousins in a small primitive tribe; there is a difference in time relations but a common impersonality. In a system in which kinship regulates marriage the limitation on personal factors in choice is set by past situations which define the range of choice for living individuals. In modern America relationships are defined, and thus the range of choice is limited, by present situations, work in the same office, attendance at the same college, membership in the same club. In a primitive society of the type mentioned individuals are required to accept a relationship because of a marriage two generations earlier. In modern America individuals accept friends and marriage partners from among those who are presented to them through the fortuitous circumstances of their contemporary work and residence arrangements.

I have stressed the way in which American companionship, partnership, and marriage arrangements, which are dependent upon ephemeral situations, resemble kinship-patterned primitive societies in order to emphasize the fact that patterning, though of a highly simplified type, develops even in a very disturbed and confused culture contact society. The apparent complexity of American culture, with its enormous number of publications, radio programs, amusements, makes of automobiles, changing styles, and so on, hides a basic simplification.* All these superficially diverse patterns are atomized in a way which makes the likenesses among them more easily perceived than the differences. It is the interchangeability of a film, a radio program, and an evening of bowling which is stressed, rather than their incomparability. As an accompaniment of this strenuous effort at simplification, ethical attitudes tend to be expressed in very black and white

* The European, to whom differences in material objects are related to a more incommensurable set of values, of course *experiences* American culture as a manifold of bewildering and unordered complexity.

terms, or to be so qualified in situational terms as to seem very cynical.*

Thus the personality type which develops where most of the rearing adults have experienced secondary culture contact reflects on the one hand the native's sense of a shattered outer world, which comes from the rapid impingement of immigration, technological change and urbanization, and, on the other, the sense of internal disorientation of the immigrant. The outer world appears atomized into meaningless units; the inner world also loses its structure and becomes fragmented and chaotic, in that the structure which usually results from the process of growing up in a human culture is often not only not strong enough to resist strain, but also not coherent enough to retain some semblance of form when the breakdown occurs. The increase of schizophrenia, in which all relationship with organized cultural reality is relinquished, is probably one symptom of this condition.

A recent intensive American study in which individuals who showed either a very high degree of hatred of socially disadvantaged groups, as measured on an elaborate questionnaire, or a very high degree of friendly sympathy toward such groups, has yielded some very suggestive results.[16] The group characterized by an unusual amount of hatred showed a type of character formation with a high amount of outer conformity, but a lack of inner order against which the outward conformity might be seen as a defense. This group contained a large number of culturally "normal" individuals and also individuals with some marked psychotic trends. The contrast group of those who were sympathetic with the disadvantaged contained many neurotic personalities, individuals with sufficient strength to maintain a difficult relationship to the world without breaking down. They had accepted the contradictions and discrepancies inherent in American culture, and, instead of handling these contradictions by denying them, they had internalized the conflict.

* Granville Hicks in his study of a small upstate New York community[15] comments extensively on the prevalence of such judgments as, "I can put up with drunkards, but I can't stomach them in church."

It may be suggested that in extreme culture contact conditions, such as now exist in the United States and will probably become more widespread over the world, these are some of the types of adjustment which may be expected to develop. We may find an extreme oversimplification, a recategorizing of cultural experience into such characteristic American forms as fraternities, clubs, and so on. Such solutions, among which gambling and betting in the United States, parts of Latin America, and Australia may also be mentioned, provide superficially coherent contexts in which the personality can act without making an attempt at any basic reorientation. Religious and political movements which base their appeal upon the existence of the disorientation and offer a single formula under which all the fragmented aspects of life can be brought together again are another characteristic form in such cultures.*

A third attempt at solution comes from efforts to increase the complexity of the broken and oversimplified culture, not by any single solution or any surface multiplication of organizational forms, but by a change in the level of organization, both in the personality structure and in the social forms. One example of such a change is the increase in awareness of social process which is

---

* Examples of the propaganda forms, which are themselves accompaniments of different forms of social organization, may be found in *Hitler Junge Quex*, a Nazi film released in 1933 (analyzed by Gregory Bateson), and in *The War for Men's Minds*, a wartime film made for the Canadian Film Board under the directorship of John Grierson.[17] The *Quex* film relies upon first invoking in the audience the deepest layers of the personality, as formed in early family relationships, and then presenting a choice between chaos and order, with order reinforced by these early family images. The Canadian film, built up of clippings from newsreels with a cut from *The Triumph of the Will*, the great Nazi film on the Nuremberg Party Rally, relies on taking the discrepancies in the contemporary world, between ideal and real, between militarization and humanity, between regimentation and individuality, and makes these the elements out of which the propaganda appeal is built. It suggests that the discrepancies, the distortions, the contradictions are the very stuff out of which a different order is to be achieved.

often, even in primitive societies, a concomitant of culture contact or migration. It is probably not without significance that the therapy which is offered to the psychotic individual, whose oversimplifications have broken down, tends to involve a *decrease* in complexity or organization, as in treatment by electric shock, insulin shock, or frontal lobotomy. The typical therapies for the neurotic, on the other hand, are the various laborious, exacting forms of psychoanalysis, in which the personality is reorganized on a *higher* level of complexity and awareness.

We are entering an era in history when an understanding of cultural change is essential. Synchronic studies have provided us with descriptions of cultural systems of varying complexity and varying types of character structure. For an understanding of the changes from one system to another we need material on the way in which individuals exposed to various forms of secondary culture contact, either directly or through the mediation of previously exposed adults, take their personality structure from the conditions of cultural instability, and become the sources of new forms of cultural order.

Social Structure, 1949.

REFERENCES

1. Mead, M., 1947e.
2. Von Neumann, J., and O. Morgenstern, 1944.
3. Bateson, G., 1949.
4. Bateson, G., 1936, 1942a; Bateson, G., and M. Mead, 1942; Benedict, R., 1946a; Erikson, E. H., 1945; Gorer, G., 1943; Mead, M., 1942a.
5. Bateson, G., 1935.
6. Mead, M., 1947c.
7. For some contemporary studies of culture contact groups, see Beaglehole, E., and P. Beaglehole, 1946; Erikson, E. H., 1939; Kluckhohn, C., and D. Leighton, 1946; Macgregor, G., 1946.
8. Mead, M., 1946.
9. Erikson, E. H., 1946.
10. Mead, M. (ed.), 1937.
11. Frank, L. K., 1940.
12. Bateson, G., 1949.

13. Abel, T. M., 1938.
14. Mead, M., 1945a.
15. Hicks, G., 1946.
16. Adorno, T. W., *et al.*, 1950; Frenkel-Brunswik, E., and
    R. N. Sanford, 1945.
17. Bateson, G., 1943a; *The Triumph of the Will*, 1934-1936;
    The War for Men's Minds, 1943.

Part II

7

The Role of the Scientist in Society*

I want to discuss the problem of how we Americans today feel about the scientist and the scientist's role, and what significance that feeling has for the contribution the scientist can make to the contemporary world crisis. This seems relevant because I am addressing an audience of practitioners. However much you may be devoting some part of your lives to research, most of you are giving most of your time to applying scientific insights to the problems of individuals, or occasionally, of groups. As practitioners, your every word and tone of voice become significant in conveying to those with whom you work, as patients, as collaborators, as members of the general public, the meaning and the promise, or the threat and the limitations of science. Perhaps even more potently than the stylizations of the scientist in the press and radio, the stage and film, the way in which the practitioner stylizes his own role, and sees his own role, tends to build up in the mind of the layman either a faith or a distrust in science. And to the degree that the practitioner sees the implications, the possible interpretations which may be placed upon his every act, he or she becomes the more aware and therefore the more effective as a communicator.

When science enters the realm of human relations, what will be the result? What, in fact, will happen to human relations and will they be seen as human at all? The

* This paper, together with papers by Franz Alexander and Lawrence E. Cole on the same subject, was presented in a symposium at the 1947 Annual Meeting of the American Orthopsychiatric Association, to an audience embracing a range of disciplines interested in problems relating to children.

problem can be approached from the standpoint of the
scientist's picture of himself, as he sees himself mirrored
in the conceptions of those around him. I would rather
reverse this picture and explore some of the reasons why
the layman entertains the various attitudes of fear, faith,
hope, and distrust toward the scientist.

Central to this problem is the question of power.
Science, as it has developed historically, has come to be
associated with the idea of power, unlimited power over
the forces of nature. Atomic discoveries have so enhanced
this picture that it is safe to say that *power* is one of the
first associations which the layman makes with the word
scientist. A second association is the word *impersonal*.
The scientist has been celebrated for his objectivity, his
freedom from bias, his cool, aloof, impersonal—and
almost by definition—inhuman behavior. This stereotype,
frightening even when applied to someone who was experimenting with unrealizable entities, is extremely repel-
lant when applied to human affairs. To treat another
impersonally, coolly, aloofly, is to be lacking in warmth,
in concern, in contact. The minute we are asked to think
of the scientist in relation to human behavior, then this
carefully built up picture of objectivity intervenes. The
desire to make a split between this coolness and the
human practitioner is seen in the contrast between the
picture of the doctor—warm, and a little shabby, who sits
by his patient's bedside—and the white-coated "scientist"
who is pictured all alone with some shining piece of
laboratory apparatus.[1] One of the tasks of interpreting
the meaning of science for human welfare becomes then
to heal this split, to reunite the tired, friendly, country
doctor, who knew and loved each patient as a person,
and the cool impersonal man in a laboratory coat.

A second conflict centers around the fear that power
over persons, even more than power over things, is blas-
phemous, is arrogating to man something which should
be left to God.[2] While this feeling is less strong in the
United States, where man has come as an adult to deal
with an unpatterned landscape, than it is in European
countries where the works of man and the natural landscape both blend together in a past to which man adjusts,

still the feeling is here. The phrase "playing God" comes readily to the lips when any specialist in human behavior seems too sure.

A third difficulty centers around the way in which the sciences of human behavior appear to restrict rather than expand the layman's sense of understanding and control of the world. The layman has no expectation of understanding, without expert help, the details of geological stratification, the movement of the stars, the wonders of embryology, or the operation of hormones and enzymes. Whatever the scientist discovers in these fields is felt to be added on to the layman's existing stock of knowledge, and the acquisition of wonderful new words like homeostasis, entropy, proton, adds to his sense of human dignity. But in the field of human relations each generation has characteristically thought of itself as well informed and well oriented. Parenthood and marriage, discipline and indulgence, love and hate, are matters which people think of themselves as "naturally" understanding. Every time a technical term, *affect* instead of love or hate, *ambivalence* for some simple phrase like mixed feelings, is developed in the sciences of human relations, the layman feels that part of his rightful inheritance as a social being has been snatched away from him, that what was simple and plain has been made mysterious and esoteric, that he is robbed of his dignity as a well-oriented human being.

This is perhaps especially likely to occur in a culture with a primary Protestant orientation, in which the insistence that each human being could read his Bible and deal directly with his God, without intervention of priest or sacrament, forms a natural background for a jealous guarding of individual choice and judgment in personal relations. The young Italian American graduate student who says "psychology is just the things my mother used to know, put in a way that no one can understand"; the jeering reaction of the press to the attempt of an educator to subsume all sorts of beatings, spankings, cuffings, ear boxings, and hand smackings under the heading of "manual discipline"—these are symptoms of this deep sense of loss and affront which the layman feels as the area of human relations is invaded, studied, classified, and labeled with new words which he must learn as he would have to learn the vocabulary of physics or chemistry.

It will probably be necessary to devise new educational methods which will set the student to wondering about human behavior first, before he is given any of this unwelcome knowledge, just as in the training of a natural scientist, the wondering curiosity of the student of natural history, of the child who holds a "cat's eye" in his hand and realizes that "this must have been alive," is the precursor of creative scientific curiosity. But too often expert knowledge in the field of human relations is offered to the layman and to the patient or client or student, not as an enlargement of a horizon which has first been opened up, but in response to what is technically called an expressed "need"—that is, a sense of individual inadequacy in solving one's psychological or social problems. If "need," a crying active awareness of trouble and inadequacy, is regarded as the appropriate setting for imparting expert knowledge in the field of personal relations, this practice is likely to reinforce the already existing sense of human outrage, that affairs which people should be able to think about and feel about as part of their adulthood, must be handed over to specialists.

The position of the human relations scientist is further complicated by the current tendency to blame science, and so scientists, for the plight to which our world has come. There is precedent in the history of human beliefs for expecting a cure from the one who causes the ailment, but when this occurs we classify it as "black magic." There are many primitive societies in which all disease, misfortune, and death are produced by men who are in special rapport with supernatural powers, and who may be persuaded by bribes, cajolery, threats or reversals of the behavior which induced them to start the train of evil, to undo what they have done. In such societies, power is to a degree undifferentiated, and reacted to with great ambivalence by those against whom it is exercised. (It is notable that witchcraft and black magic seem to increase in primitive societies in which the culture is disintegrating under contact with our civilization, and also where a village culture is giving place to an urban culture with the resulting atomization of the individual and increase in *anome*.) A world in which the disintegration of all reliable values is attributed to the natural scientist, and the resulting disintegration of personality is then referred for treatment to the human relations scientist, is of course more complicated than a witch-ridden primitive society. Nevertheless useful parallels can be drawn. If the word scientist is used both for the men who discover the laws of thermodynamics and atomic fission and for the physician who must work day by day with individual breakdown, the possibility that the scientist will be seen as both the cause and the possible magical cure is very great. In this case, the success of the psychiatrist, especially with measures such as electric shock, drug or hypnotherapy, will also tend to be read backward and amalgamated with the attitudes toward the scientists who have produced the atomic bomb. The belief in the power of science will be increased, with a corresponding emphasis upon the malign nature of that power and an enhancement of the sense of individual helplessness of the layman.

The final and perhaps the central problem of the position of the human relations scientist in society concerns manipulation.[3] Once the possibility of discovering and applying principles of human behavior is granted, what possible safeguard can society develop against the misuse of this power? The examples of recent decades in which a very little knowledge of human behavior has been used in commerce, in government, and in war to bemuse, befuddle, subjugate, corrupt, and disintegrate the minds of men, breed a very justified fear that a society with a real scientific grasp of human behavior would be a monstrous society in which no one would willingly live. It breeds the belief that it may be better to accept every human ill to which flesh is heir—disease, famine, war, insanity—than to risk the inevitable destruction of human dignity in a controlled world, in which those in absolute power have been absolutely corrupted by that power.

But while this fear is both justified and cogent, it is important to realize that the acceptance and incorporation of the science of human behavior is no longer a matter of choice. Atomic discoveries have introduced an

order of urgency which the world has not hitherto faced,
an urgency such that to neglect a single possible solution,
no matter how difficult, becomes a treachery to the human race. In addition, the developments in domestic
controls by totalitarian governments, in methods of opinion research and attitude testing by democratic governments, commercial undertakings, and in psychological
warfare, especially of the "black" * variety which intro-
duces a final corrupting note in its denial of the source
from which it emanates, have presented us with a degree
of potentially destructive uses of the science of human
behavior which we cannot eliminate by prayer or legislation or a refusal to face them. It is impossible to go back
to an age of innocence; attempted returns[5] to such earlier
states invariably assume the unlovely aspect of political
reaction and the oversimplifications of the near psychotic.[6]

Our only course is to go forward and integrate the
human sciences into the very fabric of our society. We
must invent and introduce ethics and controls which will
tie the hands of those with power, so that either by a self-
denying ordinance or by carefully devised pressures, analogous to but much more complex than the "medical
ethics" which have served mankind so well, or by controls which are in some way actually built into practice
so that any manipulative behavior becomes self-defeating,
manipulative behavior is impossible and human beings
remain free in spite of having again eaten of the tree of
knowledge. To do this, we need, most of all, a climate

* The distinction between "black" and "white" psychological
warfare is of very great importance to the whole question of
the place of the human behavior specialist in society. In "black"
psychological warfare, the source of the propaganda is con-
cealed; e.g., a manual for soldiers is written in the format and
language of the enemy and purports to come from the enemy,
and within the instruction subtle destructive suggestions are
imbedded. A vivid discussion of the dangers involved in such
purposive cultivation of systems of delusion appears in Edmond
Taylor's *Richer by Asia*.[4] "White" psychological warfare admits
its source and exhorts the enemy, or sections of the enemy,
openly in the name of its own political idealisms; e.g., the use
of Wilson's Fourteen Points in World War I propaganda
directed toward Germany.

of opinion, a sense of the role of the scientist as the responsible expression of a new kind of civilization, a civilization to which disciplined self-awareness is the very breath of life. In developing such a climate of opinion, every practitioner, in every professional word and act, can contribute.

Orthopsychiatry 1923-1948: Retrospect and Prospect, 1948.

REFERENCES

1. Lowrey, L. G., and V. Sloane (eds.), 1948.
2. Richardson, H. B., 1945, pp. 129-49.
3. Mead, M., 1945b.
4. Bateson, G., 1941a, 1943b, 1946a, 1946b; Bateson, G., and M. Mead, 1941; Mead, M., 1942a, Ch. XL, and 1942c.
5. Taylor, E., 1947.
6. Fromm, E., 1941.
7. Frenkel-Brunswik, E., and R. N. Sanford, 1945.

8

The Comparative Study of Culture and the Purposive Cultivation of Democratic Values*

One of the pressing problems in democratic living is the need to develop ways of thinking together which will not result in the formation of slavishly imitative schools around leaders, the elimination of all individuality in an attempt to find a least common denominator of theory, or an arid individualism in which each speaks for himself alone.

This paper will confine itself rigorously to suggestions as to what the comparative study of cultures can contribute to the ends to which this Conference has committed itself—its recorded belief that "modern civiliza-

---

* In its original form this paper was a collaborative effort in that it included a set of comments by other anthropologists— Gregory Bateson, Ruth Benedict, Geoffrey Gorer, Clyde Kluckhohn, and Dorothy Lee. It was one of a group of papers on "The Natural and Social Sciences in Their Relation to the Democratic Way of Life," prepared for the Second Conference on Science, Philosophy and Religion, held in New York, September 1941. By then, two years after the outbreak of World War II, it was abundantly clear what the nature of the struggle was; particularly, it had become clear that the resources of science and technology could be used to destroy as well as to create an ordered world. It seemed the more important, therefore, to consider not merely the short term but especially the long term commitments necessary for the building of a democratic way of life. Eight years later, in 1949, I wrote a second version of this paper for the Tenth Conference, the papers for which were published in a volume, *Perspectives on a Troubled Decade, 1939-1949*. Taken together, they provide a view, both retrospective and anticipatory, of some of the problems to which social scientists can make a contribution.[1]

tion can be preserved only by a recognition of the supreme worth and moral responsibility of the individual human person." The Conference has set up this touchstone, and every cultural institution which it surveys or envisages must be tried and tested by it.

What, then, can the comparative study of cultures signify to those who have taken this firm stand, who have selected and acclaimed this particular standard? I would suggest several possible functions: It can demonstrate, from data on other cultures (and, by virtue of their relative simplicity and the extent to which they differ from our own culture and represent parallel developments rather than ancestral or divergent forms of our own culture, particularly from primitive cultures) that every culture must be seen as a whole, with its value system as an inextricable component. It can refute and brand as unscientific, irresponsible, and dangerous the use of cross-cultural data for purposes of devaluing any given cultural system by the demonstration that other cultures have placed different emphases and different values on some isolated detail of behavior. Historically, those who are desirous of breaking down some particular traditional value in our society have arrayed a miscellaneous assortment of divergent practices, showing that this and that other people, or indeed ourselves at some other period in history, regarded a given practice in a different moral light, arguing that, therefore, all moral practices are limited in time and place and lack any ultimate validity. This mischievous and uninformed use of cultural material is often mistakenly called cultural relativity, but that is exactly what it is not, for cultural relativity demands that every item of cultural behavior be seen as relative to the culture of which it is a part, and in that systematic setting every item has positive or negative meaning and value. Even where items of cultural behavior, so-called cultural traits, have been so easy to identify and so alluring to the members of other cultures that they have diffused—have been progressively borrowed by the members of different cultures in contact one with another—modern social anthropology has shown how a trait which appears to be objectively the same may have markedly different meaning and function in different cultural settings. The science of culture can insist, therefore, that when we consider contrasting types of behavior we shall attend always to the complete system, and that random, indiscriminate citations of cultural contrasts in detail be strictly recognized for what they are, iconoclastic polemic material, ammunition for agitators, but with no scientific validity.

The precise and detailed data which have been accumulated on some of these alien cultural systems provide an exercise in the appreciation of the degree to which every detail of a culture is interdependent with every other detail, so that items of behavior which have not historically been considered to be in the same sphere of discourse—the way a mother handles her baby, the attitude toward the supernatural, methods of classifying relationships, the style of literary composition, the rambling scribblings of children in the sand, and the type of self-control toward which the will power of the dying is directed—that all of these are systematically related to the whole. Such a consideration of cultural data may lead to a recognition of the extent of our problem, that the system of values involves in the end the whole culture. It makes the problem of values at one time more difficult, demonstrating the width and depth of their ramifications, and more exigent, in that it constitutes further documentation of the dependence of any people upon their culture—their system of values—a sort of primitive atlas on the theme that man does not live by bread alone.

The discipline of looking objectively at other cultural systems, i.e., seeing them as systems with their own coherent and self-contained ethic and not introducing into them intrusive ethical considerations from our own system, can also be used in maintaining perspective when a group such as this Conference meets to affirm a faith and to attempt to lead a whole civilization in a given direction.

By insisting upon the systematic interrelationship of different elements of culture, anthropology can warn against any planning which disregards essential components whose relevance may not be immediately apparent to those whose eyes are directed along more special lines. It can provide the underpinning and groundwork for an understanding, which must otherwise remain intuitive, of the importance of certain social trends, of the relevance of certain moves. It can insist upon the necessity of devising psychological-cultural equivalents for traits or practices which social thinking decides should be altered or abolished.

As an illustration, I should like to cite here the question of compulsory sterilization of the unfit, seen as a measure to save the community the expense and social waste of a large subnormal population. Although legislation providing for such sterilization has been passed in a great proportion of our states, it is still almost entirely uninvoked. Controversies have tended to rage about the absolute right or wrong involved in such a measure. A comparative science of culture would shift the issue to the relationship, today, between the attempt to save and augment the emphasis upon the "supreme worth and moral responsibility of the individual human person" and the forces within our society which seek to put the efficiency, economy, and rationale of the state above the importance of the individual. Legislation permitting any governmental body to exercise such a discretionary power in an area in which there is still such popular uncertainty and difference of opinion as to the ethics involved will be seen as dangerous—at present—and the cost of maintaining institutions for the feeble-minded as a most minimal individual tax, seen in the light of what might be endangered by this method of abolishing them. Such legislation, with its arbitrary character and its emphasis upon sacrificing the admittedly innocent for the sake of Society—and particularly of Society's pocket—opens the way for the types of state euthanasia which were preached as part of Fascist dogma. But such a judgment as this would have nothing whatsoever to say about the ultimate rightness and wrongness of putting legislation of this type into full practice at some other time. It would consider it quite possible for our culture to develop a form of society in which government is so morally responsible and so committed to the furtherance of democratic values, that the exercise of such governmental power might have no morally detrimental effect upon those who exercised it, just as the judge who today sentences to death a man convicted of cold-blooded and calculated murder is not morally endangered by such an exercise of power, since he acts as the executive of a convinced community which regards murder as behavior for which the murderer is presumably responsible.

Among the Arapesh of New Guinea, children are valued and welcomed. Parents make every sacrifice that their children may thrive and grow, and the whole culture is oriented toward the needs of the next generation. Yet infanticide is part of the standard cultural behavior. If, in spite of rigorously observed lactation taboos on sex relations until at least a year after each child's birth, a woman bears more children than she and her husband can care for, or if the next oldest child is still sickly and needs great care, then it is the duty of the parents to put the new baby to death. Living on very poor land, with a most meager technology, infanticide is a moral act for the Arapesh. If, however, they were transplanted to more fertile land, their scanty supply of food crops augmented with new and more nourishing food plants, their inadequate technology improved, infanticide would cease to be compatible with the central value in their culture, the stress on the importance of producing and raising children. Unless the practice of infanticide were abandoned, under these changed conditions, it is probable that the whole generous ethic of the Arapesh would undergo an alteration compelled by the incongruity between a practice no longer consistent with the exigencies of Arapesh life and the avowed Arapesh ethical ideal.

The fashion in which a nomadic people, who have traditionally abandoned their aged because they hindered the absolutely essential search for food, altered this practice when new means of transportation or storing food were discovered, is another instance of the way in which an item of behavior may alter its moral implications as the context alters. These are, it is true, very simple examples of simple peoples, whose ethics were necessarily adjusted to a precarious existence. But in a complex society like ours, there is as exigent a relationship between one institutional pattern and another as there is in the relationship between a nomadic culture and the food supply. It should be the special contribution of anthropologists to identify points of interdependence which are in danger of being overlooked, and to warn those who would give us ethical leadership whenever they ignore vital patterns or fail to provide new patterns to meet needs which their leadership will inevitably create. Anthropologists can underline the need for a critical re-evaluation of our culture in the light of the changes resulting from the extraordinary advances in technology which have introduced so many discordances into our way of life and our value system.

An illustration might be taken from the relationship between parent and child, a subject which is particularly crucial to the maintenance of the type of character structure upon which any system of values depends. Leaders in ethical thinking might question the extent to which the parent has assumed moral responsibility for the commands which he gives the child, and claim that it is more compatible with the trends of a relativistic culture for the parent to abrogate his historic claims to know what is right and what is wrong. A cogent case can be made for such a position, but, before setting the stamp of approval upon our increasingly confused system of child rearing, we may well pause and ask: From whence comes our belief in the importance of moral responsibility? An examination of the child-rearing systems of other cultures will reveal that the degree to which parents among us assume the onus of making moral choices and standing by them in the face of their child's rebellion, even hatred, is a special characteristic of our culture. In other cultures we find, as standard procedure, that parents rely upon a shared fear of the supernatural, or inculcate in their children a devastating fear of public opinion, or teach them that the only absolute is anger. It is rare, however, for parents to face their willful small children and say, "I insist upon this because I believe it is right." It is very possible that our peculiar dedication to moral values is specially fostered by such a system of child rearing, and that that dedication could not survive if this system were rudely torn away. However, it is necessary to distinguish sharply between taking moral responsibility before one's child in condemning his act and the old-fashioned authoritarian position in which the parent said, "You are bad. You do not obey me." By assuming moral responsibility, I mean that the parent will be willing to stand by his own code of ethics, that he will insist that ethical choices are important, that he will not "spoil" his child by giving or permitting him that which he himself believes to be wrong in order to buy peace, and that he will not woo the child's affection by moral concessions or trick him by some imaginary outside sanction. The line between this position and the authoritarian one of a single ethical system, ruthlessly enforced upon each generation, is a difficult one to draw. But it is possible that a system of child rearing, essentially democratic, in which the child is left free to choose, but is left in no doubt as to the moral necessity of choice, can develop more easily out of the older system of complete parental control than if we wait for the development of a system in which the parent has abrogated all sense of moral responsibility. Unless we democratize family life it is idle to talk of democracy. We have heard much of the way in which faithless ages live upon a residue from an age of faith, a residue which they are, however, powerless to transmit to their children. A comparative anthropologist who sees the system of child training as an integral part of any cultural system would point out the importance of this problem and warn the ethical leader to pause and consider.

The anthropologist must, furthermore, take into account even the special value of seeming discrepancies, infelicities, and contradictions in the culture which we are seeking to shape. Adolescent revolt against parental values, which appears to be a minus value in our civilization, might then be seen as a nevertheless necessary component of a belief in progress and an impetus to work actively for a better world.*

* Scientific inquiry may appear to many to be merely an instrument for undermining established beliefs, but it may also be seen as producing a ferment out of which a far greater degree of human enlightenment will develop. On the other hand, many cultural practices which are at present viewed with complacency by ethical leaders, such as the intense emphasis upon the importance of competition, or the way in which adolescents are debarred from any meaningful participation in the community under the guise of "education," may be found to be completely incompatible with democratic goals.

He should also be sure to identify obscure connections which are not immediately apparent to those whose vantage ground is merely a point of moral elevation inside the system they desire to improve. So, where the ethical leader who wished at all costs to encourage gentleness and respect and regard for human life and hatred of cruelty might think offhand that anti-vivisection campaigns could not but make for a general and desirable hatred of cruelty, the student of culture might be able to show the way in which such campaigns actually arouse and stimulate sadistic impulses and prepare people for outrages, rather than for gentleness. In this connection it is interesting that in the 1930's an elaborate anti-vivisection campaign was run in the government-controlled press in Germany just a short time before the officially stimulated pogroms.

In all the contributions which I have sketched so far, the anthropologist has played the role of placing items of culture in proportion, of relating disparate items to whole systems, utilizing the comparison of one system with another to enhance appreciation and knowledge of the way in which such systems are internally consistent and interrelated, issuing warnings and pointing out the implications of various changes or trends within our chaotic, heterogeneous culture. All of these possible contributions rest upon the hypothesis that cultures are systems of greater or less degrees of coherence and integration, but that even in the most fragmented and incoherent culture there exists a degree of intricate interdependence far in excess of that which is usually recognized.* This proposition cannot be demonstrated in the space of this paper; its final acceptance rests, in most cases, upon the willingness of students from other fields to undertake the labor and the discipline of mastering the record of at least one simple primitive culture in its entirety. I am in no authoritative position to require such

* Because of this intricate interdependence men cannot live in a culture as full of discrepancies and contradictions as our present culture without paying very heavily in terms of isolation, impaired ability, ill-health, unhappiness and loss of human dignity.

an exercise from every member of this Conference, and I can only, therefore, speak as one who has undergone this discipline in the more extreme form of being charged with the responsibility of recording entire cultures, and who has found them systematic. Anthropologists with other interests might offer a contrasting, but perhaps equally valuable contribution by using cross-cultural data to show the universal needs of man, which every culture has met. I feel, however, that we are concerned, not with the universal needs of man which cultures must somehow meet—except in so far as they set a minimum, a lower limit below which a culture cannot fall and survive—but with the universal potentials in mankind, which is the task of culture to develop. Comparison of different cultures demonstrates that man may set his spiritual goal low or high, that he may cast himself a cheap or a heroic role, and that as he casts himself, so will he live and his children after him. To the extent that we are concerned with minimums, we are tied closely to the way in which culture meets and is limited by man's basic biological make-up. To the extent that we are concerned with maximum human development, we are concerned with what human cultures are able to make of that most precious material, the human being, after—long after—the simple universal needs have been met. An emphasis on needs alone confines us to an acceptance of any number of makeshifts, which pass for spiritual food and drink and which, by stressing the common solutions that mankind has reached at different times and in different places, loses sight of the uncommon solutions. Among them may be counted the great religions of the world, by which the dignity of man in his quest for spiritual values has been reinforced and enhanced. The emphasis upon cultural systems as creations of man's imagination, conforming to law but subject to any number of fortuitous events, including the insights of spiritual geniuses and the happy accidents of combinations of values from different cultures, defines the area of inter-action between the anthropologist as scientist and the spiritual leader. The leaders say: "These are the values which we would foster." The anthropologist then places them in their cultural context and makes his contribution accordingly.

So far, in this role for which we have been casting the anthropologist, there has been no conflict between the idea of free moral responsibility for the individual and the contribution of the scientist. If, however, we push the question one step further and say: "We have established the direction in which we want to move. Now you social scientists, specialists in culture, tell us how to get there. You implement our spiritual program for us!" Have we then reached a point at which freedom of the individual will and scientific procedure clash? Does not the implementation of a defined direction call for control, and does not control—measured, calculated, definite control, control which really attains its ends—by its very existence invalidate democracy, necessarily raising up some men to exercise the control and degrading all others to be its victims? You can implement loyalty to the state or rigid conformity to law, habits of uncomplaining industry or absolute obedience to a religious functionary. This has often been done without the aid of science. Fascism showed how much more efficiently it could be done with scientific aid. But to implement moral responsibility for the individual means, in effect, the development of a kind of social order within which moral responsibility will be developed in every child and given free flexible play in every adult. This task is a far more complicated one, yet I think it is possible.

Before the social scientist is called upon to implement a program of greater democracy, however, it is necessary for those who invoke his help to recognize one essential difference between social science and natural science. In the natural sciences, progress has been made by the systematic exclusion of the observer, his errors, his biases, and human fallibility, from any experimental observation which was made. In the social sciences, every effort to repeat this performance has met with sterility, producing a pseudo-social science hollowly imitating the natural sciences. Advance in the social sciences depends upon the systematic inclusion of the human experimenter within the experiment, in terms of his constitution, culture, idiosyncratic life history, and the constellational significance which he has for his subjects. Instead of attempting to rule these out, in which case we are confronted with a vacuum, the position of the experimenter in these various respects becomes the point of reference from which we define a field of observation, and only as his position is known can the field be known.

This leads us to a further step in cultural relativity which is too infrequently taken, to the realization that were the world we dream of attained, members of that new world would be so different from ourselves that they would no longer value it in the same terms in which we now desire it. In order to implement a spiritual future which transcends our present cultural values, we need humility to realize that we would no longer be at home in such a world; that we who have dreamed it could not live it. The very imperfections which gave impetus to our dream would unfit us for its execution. Yet cultures have no real existence outside the habituated bodies of those who live them. Here, then, is a dilemma which must be squarely faced. It involves the scientist, who is the executant as well as the planner, for he is, of necessity, a part of his culture and its aspirations at the same time that he would bend his skill to serve it. It means that implementation can never take the form of finished blueprints of the future, but must involve direction, an orientation of the culture in a direction in which new individuals, reared under the first impetus of that direction, can, and *will*, take us further. It means that the student of culture realizes that culture is limited in its development by the individuals who must administer it, and so makes his plans for an interaction between altered institutions and altered individuals which will proceed slowly enough to maintain the direction which he has determined upon. He must lay his hand upon a process with a control none the less sure, none the less adjusted to everything that he knows about the processes of culture and the peculiar nature of his own culture, for all that he cannot, nay he must not, envisage the end toward which he is setting that process in motion.

For a detailed picture of the end, a finished blueprint

of the future of the absolutely desirable way of life, has always been accompanied by the ruthless manipulation of human beings in order to fit them, by the use of wrack, torture and concentration camp if necessary, to the decreed pattern. When such attempts have been merely the blind intuitive gropings of the fanatical and the power-driven, they have been sufficient to destroy all the values upon which the democratic way of life is based. Implemented by science, as they could be implemented, a new hideousness is created unguessed at in the darkest torture chambers of the past. The victims of such a process become progressively more apathetic, passive, and lacking in spontaneity. The leaders become progressively more paranoid. Only by devoting ourselves to a direction, not a fixed goal, to a process, not a static system, to the development of human beings who will choose and think the choice all important and be strong, healthy and wise in choosing, can we escape this dilemma.

This conclusion may sound like a pronouncement on spiritual values; it is also, I believe, a conclusion that can be supported by the findings of social science. The history of revolutions fully documents the dependence of any Utopia upon the human executants and the inability of those who dreamed and fought and guillotined for their Utopia to carry it out. The comparative science of character formation demonstrates the dependence of the child upon the culture which is mediated to it by those who handle it in infancy, and the absolute dependence, therefore, of any cultural system upon those who transmit it. The most complete implementation social science can then offer those whose aim is the increase in appreciation of the supreme worth and moral responsibility of every individual human being is an understanding of the techniques for preserving the spontaneity and initiative of each new generation. For the implementation of these aims depends on the creation of a cultural frame progressively better suited to the realization of ideals which a people are progressively better suited to live out and pass on, with moral impetus, to their children.

Science, Philosophy and Religion: Second Symposium, 1942.

REFERENCES

1. See the two volumes, Bryson, L., and L. Finkelstein (eds.),
   1942, and Bryson, L., L. Finkelstein, and R. M. MacIver
   (eds.), 1950; also Mead, M., 1950.

9

The Application of Anthropological Techniques to Cross-National Communication

During World War II, anthropologists addressed themselves to various ways in which their discipline could be put at the direct service of their society, attempting to short-cut the lag which normally obtains between the development of abstractions based upon laboratory and field research and their applicaton to contemporary problems. One part of this anthropological effort was concerned with delineating significant aspects of the national character, or culture pattern, of enemy peoples or peoples of occupied countries about whom our knowledge was wholly inadequate.[1]

A second use of anthropological techniques was found in the attempt to select salient aspects of our own cultures and describe them in such a way that they could be used for various sorts of rapid training or morale building.[2]

The use of anthropological knowledge in operations directed toward the enemy involved only a limited analysis of our own culture, except when a policy had to be carried out by large numbers of Americans whom it was impossible to train in detail to act in any way antithetical to their usual behavior, or when, as in our formal treatment of the Japanese emperor, widespread public support of a national policy was necessary. The use of similar anthropological knowledge within the limits of our own culture raised all the ethical problems of the responsibility of leaders of a democratic society not simply to manipulate but to appeal openly to existing and cherished strengths.

When an attempt is made to use anthropological

methods to strengthen a relationship between peoples of two contemporary cultures, still different problems arise. Here, the focus is not upon points of vulnerability (which may be breached, as with the enemy, or strengthened, as for members of occupied countries), nor upon traditional strengths and coherencies to be enhanced and weaknesses and contradictions to be guarded against, as in work in one's own culture. Instead, our efforts have to be directed toward finding areas of agreement which can be used as a background for the acceptance of differences which are causing specific friction and tension. Research and resulting communications are focused upon a relationship, and the nodes selected for emphasis are defined in terms of that relationship, not in terms of the emphasis within the whole culture pattern of each society. For instance, if foreign policy is to be discussed and the foreign policy of one culture is most congruent with upper-class values, while in the other it is most congruent with middle-class values, this asymmetry would be consciously explored, perhaps to the neglect of any exploration of the exactly corresponding class in the other country, because of its lack of immediate relevance to the problem in hand.

As illustrative material for such an operation, I shall draw upon my own experiences in working on Anglo-American relations. I particularly propose to use data upon the areas of friction and misunderstanding between American troops and British civilians in Britain in 1943. My case is unusual because I had the opportunity to participate in framing the hypotheses with which I went to Britain, to combine field work on these hypotheses with lecturing all over Britain, under the auspices of the Ministry of Information and, later, through the United States Office of War Information in London, to prepare various sorts of materials, both as background and as immediate communication, for circulation among Americans and Britons. Thus, activities which would more usually be divided among a large number of individuals with different skills—research, field work, analysis, interpretation, preparation of directives, writing, rewriting, broadcasting, presentations, etc.—and which would be subject to all the hazards which attend communication within such a diversified group, were embodied in the work that I did. This is an accident which we have no reason to believe will be repeated often. Analysis of such an experience bears the same relationship to thinking about cooperative operations that an analysis of the functions of the vanishing general practitioner bears to an attempt at constructing modern medical services in which many disciplines participate. This experience also provided a unique opportunity to explore some of the problems involved, and to test our hypotheses on the spot.

I plan to discuss examples of a variety of the procedures and problems which arose, so as to give as broad a picture as possible of the way in which anthropological methods may be applied to relationships between any pair of peoples. The analysis of such binary relationships is a necessary step toward an understanding of more complicated patterns of relationship on which a world order will have to be built.

I have used the term, cross-national, deliberately, to indicate that I am dealing not with relationships between *nations*, self-maximating competitive national units, but between the *peoples* of different nations, whose effective communication is a compromise of both differences in culture and the circumstance of different nationality, which gives a special competitive coloring and significance to these differences. To the extent that local allegiance is an important ingredient of the picture of the own group, the acceptance of differences in culture will vary enormously, according to whether any sort of boundary, even a state or county line, intervenes. In wartime, uniforms and all the paraphernalia of nationalistic warfare exacerbate the sensitivities of the populations involved.

In the initial steps, I depended upon the formulations of symmetrical and complementary schismogenesis, developed by Gregory Bateson,[3] in which the United States and Britain were both diagnosed as relying upon the stimulus provided by greater strength in the opponent, while Germany seemed to rely upon greater weakness. With this approval of symmetrical relationships shared by both countries, there was associated a common moral disapprobation of bullying, picking on someone who was smaller, throwing one's weight around, etc. In addition to the original statement of this diagnosis, I had elaborated, before going to England, the American version of adequate provocation to attack, under the formulation of "the chip on the shoulder." [4] In this, I stressed that the American boy, reared by women, was given a deep doubt of his essential aggressiveness, combined with a lack of pattern for exercising it, in contrast to the British boy, reared by older boys and men to combine a belief in his innate aggressiveness with an obligation never to use his full strength unless pushed into an extreme position in which he could turn at bay. The famous "Back to the Wall" order of Haig in World War I to the British, and reported exhortations of General Patton to his men, emphasizing the difficulty of the task but also the fact that the enemy was on the run and the United States Army had the best equipment in the world, are conspicuous examples of the way in which military leaders have intuitively relied upon these different patternings of a basically symmetrical schismogenic attitude. Phrased colloquially, the underlying similarity became, "Both British and Americans believe that the strong have an obligation not to abuse their strength. We both hate bullies and, conversely, those who cringe to bullies."

The second theoretical formulation was the hypothesis of *end linkage* (Bateson[5]) that the way in which parent-child relationships are patterned in respect to succoring-dependence, dominance-submission, and exhibitionism-spectatorship, provides a learning situation for the child which patterns his subsequent behavior in situations where these behaviors are involved. Specifically, in Anglo-American relationships, the exhibitionism is reversed. In Britain it is Father who exhibits to his children: he is the model for their future behavior. Father does the talking and provides the model, before a very quiet and submissive audience, in accordance with the deep ethical disapproval of overuse of strength. He underplays his strength, understates his position, speaks with a slight appearance of hesitation in his manner, but with the cool assurance of one who knows. In the United States, this position is reversed: at the American breakfast table, it is not Father but Junior who talks, exhibits his successes and skills, and demands parental spectatorship and applause with an insistence that can be clamoring and assertive because, after all, he is speaking from weakness to strength. The American background for this reversal was explored[6] and, in the spring of 1943, we tried an experiment of using the contrast in a radio program in which samples of parent-child behavior at the breakfast table were followed by excerpts from American and British public speeches.* [7]

These two formulations of symmetrical schismogenesis and end-linkage provide both a theoretical background for understanding and material for interpreting one of the acute points of friction between British and Americans. This point of friction was the British repudiation of American "boasting" and the American repudiation of British "arrogance." It lent itself particularly well to use on the lecture platform and over the radio, as tone of voice was the principal medium in the demonstration. By a little careful interviewing in each new area in Britain, I could get *verbatim* (and, therefore, acceptable) statements of the British objections: "The trouble with the Americans is that when they are good at something they

---

* The two speeches ran as follows:

British Lecturer: "Ladies and gentlemen—I have been asked to talk to you tonight about British war production. We have, of course, improved. Our over-all figures for the past year show a definite increase. But it is, I think, in planes that the picture is most striking. Our largest bombers, which incidentally carry four times the bomb load of yours, are now coming quite satisfactorily into production."

American Lecturer: "Well, ladies and gentlemen—I see I'm down on the program to talk to you tonight about Alaska. I can think of one good reason why I know something about that country. It's because I've had to make upwards of 20 to 30 trips there, summer and winter in the past fifteen years. Two or three of these trips, I might add, were by dog sled, far off the beaten track. On at least one of them, I nearly lost my life. But the thing I want to tell you folks about tonight, is the change that's come over Alaska since our boys went in there. Yes sir . . . mass production methods and the Good Old American qualities of hard work and initiative are showing results up there these days. (fading) I predict that five years after this war finishes, we'll be spending Summers in Alaska the way we used to spend winters down in Florida. That's a tip, folks."

say so," or "The trouble with the Americans is that they talk so much about what they are going to do; we don't talk, we just *do* it" (from the Scots), etc. I could then rely upon the lecture situation, itself one in which the exhibitionistic role of the lecturer and the spectatorship role of the audience was defined, to provide me with additional illustrative material. I could quote from the chairman who, in presenting me—putatively in the parental role on a British stage—to a great tired audience who had come out in the blackout on a freezing Sunday night in Scotland, said: "Be as kind to the audience as you can, Dr. Mead." Or I could refer to the whole institution of the "vote of thanks," in which the British audience, after sitting docile and respectful while the lecturer plays Father, re-establishes the balance by the paternalistic tone in which the proposer of the vote of thanks addresses the now seated lecturer. Explanations of behavioral differences which stressed upbringing were easily acceptable to the British, because of the strong cultural emphasis upon "character" as something which is acquired in the course of the right education rather than as an innate possession of any individual or class of individuals. It was possible to show that, whenever an American spoke, he spoke as he had learned to speak when he was small, and so would put that irritating overstatement into his voice which the British called "boasting"; while, whenever a Briton spoke, he spoke as he had heard his father and other elders speak, as the strong and assured, carefully pulling his punches, with that irritating understatement in his voice which the American called "arrogance." It was possible to show how the words *understatement* applied to the British and *boasting* applied to the Americans emphasized the virtues of British behavior and devalued American, while by using the parallel words *understatement* and *overstatement*, both British and American behavior could be put in a common frame, *viz.*, that of habits learned in childhood.

When I reached Britain, our troops were still pouring into the country, there were still many British troops around, and very few American girls had, as yet, reached Britain. The relationships between American men and

British girls were providing an acute point of misunderstanding among both nationalities.

The friction took many forms, which required quite different types of treatment. It was necessary to explain to British authorities that an American boy would have difficulty in judging the age and degree of discretion of a girl who told him she had been out of school and working for two years, and to construct ways in which the Americans could spend their disproportionately large pay on British girls without using up goods or creating new social problems. But there was the much more basic problem of the way in which disturbed heterosexual relationships were festering beneath the surface of Anglo-American relationships in general. The problem was not primarily a police problem involving the reduction of illegitimate births, which seemed to be following a pretty uniform curve whichever troops and nationalities were involved, but rather to reduce the disorientation which expressed itself in the British statement that the American men were "immoral" and the American insistence that the British girls "had no morals." Accusations of this sort might, of course, have been mere expressions of symmetrical friction, in which case it would have been necessary to look elsewhere for more basic areas of discrepancy. However, there is always a good possibility that, under identical accusations, there will be expressed some profound and unrealized difference which has become the more dangerous because it is so completely masked.*

I set about to explore the relationships between American men and British girls. A key to the misunderstanding lay in the differences in the location of responsibility for sex advances and sex refusals; in fact, for the whole modulation of sex behavior. The American girl is trained

* Early in the war, the British were frequently advised, by American expatriates and Anglophiles, to retaliate against American comments about India by remarks about the treatment of Negro Americans in the United States. This *tu quoque* phrasing only increased the bitterness and intolerance on both sides, as the two cases were felt as basically dissimilar by the Americans, who equated Indian problems with American pre-revolutionary problems as a country, and racial problems in the U. S. as equivalent to the slum problem inside Britain, a purely domestic matter.

to look after herself, unchaperoned and without any insistence upon rules of etiquette which will insure her person immunity from physical advances. She is taught that her behavior is in her own keeping, and the boy learns to make advances and rely upon the girl to repulse them whenever they are inappropriate to the state of feeling between the pair. In Britain, the situation is reversed: the girl is reared to depend upon a slight barrier of chilliness and frostiness which the boys learn to respect, and for the rest to rely upon the men to approach or advance, as warranted by the situation. Both systems give about the degree of satisfaction which can be expected in any pattern which locates initiative formally in one sex, without reference to temperament, in the respective countries concerned. In wartime Britain, however, it meant that American boys, taught to ask with a full expectation of being refused effectively most of the time, were confronted by British girls, taught to accede to every forceful invitation. Several characteristic patterns of response developed. Some British girls became even chillier and repelling even American optimism, succeeded in keeping the Americans at arm's length and sending them away to complain about everything in Britain. Some responded to the first stylized wisecrack with an impassioned surrender which was thoroughly disconcerting to the American in its intensity and implications. Some, finally, succeeded in maneuvering a middle course for a few hours, until the Americans who seemed to be "serious" could be presented at home as future sons-in-law—which annoyed a great many Americans very much. The interpretation of this difference to the men themselves, and to those who were charged with youth and protection programs, gave a working basis for improved relationships, and a phrasing under which the mutual accusations of immorality could be reduced.[8]

The problem of communication in a language which was theoretically mutually intelligible and "one language," presented a number of difficulties which could be partially resolved by reference to cultural differences. In all probability, the greater the difference between the languages of the pair of cultures with which one is attempting to work, the more automatic warnings are provided to the translator. Between English and American, however, and between other cultures similarly related through a common tradition and a still somewhat intelligible pair of languages, language confuses rather than clarifies, and other sorts of clues are necessary. Two systematic observations made it possible to communicate better. The first was analysis of the difference between the American and British sense of a scale of values. Americans tend to arrange objects on a single scale of value, from best to worst, biggest to smallest, cheapest to most expensive, etc., and are able to express a preference among very complex objects on such a single scale. The question, "What is your favorite color?" so intelligible to an American, is meaningless in Britain, and such a question is countered by: "Favorite color for what? A flower? A necktie?" Each object is thought of as having a most complex set of qualities, and color is merely a quality of an object, not something from a color chart on which one can make a choice which is transferable to a large number of different sorts of objects. The American reduction of complexities to single scales is entirely comprehensible in terms of the great diversity of value systems which different immigrant groups brought to the American scene. Some common denominator among the incommensurables was very much needed, and oversimplification was almost inevitable.[9] But, as a result, Americans think in terms of qualities which have unidimensional scales, while the British, when they think of a complex object or event, even if they reduce it to parts, think of each part as retaining all of the complexities of the whole. Americans subdivide the scale; the British subdivide the object. Americans are able to describe a room in terms of its "color scheme," where the British eye would retain a sense of some fifty elements involved in the whole interior pattern, even when speaking of a square inch of the rug. From this British insistence on complexity there flows, naturally enough, an insistence upon uniqueness and an unwillingness to make comparisons. Discussions as to the relative virtues of cities, which Americans make happily in terms of size, wealth, or some other common denominator, appear to the British either as meaningless or as irrelevant boasting. In turn, the British refusal to provide statistics on the size or wealth of a city seemed to the Americans to be either obscurantist or unfriendly. In Anglo-American contacts of all sorts, committee meetings, teaching situations, etc., it was important to watch the misunderstandings which arose along these lines, since the British voted the Americans as oversimplifying when they harped on some exact statement of a position on a numerical scale, and the Americans voted the British as inaccurate, if not engaged in deliberate falsification, when they quoted the population of Bengal with an error of ten million, with the statement that it "didn't matter," because they were concerned with the relative, not the absolute size of one Indian province.

Another sort of misunderstanding which influenced communication was the difference between the British and American sense of the real world. The Americans see the world as man-controlled, a vast malleable space on which one builds what one wishes, from blueprints one has drawn, and, when dissatisfied, simply tears the structure down and starts anew. The great sense of mechanical control of the environment—product, at least in part, of an empty continent and the machine age— extends to American attitudes toward crops and animals, which are again something to be planned for, streamlined, increased or decreased at will, and even, to a certain degree, to human beings, who can be, if not completely molded by man-made devices, at least sorted mechanically into simply defined pigeonholes. The British, in contrast, see the world as a natural world to which man adapts himself, in which he assumes no control over the future but only the experienced foresight of the husbandman or the gardener, who plants the best seed and watches carefully over the first green blades. Man is seen as the junior partner of God (expressed in either conventional or more contemporary forms, but still as the junior partner of forces to which he can adapt himself but which he cannot control). He can "only handle one link in the chain of destiny at a time." The humility of this phrasing has its own forms of arrogance, as in Milton's: "God is decreeing to begin some new and great period . . . what does he then but reveal Himself to his servants, and as his manner is, first to his Englishmen." Vis-à-vis this state of mind, ordinary American figures of speech implying control and mechanism not only fail to communicate but actually establish barriers. It was necessary to drop the familiar figures of an America converting for full production, laying down blueprinted acres of factories, six months ahead of schedule, and streamlining labor-management relations, and to use instead the figures of speech of horticulture, to speak of "planting the seed" in "carefully prepared ground," of an effort which, even when skill and experience were used to their utmost, still depended in final outcome on forces with which man could cooperate but which he could not control.

Roads and buildings in Britain which have been there a long time, become part of the natural world, not something to be swept aside lightly for a new plan. This was difficult to understand for Americans who often found that a badly bombed city, which was still a wounded landscape to the British once the rubble had been cleared away, looked to them very much like any American city, in the eternal process of rapid transformation in which the old was torn down with hardly a sigh of regret.

The very different sorts of self-consciousness about all social process also had to be analyzed and allowed for: the American's willingness to think about the immediate future and his unwillingness to think very far ahead; the British unwillingness to let too great a degree of self-consciousness interfere with the smooth flow of highly disciplined habitual behavior but their greater willingness to think ten years ahead; the sudden shift in British attention which permitted them to attribute to themselves, retrospectively, a degree of planfulness which they would have repudiated, at the time, as paralyzing. I was at first confused by these contradictions, by being told in one breath that to think about next week's plan would be unthinkable, and that, in some earlier operation of exactly the same nature, "we were very clever" and infinitely cunning. Once the contrast was clear, it was possible to discuss the past when any detailed dissection of motive and behavior was desired, and the far future if articulate goals came into question.

During the next two years, I had occasion to lecture on

Britain to various types of professional and popular audiences in the United States, as well as to write, and to teach selected groups of American personnel destined for the Far East where they would come into frequent and friction-laden contact with the British. The problems of addressing members of one's own culture about their relations with members of another culture presented some distinct features and led to formulations of significant differences which had not been pointed out during my British experience. These differences in insight are to be laid primarily, I think, to the inevitable shift in one's type of participation under the two circumstances. In Britain, I was a friendly visitor, using my professional skill to facilitate relationships between two wartime allies. In the United States, particularly in my teaching role in the various outpost schools, I was concerned with the strengths and weaknesses of Americans for the tasks of cross-cultural understanding which they were going to face. I had to find, if possible, approaches which, in clarifying their own cultural attitudes, would make it possible for them not merely to be more understanding but to act in cross-cultural situations. Furthermore, one faces, in discussing one's own culture with fellow members, a different sort of cross fire of criticism and is likely, occasionally, to abandon sympathetic impartiality for a note of urgency, if not astringency. In closed classes, designed for war purposes, there were no members of other nationalities, and it was sometimes difficult to convince the students that I would have used the same words and made the same points had there been British in the audience. In all work of this sort, it is essential to speak in terms which envelop the two or more peoples being discussed, and which represent the differences in ways acceptable to both. However, this necessity is more vividly demonstrated if actual human beings of each group are present in the flesh.

An American addressing an American audience about Britain is speaking to people who have strong and partly unconscious attitudes about Britain which go very deep —much deeper than any attitudes which the British, as a group, had about America in 1943. The American sense of national identity contains the earlier and severed relationship with Britain as an intrinsic part, while the British do not use the loss of America as a component of their sense of national identity. Furthermore, in the United States the Anglophile position is traditionally associated with that of the upper-class, the conservative, the wealthy, and the more easterly part of our population —added to the circumstance that the bulk of American tourists before the war were women devoutly following the footsteps of one or another bard. The Anglophobe position contains a mass of assorted elements, Middle West against the East, European ancestry against the older Anglo-Saxon stock, the plain man against the would-be aristocrat, etc. To discuss Britain dispassionately, it was necessary for the lecturer to face and deal with these strong currents of feeling, sometimes existing simultaneously in the same individual. I finally solved this problem, satisfactorily for myself at least, by beginning a lecture with a caricature* of the pro-American British woman, who represents, in capsule form, a way of repudiating the snobbish note which oversweetened the voice of the Anglophile and of startling the Anglophobe into a provisional (British) identification with the kind of Britons who would not like the type of Americanphile whom I presented. This produced a loosening of traditional identifications, which permitted the clarification material to get a hearing.

A second difficulty arose from the inveterate American habit of asking about every piece of behavior, "Is it better or worse than ours?" This contrast with the British insistence on complexity and, hence, uniqueness, has been discussed above, but it presented itself in a new form as I lectured on British wartime arrangements for community feeding, advising disoriented citizens through the Citizens' Advice Bureaus, or caring for the children of working mothers. Invariably, the American audience wanted to know, "Is their system better or worse than ours?" Behind this question were two unexpressed attitudes: one, the hope that ours would be better and, second, the tacit acceptance of the obligation to copy theirs if ours was worse. As most of the audience vigor-

* It should be noted that caricatures contain a strong hostile element, which has to be recognized whenever they are used.

ously resented any suggestion that they copy Britain, these presentations were always charged with rapport dangers. It was necessary to stress, over and over again, that the British solution was different, not better or worse. While this point might be surmounted temporarily in a lecture, it usually did not survive in next day's newspaper headlines, and actually represents one of the most serious hazards to any sort of comprehension of other peoples by Americans. A simple sense of either inferiority or superiority would be easier to deal with than this belief that all institutions can be placed on a single scale, and that it becomes the American's obligation to choose the best. The pleasure derived from the study of foreign behaviors which can be voted as inferior is alloyed by the discomfort of encountering those which are superior.

American audiences also raised a question whose counterpart I never met in Britain. It illustrates how valuable each side of such a relationship is in drawing attention to parts of the whole which the other side might neglect. "Why is it the British always insist on their own way in international affairs and we always lose?" "Why do the British always pull the wool over American eyes?" were frequent questions. In comments upon our international negotiations, the terms "the poor little United States" cropped up with amazing frequency. In working out a clarification of these questions, of this American belief that we always lost, I again sought for a common element in the two cultures against which the differences could be highlighted. Americans share with the British a common tradition in regard to the appropriate behavior of minorities who are minorities because they are in some way more right than the majority. Such minorities, best represented by the long line of dissident Protestant sects, but today also represented by the Roman Catholic minority in England, have been accorded, as part of the whole picture of our form of government, the right to differ and the duty to stand up for their positions. A virtuous minority in both countries is virtuous just because it does not compromise. Here, however, the parallel ends, because the British, speaking from strength, from the paternal position, do not identify government negotiations as made from a minority position. The government acts from strength and, being strong, can *include* some of the minority demands in any proposal. To compromise is the act of the strong and the entrenched, an act of graciousness, expediency, and a recognition that the heresies of today become the orthodoxies of tomorrow. Thus, in Britain, the word "compromise" is a good word, and one may speak approvingly of any arrangement which has been a compromise, including, very often, one in which the other side has gained more than fifty per cent of the points at issue. On the other hand, in the United States, the minority position is still the position from which everyone speaks: the President *versus* Congress, Congress *versus* the President, the State government *versus* the metropolis, and the metropolis *versus* the State government. This is congruent with the American doctrine of checks and balances, but it does not permit the word "compromise" to gain the same ethical halo which it has in Britain. Where, in Britain, to compromise means to work out a good solution, in America it usually means to work out a bad one, a solution in which all the points of importance (to both sides) are lost. Thus, in negotiations between the United States and Britain, all of which had, in the nature of the case, to be compromises, as two sovereignties were involved, the British could always speak approvingly and proudly of the result, while the Americans had to emphasize their losses. Out of the same ethic, but as contrasting interpretations of our position, came these mutually reinforcing estimates of a document or treaty.

Closely related to this sense of being weak but on the side of the right, and therefore committed to demanding a hundred per cent victories, is the American fear of being exploited by other groups, best summed up in the vernacular phrase, "Don't be a sucker." This is so deeply seated and has been so heavily exploited in discussions of our relationship to other countries, both those who are believed to outwit us in the diplomatic game and those who ask us for help, that it seemed important to analyze it. First, it was necessary to work out the interpersonal dynamics of the conception. A "sucker" in America, who is not to be given an even break, is anyone who enters a game in which he does not have the skill, or wit, or strength, to compete. Superficially, the American ethic that a sucker should be trimmed seems discrepant with the ethic that it is wrong to bully. However, seen against the way in which American boys are reared it becomes intelligible. Instead of the British father who supports the eldest son, as a surrogate of himself, against the competition of the younger sons, and at the same time exhorts the eldest to be gentle but firm, the American boy is reared by a mother who defends the younger against the elder and continually uses the success of the younger to goad the elder toward achievement. The slightly younger brother, backed up by the mother, becomes a threat, especially to the young boy whose games are continually subject to the intrusion of the younger. This contemporary child-rearing tradition combines with the frontier tradition in which the tenderfoot is a threat to the whole community. Older frontiersmen, alert to the dangers which one careless act may precipitate, and older brothers alert to the way in which the younger may spoil their games, both find refuge in the ethic, "Never give a sucker an even break," an ethic which is also honored by the admission of the American who loses, "I was a sucker, I asked for it."

At the same time, the word, sucker, is used in another and positively toned sense, to describe the man who is generous, enthusiastic, willing to give of his time and energy, as when a physician remarks in a public speech, "You know doctors always head the sucker list." This is said with approval of the doctor's kind heart and is tantamount to saying, "We are admirably tenderhearted people." Or, the student, cited in a psychological study as a normal, well-adjusted young American, will remark on the offices which he has held in organizations, and add, "I'm a sucker for work." This dual attitude toward the sucker position further complicates the American attitude toward other peoples, because it is just when Americans are behaving well that they are most likely to suspect that they are being made suckers against their will. Then the whole negative set of sanctions comes into play, and the ethic of never giving a sucker an even break is projected on to the other national group. The formula reads that we are suckers in the international game, either when we compete or when we are generous, that we aren't up to it, either way, that we are playing a game we do not understand and that, therefore, we will be trimmed. A perfect instance of this interpretation when confronted by the British insistence on the assumption of an appearance of model, self-controlled parental behavior, was provided in an article by Senator Brewster: [10]

"A number of different diplomatic, commercial, and financial moves will be necessary if we are to hold our rightful place in world commerce, but one of the most important is this: We must stop being out-traded by our good friends the British, the world's greatest experts in economic diplomacy.

"One day I was talking with Sir Gerald Campbell, Lord Halifax's right-hand man in the British Embassy in Washington, and I told him I believed our statesmanship is so bad that in nearly every negotiation with the British we came out second best.

"Sir Gerald smiled. 'Of course, we put it over on you,' he said. 'But not half as often as we could!' . . ."

This passage sums up the whole position, the American fear of being trimmed as suckers who do not know the game, the British failure to recognize the issue which is being raised, and their response first with a jocular acceptance of the stated inferiority, which from their point of view takes the sting out, coupled with a statement of the high ethical behavior which all fathers, governors, and persons in authority are supposed to display. The unpalatability of the British reply to the ordinary American can best be stated by referring to the Fijian form of insult in which most enemies were eaten but those who were to be most insulted were cooked and left uneaten. The jocular, Olympian assumption of restraint in the British answer simply exacerbates the American feeling of being treated negligently and condescendingly.

Another pretty example occurred in an article in the *Washington Star*, in 1945, under the heading, "Critics Air U.S.-British Views." [11] One author, Sir John Wardlaw Milne, wrote: "In this country we are thankful and *indeed proud* of the great United States, but we heartily dislike the tendency to suggest that America's intervention is a kind of act of grace from some superior beings who need not have engaged in the war at all." (The italics are mine.) Senator Burton Wheeler wrote, in the other column: "America wants no more deceptive slogans such as 'Give us the tools, we'll finish the job.' We are not going to tolerate any condescending attitude on the part of anyone that implies or assigns us the status of 'poor relations.' " Here, we see the British tone of speaking from an established position, and discouraging any upstart claims, the American tone of maintaining their rights against those who would put them down.

The phrase *proud of*, so galling to American ears, was a British way of boasting on behalf of the Americans. The whole problem of how Americans should speak of British achievement and British of American was a particularly ticklish one all through the war. After repeated instances of the degree of misunderstanding which was generated by the way in which each ally spoke of its own and allied efforts, Geoffrey Gorer and I worked out a phrasing in terms of the conceptions of partnership which provided a form of clarification suitable for lecturing and teaching. All through the war, the United States and Britain were spoken of as "partners," a word which is common to both languages. But the British associated the word, when applied to international affairs, with a sports concept, with the tennis partner who, for the duration of the game, is treated as like oneself, whose successes one acclaims and whose failures one grieves over. It was possible to invoke from the memories of anyone who had played deck tennis with British partners the continuous, "Good shot, partner!" "Hard luck, partner!" which is an inseparable part of the verbal etiquette of the game. The American, however, seeing international relationships primarily in a business context, associated the word with a business partnership, in which the relationship is conventionally asymmetrical—one partner putting up the funds, the other providing the brains or the entry, but neither committed to a social relationship with the other, with an expectation of the partnership lasting until it is disrupted by disagreement or death, and with no obligation on either to boast or grieve for the other partner. Therefore, a careful British attempt to boast for their partners (as in the case of the great emphasis given to the American contribution to bringing down the buzz bombs) was met by the Americans, not by a little piece of symmetrical vicarious boasting, about, say, the landing platforms, but instead by blow-ups in the American papers of what the British had said about the buzz bombs. This produced inevitable confusion, and even some abortive attempts on the part of the British to do their own boasting.

The methods described in this paper are anthropological methods. That is they rely upon an understanding of the cultural patterns of the peoples involved, and they invoke regularities for purposes of clarification. It is, however, important to recognize that clarification alone will not promote understanding—that it is still necessary to set some tone within which feeling may flow freely. In the presentations and teaching described in this paper, I relied on several methods which invoked feeling: first, emphasizing symmetries and, when possible, reducing to symmetrical terms what looked like complementary contrasts; second, giving a description of the other peoples' behavior in terms which made *identification* possible (e.g., in the description of the breakfast table, it is possible for listeners of each nationality to imagine what it would be like to be in the reciprocal exhibitionist position); and, third, on arousing the kind of laughter which comes from the exactitude of the cultural statement. Members of an audience invariably laughed hardest at the description of their own cultural behavior, not at that of the others. To obtain this effect, it is very important to avoid caricature, which is self-defeating. The device also fails if there are many expatriates in an audience, since these are likely to see their home culture with a degree of distortion that makes any exact description, which will invoke the laughter of recognition from others, seem to them a caricature—usually a hostile caricature. In other words, the method failed when it was used with those who were themselves highly ambivalent about their own culture, and overaccepting of the other. Significantly enough, attempts to give equally exact descriptions of German behavior have usually failed to evoke the same sort of recognition from Germans in this country. It is possible that this method is best suited to cultures and situations in which ambivalence toward the own culture is least in evidence.

Undoubtedly, in other interpretative hands or in different media, other ways of evoking feeling would be more appropriate than the deliberate attempt to embody the clarifying statement in exact, laughter-producing *verbatim* vignettes. That the method is suitable for more than one culture is evidenced by the very similar response which I received from British and American audiences when I gave the same material, in the same way. At the same time, the evocation of pity, or eager purposive aspiration, may also be feeling states which might appropriately accompany the type of clarification which an initial objective anthropological analysis of cultural patterns provides. Evoking either fear or anger runs, I believe, into the danger of stirring up, in the audience, feelings which interfere with acceptance of the clarification. Strong identification is possible with an evocation of fear or anger, but the identification tends to be so strong as to interfere with the degree of distance which is necessary both for laughter and for an understanding of difference.

If we are to build a world in which a variety of cultures are orchestrated together so as to produce a viable social order, we need intensive exploration of the types of clarification and types of presentation which will increase understanding between pairs of cultural groups and then among more complicated groupings.

Transactions of The New York Academy of Sciences, Ser. 2, Vol. 9, No. 4 (1947), 133-152.

REFERENCES

1. Bateson, G., 1943a; Bateson, G., and M. Mead, 1941; Benedict, R., 1946a, 1946b; "Germany after the War, Round Table—1945" 1945; Gorer, G., 1943; Mead, M., 1943a, 1944a; Parsons, T., 1945.
2. Bateson, G., and M. Mead, 1941; Mead, M., 1942a, 1943e; Report of the Committee on Food Habits, 1943, and 1945.
3. Bateson, G., 1942a, 1942c.

4. Mead, M., 1942a, Ch. IX.
5. Bateson, G., 1942a.
6. Mead, M., 1942a.
7. Dyer, A. M., and M. Mead, 1944.
8. Mead, M., 1942e, 1943b, 1943f, 1944a, 1944b, 1944d, 1944e, 1944f.
9. Mead, M., 1942a, Ch. IV.
10. Brewster, O., 1945.
11. *Washington Star*, 1945 (see Wheeler, B. K.).

10

Warfare: An Invention—Not a Biological Necessity

Is war a biological necessity, a sociological inevitability or just a bad invention? Those who argue for the first view endow man with such pugnacious instincts that some outlet in aggressive behavior is necessary if man is to reach full human stature. It was this point of view which lay back of William James's famous essay, "The Moral Equivalent of War," in which he tried to retain the warlike virtues and channel them in new directions. A similar point of view has lain back of the Soviet Union's attempt to make competition between groups rather than between individuals. A basic, competitive, aggressive, warring human nature is assumed, and those who wish to outlaw war or outlaw competitiveness merely try to find new and less socially destructive ways in which these biologically given aspects of man's nature can find expression. Then there are those who take the second view: warfare is the inevitable concomitant of the development of the state, the struggle for land and natural resources of class societies springing, not from the nature of man, but from the nature of history. War is nevertheless inevitable unless we change our socal system and outlaw classes, the struggle for power, and possessions; and in the event of our success warfare would disappear, as a symptom vanishes when the disease is cured.

One may hold a compromise position between these two extremes; one may claim that all aggression springs from the frustration of man's biologically determined drives and that, since all forms of culture are frustrating, it is certain each new generation will be aggressive and the aggression will find its natural and inevitable expression in race war, class war, nationalistic war, and so on.

All three positions are very popular today among those who think seriously about the problems of war and its possible prevention, but I wish to urge another point of view, less defeatist perhaps than the first and third, and more accurate than the second: that is, that warfare, by which I mean organized conflict between two groups *as groups*, in which each group puts an army (even if the army is only fifteen Pygmies) into the field to fight and kill, if possible, some of the members of the army of the other group—that warfare of this sort is an invention like any other of the inventions in terms of which we order our lives, such as writing, marriage, cooking our food instead of eating it raw, trial by jury, or burial of the dead, and so on. Some of this list any one will grant are inventions: trial by jury is confined to very limited portions of the globe; we know that there are tribes that do not bury their dead but instead expose or cremate them; and we know that only part of the human race has had a knowledge of writing as its cultural inheritance. But, whenever a way of doing things is found universally, such as the use of fire or the practice of some form of marriage, we tend to think at once that it is not an invention at all but an attribute of humanity itself. And yet even such universals as marriage and the use of fire are inventions like the rest, very basic ones, inventions which were perhaps necessary if human history was to take the turn it has taken, but nevertheless inventions. At some point in his social development man was undoubtedly without the institution of marriage or the knowledge of the use of fire.

The case for warfare is much clearer because there are peoples even today who have no warfare. Of these the Eskimo are perhaps the most conspicuous example, but the Lepchas of Sikkim are an equally good one. Neither of these peoples understands war, not even defensive warfare. The idea of warfare is lacking, and this idea is as essential to carrying on war as an alphabet or a syllabary is to writing. But whereas the Lepchas are a gentle, unquarrelsome people, and the advocates of other points of view might argue that they are not full human beings or that they had never been frustrated and so had no ag-

gression to expend in warfare, the Eskimo case gives no
such possibility of interpretation. The Eskimo are not a
mild and meek people; many of them are turbulent and
troublesome. Fights, theft of wives, murder, cannibalism
occur among them—all outbursts of passionate men
goaded by desire or intolerable circumstance. Here are
men faced with hunger, men faced with loss of their
wives, men faced with the threat of extermination by
other men, and here are orphan children, growing up
miserably with no one to care for them, mocked and
neglected by those about them. The personality necessary for war, the circumstances necessary to goad men to
desperation are present, but there is no war. When a
traveling Eskimo entered a settlement he might have to
fight the strongest man in the settlement to establish
his position among them, but this was a test of strength
and bravery, not war. The idea of warfare, of one *group*
organizing against another *group* to maim and wound
and kill them was absent. And without that idea passions
might rage but there was no war.

But, it may be argued, isn't this because the Eskimo
have such a low and undeveloped form of social organization? They own no land, they move from place to place,
camping, it is true, season after season on the same site,
but this is not something to fight for as the modern nations of the world fight for land and raw materials. They
have no permanent possessions that can be looted, no
towns that can be burned. They have no social classes to
produce stress and strains within the society which might
force it to go to war outside. Doesn't the absence of war
among the Eskimo, while disproving the biological necessity of war, just go to confirm the point that it is the
state of development of the society which accounts for
war, and nothing else?

We find the answer among the Pygmy peoples of the
Andaman Islands in the Bay of Bengal. The Andamans
also represent an exceedingly low level of society; they
are a hunting and food-gathering people; they live in tiny
hordes without any class stratification; their houses are
simpler than the snow houses of the Eskimo. But they
knew about warfare. The army might contain only fifteen
determined pygmies marching in a straight line, but it

was the real thing none the less. Tiny army met tiny army in open battle, blows were exchanged, casualties suffered, and the state of warfare could only be concluded by a peace-making ceremony.

Similarly, among the Australian aborigines, who built no permanent dwellings but wandered from water hole to water hole over their almost desert country, warfare—and rules of "international law"—were highly developed. The student of social evolution will seek in vain for his obvious causes of war, struggle for lands, struggle for power of one group over another, expansion of population, need to divert the minds of a populace restive under tyranny, or even the ambition of a successful leader to enhance his own prestige. All are absent, but warfare as a practice remained, and men engaged in it and killed one another in the course of a war because killing is what is done in wars.

From instances like these it becomes apparent that an inquiry into the causes of war misses the fundamental point as completely as does an insistence upon the biological necessity of war. If a people have an idea of going to war and the idea that war is the way in which certain situations, defined within their society, are to be handled, they will sometimes go to war. If they are a mild and unaggressive people, like the Pueblo Indians, they may limit themselves to defensive warfare; but they will be forced to think in terms of war because there are peoples near them who have warfare as a pattern, and offensive, raiding, pillaging warfare at that. When the pattern of warfare is known, people like the Pueblo Indians will defend themselves, taking advantage of their natural defenses, the *mesa* village site, and people like the Lepchas, having no natural defenses and no idea of warfare, will merely submit to the invader. But the essential point remains the same. There is a way of behaving which is known to a given people and labeled as an appropriate form of behavior. A bold and warlike people like the Sioux or the Maori may label warfare as desirable as well as possible; a mild people like the Pueblo Indians may label warfare as undesirable; but to the minds of both peoples the possibility of warfare is present. Their thoughts, their hopes, their plans are oriented about this idea, that warfare may be selected as the way to meet some situation.

So simple peoples and civilized peoples, mild peoples and violent, assertive peoples, will all go to war if they have the invention, just as those peoples who have the custom of dueling will have duels and peoples who have the pattern of vendetta will indulge in vendetta. And, conversely, peoples who do not know of dueling will not fight duels, even though their wives are seduced and their daughters ravished; they may on occasion commit murder but they will not fight duels. Cultures which lack the idea of the vendetta will not meet every quarrel in this way. A people can use only the forms it has. So the Balinese have their special way of dealing with a quarrel between two individuals: if the two feel that the causes of quarrel are heavy they may go and register their quarrel in the temple before the gods, and, making offerings, they may swear never to have anything to do with each other again. Under the Dutch government they registered such mutual "not-speaking" with the Dutch government officials. But in other societies, although individuals might feel as full of animosity and as unwilling to have any further contact as do the Balinese, they cannot register their quarrel with the gods and go on quietly about their business because registering quarrels with the gods is not an invention of which they know.

Yet, if it be granted that warfare is after all an invention, it may nevertheless be an invention that lends itself to certain types of personality, to the exigent needs of autocrats, to the expansionist desires of crowded peoples, to the desire for plunder and rape and loot which is engendered by a dull and frustrating life. What, then, can we say of this congruence between warfare and its uses? If it is a form which fits so well, is not this congruence the essential point? But even here the primitive material causes us to wonder, because there are tribes who go to war merely for glory, having no quarrel with the enemy, suffering from no tyrant within their boundaries, anxious neither for land nor loot nor women, but merely anxious to win prestige which within that tribe has been declared obtainable only by war and without which no young man can hope to win his sweetheart's smile of approval. But if, as was the case with the Bush Negroes of Dutch Guiana, it is artistic ability which is necessary to win a girl's approval, the same young man would have to be carving rather than going out on a war party.

In many parts of the world, war is a game in which the individual can win counters—counters which bring him prestige in the eyes of his own sex or of the opposite sex; he plays for these counters as he might, in our society, strive for a tennis championship. Warfare is a frame for such prestige-seeking merely because it calls for the display of certain skills and certain virtues; all of these skills—riding straight, shooting straight, dodging the missiles of the enemy and sending one's own straight to the mark—can be equally well exercised in some other framework and, equally, the virtues—endurance, bravery, loyalty, steadfastness—can be displayed in other contexts. The tie-up between proving oneself a man and proving this by a success in organized killing is due to a definition which many societies have made of manliness. And often, even in those societies which counted success in warfare a proof of human worth, strange turns were given to the idea, as when the Plains Indians gave their highest awards to the man who touched a live enemy rather than to the man who brought in a scalp—from a dead enemy—because killing a man was less risky. Warfare is just an invention known to the majority of human societies by which they permit their young men either to accumulate prestige or avenge their honor or acquire loot or wives or slaves or sago lands or cattle or appease the blood lust of their gods or the restless souls of the recently dead. It is just an invention, older and more widespread than the jury system, but none the less an invention.

But, once we have said this, have we said anything at all? Despite a few instances, dear to the hearts of controversialists, of the loss of the useful arts, once an invention is made which proves congruent with human needs or social forms, it tends to persist. Grant that war is an invention, that it is not a biological necessity nor the outcome of certain special types of social forms, still, once the invention is made, what are we to do about it? The Indian who had been subsisting on the buffalo for generations because with his primitive weapons he could slaughter only a limited number of buffalo did not return to his primitive weapons when he saw that the white man's more efficient weapons were exterminating the buffalo. A desire for the white man's cloth may mortgage the South Sea Islander to the white man's plantation, but he does not return to making bark cloth, which would have left him free. Once an invention is known and accepted, men do not easily relinquish it. The skilled workers may smash the first steam looms which they feel are to be their undoing, but they accept them in the end, and no movement which has insisted upon the mere abandonment of usable inventions has ever had much success. Warfare is here, as part of our thought; the deeds of warriors are immortalized in the words of our poets; the toys of our children are modeled upon the weapons of the soldier; the frame of reference within which our statesmen and our diplomats work always contains war. If we know that it is not inevitable, that it is due to historical accident that warfare is one of the ways in which we think of behaving, are we given any hope by that? What hope is there of persuading nations to abandon war, nations so thoroughly imbued with the idea that resort to war is, if not actually desirable and noble, at least inevitable whenever certain defined circumstances arise?

In answer to this question I think we might turn to the history of other social inventions, inventions which must once have seemed as firmly entrenched as warfare. Take the methods of trial which preceded the jury system: ordeal and trial by combat. Unfair, capricious, alien as they are to our feeling today, they were once the only methods open to individuals accused of some offense. The invention of trial by jury gradually replaced these methods until only witches, and finally not even witches, had to resort to the ordeal. And for a long time the jury system seemed the one best and finest method of settling legal disputes, but today new inventions, trial before judges only or before commissions, are replacing the jury system. In each case the old method was replaced by a new social invention; the ordeal did not go out because people thought it unjust or wrong, it went out because a method more congruent with the institutions and feelings of the period was invented. And, if we despair over the way in which war seems such an ingrained habit of most of the human race, we can take comfort from the fact that a poor invention will usually give place to a better invention.

For this, two conditions at least are necessary. The people must recognize the defects of the old invention, and some one must make a new one. Propaganda against warfare, documentation of its terrible cost in human suffering and social waste, these prepare the ground by teaching people to feel that warfare is a defective social institution. There is further needed a belief that social invention is possible and the invention of new methods which will render warfare as out-of-date as the tractor is making the plow, or the motor car the horse and buggy. A form of behavior becomes out-of-date only when something else takes its place, and in order to invent forms of behavior which will make war obsolete, it is a first requirement to believe that an invention is possible.

Asia, Vol. 40, No. 8 (1940), 402-405.

11

World Culture*

The term "world culture" may be defined as the patterns of technology, language, custom, and values prevailing among the peoples of the world and the tendency for these patterns to become more or less alike. We may ask what effect will increasing homogeneity of cultures have upon material contacts? Upon loyalties? Upon institutions? The following significant sentences are taken from the committee's statement, "The World Community":

"In general, the more uniform cultures are throughout the world, the more the world's people is a community."

"In general, the more all people are aware of, and identify themselves with, the same symbols and purposes, the more the world is a community."

"In general, the more the people of the world are organized into universal institutions, the more the world is a community."

As an anthropologist, I would rephrase these statements as follows: "In general, the more the people of the world recognize *certain* symbols, values, and purposes

* This paper, which was prepared for the Twenty-third Institute of the Norman Wait Harris Memorial Foundation, held in Highland Park, Illinois, March 1947, was one of a set of papers prepared and discussed by members of eleven disciplines on the subject of the World Community. The three statements which provide a point of focus for this paper appeared in a preliminary memorandum by Quincy Wright and other members of the Committee on the Harris Foundation circulated among the participants. The primary objective of the conference, as stated by Wright in his introduction to the published volume, to "enlarge the understanding of the fundamental problems with which both the statesmen and the people of the world are faced" in bringing about a world community, is now, as then, a crucial issue.[1]

as both their own and those of all the other peoples of
the world, and give to those symbols, values, and purposes a high place, the more the world is a community."
The shifts involved in this rephrasing are three.

The word "uniform" is removed, because attempts to
see analogous values and institutions, in different cultures,
as uniform have proved to be extraordinarily self-defeating. The very words "uniform" and "uniformity" are
incongruous with the complex nature of cultural phenomena and with a recognition of the importance of
pattern. A culture is characterized not only by uniformities in the behavior of its members but also by *regularities*
which may be seen in the non-uniform and dissimilar behavior of its members as well as by the contrasting contrast habits and beliefs of different groups which are
nevertheless systematically related to each other, so that
even the criminal and the insane will be found to express,
in some recognizable form, the cultural emphases.[2] A
single culture may comprise a very large number of deeply
contradictory, contrasting, discrepant themes, provided
some over-all recognition of commonality or community
makes each individual member feel that all these behaviors, in spite of their diversity, are parts of the same
over-all culture to which he gives allegiance. This is true
at the simple and obvious levels of the differentiation
between men and women and by age groups, even in
the simplest primitive culture, and it is also true when
we reach the enormous differentiation of religion, style
of life, occupation, and philosophy which characterizes
any great complex culture.

How far such differentiation can go without a breakdown, what the order of breakdown is which may occur,
and how it may be forestalled are all questions on which
we have as yet very little data, but they are questions
which can be investigated. We can say, given our present
data, that it is possible to build strong, well-integrated
cultures in which differences of great extent are recognized as parts of a whole. And we can, furthermore, say
that those cultural trends which occur during periods
of rapid culture contact and intermixture of peoples,
which are trends toward uniformity—as complex and
apparently irreconcilable value systems characteristic of

different cultures are atomized and simplified during periods of culture contact—themselves breed competition and various sorts of conflict. The idea of nationalism is a conspicuous example of a "uniformity" within which societies incomparable in almost every respect can compete in maximizing their national prestige.[3] The idea of the "one true God" for whom a single religious system speaks is again a uniformity, within which two competing world religions can communicate, compete, and struggle for dominance, but it is not an idea within which several religious systems can live in harmony.

The emphasis on the peoples of the world identifying themselves with the same symbols, values, and purposes is shifted to an emphasis on the need for them to recognize *certain* symbols, values, and purposes. This opens up the whole question of which symbols, values, and purposes they should so identify as both their own and those of others. In general, it may be said that it is important that these symbols be symbols of the wider general framework within which the various systems of the world can be seen as differentiated but integral parts rather than as unrelated or competing or contradictory elements. Certain characteristics of this framework, which will in turn partially define the nature of the symbols, values, and purposes with which it must be associated, may be suggested. The framework of ideas should be of a sufficiently high level of abstraction to include cultural values which are at the present time seen as competing or, at the best, incompatible and irreconcilable.[4] For the idea of one true God, with a specific prophet and institutional forms which are superior to all others, there would be substituted a belief in the value of religion, so phrased that all religious systems would be able to identify with it, plead their causes in terms of it, and communicate with each other through the symbols which would develop. For the idea of national sovereignty, which decrees that all nations will compete with one another on a single scale, ideas of cultural integrity would provide a framework within which such competition could be dissolved. For the ideal that every people in the world should have "three square meals a day," or 2,600 calories a day, would be substituted the ideal of adequate nutrition within a given physical and social environment for peoples with given constitution and occupation. Each purpose would be so phrased that the very different aspirations and practices of the people of the world could fall within it.

The third shift in phrasing involves changing the word "same" to the phrasing "recognize . . . as their own and those of all other peoples." This shifts the emphasis from the demand for similarity in the *content* of the values and purposes to the *relationship* between each people and the over-all set of values.[5] Such an emphasis would enable each people of the world, whatever their political arrangements, their major religious orientation, or their current political ideology, to use different and locally appropriate ways of establishing loyalty and enthusiasm for the set of world values without doing the violence to their own cultural tradition which is involved in an arbitrary acceptance of an as yet unrealized and alien content. "Freedom of religion" in a country like the United States means one thing to Protestant peoples and another to Catholic people, and yet, within that stated value, a certain minimum of peace is preserved. If we could realize such a degree of peace for the world, it would take us a long way in the direction of a world system within which war would be a lessening threat. Perhaps the importance of this point can be best illustrated from the field of art, when there is an attempt to establish the value of art as background for greater understanding among peoples. For any people to learn to value the art product or the art canon of a people very different in culture is a long and difficult task. But to teach the people of each country who are interested in using paint and pallet, chisel and wood-carving tool, that the artists of other countries have a comparable relationship between hand and tool and finished work of art, even though the finished works of art seem so incomparable, is a much easier task and one which does not risk alienation from one's own cultural values which are necessary to give depth and strength to the work of the artist within each country. Artists from different cultures can then communicate among themselves as artists recognizing a single value but many different styles.

Thus, in order to further the development of a world

culture, we would work toward the development of over-all values, within which each people could see both themselves and all other peoples as understandable and tolerable parts of a whole, to which each, in a *different* way, owed a comparable and reliable but not uniform, identical, or necessarily even similar loyalty.

If we consider the term "community" to apply to a group of persons, so that we are dealing with a scientific abstraction in which the units are individuals rather than units of human behavior, as they are when we use the term "culture," the same principles can be shown to apply.

In the statement on "The World Community" this sentence occurs: "Through co-operative living plus common habits and loyalties men come to feel and act as though they belong together." Here the key words are "cooperative" and "common." Analyses of the cooperative behavior of different primitive societies have made it possible to compare those situations where individuals cooperated for a common goal, each performing an identical and similar function, or performing complementary and diversified functions.[6] The strongest co-operative systems, and the one which would seem least likely to break down into destructive competition, are those in which individual contributions to the common goal are differentiated in many ways. The word "common" may be also construed as uniform, identical, similar, or as involving quite diversified roles. We can think of a society in which all individuals have in common the same kind of assertiveness, or of societies in which one age group, one sex, or one caste or class has a set of habits which are complementary to those of another, where one assertively initiates and the other compliantly performs;[7] or we can think of the even more complex situation in which there is a large variety of different kinds of habits, all used sometimes by each person in the society, in situations where it is agreed that they are appropriate. The word "common" would then apply not at a simple level to a certain sort of assertiveness or accommodation but rather to a *common* recognition of the appropriateness of a variety of interrelated types of behavior. The word "cooperative" would cover different as well as similar contributions to an end valued in common, though nevertheless perhaps valued in different terms.*

Our material on the constitution of functioning communities also reinforces this emphasis upon the value of diversity rather than upon uniformities within a community. The one-class suburb, the dreary expanses of "homes for heroes" without shops or churches or community facilities laid out in Britain during the last war, the undesirable qualities of housing projects where all the residents come from one income group, the one-industry town—all provide abundant data on the unsatisfactory quality of these ways of living. It is rather the highly diversified community, in which living and making a living, at many different economic levels, in many different ways, are fitted together, which is today the goal of the town planner and the sociologist. Such uniformity of habit as makes it possible for traffic to flow, for pennies to be left on unguarded newsstands, for children to wander safely on any street at dusk—yes, but these are the uniformities which make it possible for the doctor and the laborer, the housewife, the teacher, the plumber, the electrician, the factory worker, the waiter, the market gardener, the policeman, and the preacher each to perform different roles part of the time and similar roles at

* There are interesting reports on the various efforts which were made to help and hinder the return of Japanese-Americans to the Pacific Coast after the war. Careful research has shown that, while the groups who felt it most important that the Japanese-Americans should return and the groups who opposed their return were, in these separate terms, completely irreconcilable, if an emphasis was placed on the good name and good standing of the city or town, a common denominator could be found. This community loyalty was sufficient to muster community support from all but a fringe of extremists whose opposing attitudes were no longer significant, either for the overall smooth functioning of the community or for the specific goal of a peaceful return of the Japanese-Americans. Many individuals who could be appealed to in terms of the over-all community value cared for their community in ways which others who answered the appeal would have felt as most uncongenial, and yet it was possible to muster the support of both groups.

other times, within the framework of a highly complex, diversified community.

However, if we were to accept the principle of the diversification of cultures within an over-all set of world values, which, while differently interpreted and differently executed, were all valued by the peoples of the world, there would still be questions left unanswered. Even if we admit that uniformities are not a desirable goal and may in fact seriously impair the attainment of the goal of a world community, because they not only impoverish but also lead to competition (where competition is destructive) rather than to cooperation, we are still faced with the question: What uniformities *are* occurring and what is their probable contribution to the possibility of attaining a world community?

We may first consider such uniformities as the use of money, with the possibility of adopting a single currency, only modified to suit the unit needs or the carrying or shopping habits of different peoples; * telephone systems which work in the same way; airplanes, trains, and boats, hotels and post offices and banks, food service places and barber shops. What is the difference between having these thin networks of very similar facilities spread over the world, in which the traveler and the immigrant can make initial moves with great ease but from which, however, the step to the local intricacy of custom is very great, and having a growing similarity but not identity of technology, such that the traveler and immigrant knows that there will be money and telephones, trains, planes, hotels, post offices, and banks, but must expect to find them very differently set up. The network of identical hotel dining rooms for the moneyed American and European traveler in the past facilitated travel and reduced immediate hostilities to the strangeness of new environments but interposed a wall between the traveler and any understanding of the peoples among whom he

* New Guinea peoples like to carry money in the ear, and any money smaller than a shilling is unsuitable. In Bali the market-going woman changes Dutch coins into long strings of Chinese cash, because the Dutch cent is too large a unit for buying most of her supplies, etc.

journeyed and sojourned. If, instead, the details of living are at the same time identifiable but different, then as he learns to find a mailbox under a tobacconist's shop in France or to "push Button B and get your money back" in a British telephone booth, the traveler or immigrant is enabled both to function well enough so that he is not hopelessly alienated by this environment and to learn, as he makes change, mails a letter, or makes a telephone call, something about the style and tempo of the people among whom he is living.

So it may be argued that the greatest facilitation of growth toward a world community will come if the technological revolution proceeds in such a way that each culture, or at least each culture area (Spanish-speaking South America, as opposed to each South American country), is able to embody some of its distinctive values even in the material details of structure and function. At the same time the very fact of technology—lights which will turn on if only the switch can be located and if it can be ascertained which way it moves; stoves which can be lit or switched on; telephones which ultimately connect one with someone at a distance—can provide a familiar and reassuring medium within which the incurious can learn more about other peoples and so communicate better with them.

A second aspect of this question of growing technological uniformities centers about the danger that technological changes (especially when they begin to affect deep-seated working and living habits of a people by, for example, individual wage scales instead of family labor, altering the method of food preparation or childbirth, or substituting the automobile for the family parlor for courtship purposes) may, if introduced without time for adjustment and assimilation to local patterns, invoke resistances which will express themselves in retroactive movements, nativistic cults, minor and atavistic nationalisms, separatist movements, impoverished and unstable personalities, etc., which in turn will impede the development of world community. An insistence that each idea which is to be exported, whether it be the setting-up of a telephone system, a bank, a spinning mill, or a child welfare clinic, pass through the hands of specially trained persons who are thoroughly representative of the culture of the locality which is to receive the new piece of technology or applied science is the only effective device of which I know to insure that its introduction will not impede rather than advance the approximation to twentieth-century technology which is an aspiration of the more advanced peoples for the dependent peoples and an aspiration, too, of those high civilizations which did not participate in the first stages of the technological revolution.

In the third place, uniformities, especially of material objects and the habits which are related to them, have been extremely valuable in the United States, where the problem was the development of a culture to be held in common by adults coming to a new physical and social environment from many very different environments. Understandably, Americans are bound to feel that a pattern which turned millions of diversely speaking newcomers into loyal Americans in such a short time must be a very valuable and useful one. But two cautions are necessary here. In areas of extreme immigration some uniformities, either material or nonmaterial, will almost invariably be invoked. But the needs of a receiving country are quite different from the needs of peoples, who though they remain at home in their own countries, nevertheless wish to become part of a commonly valued world. There will be a danger that Americans will overvalue technological similarity—as when, after the war, German culture tended to be valued above French culture because of the superior sanitary arrangements in Germany. Wherever they find them, Americans may acclaim those people who appear to have or want most the same technology, as advancing most rapidly toward membership in a world community, and they may back up with disproportionate enthusiasm the efforts of those groups in other countries who may be alienated from their own culture in their effort to force Westernization upon their peoples prematurely. Useful correctives to this American tendency may be a vigilant awareness that, while it is natural, it is also ethnocentric and a conscious emphasis on the quite different sets of uniformities which France or an Islamic country, for example, might seek among other peoples of the world.

It is necessary for this generation to work at high speed if the whole of the modern world, if not the whole of humanity, is to be rescued from destruction. It has been found most efficient where science is to be applied to human affairs—dependent as it is upon human nervous systems and human learning for implementation[8]—to work simultaneously on a clarification of our major sense of direction, on basic research which will increase both the clarification and the methods for directing social change, and on immediate practical steps which will develop a supporting climate of opinion and will also facilitate the directions in which we are seeking to move.

In this connection it seems important to emphasize some of the steps which may be taken to develop a world climate of opinion favorable to the development of world community—a better phrase I feel than "*The* World Community," for there is no need for a definite or an indefinite article when there is known to be only one such phenomenon in the universe. Each step should be inspected in terms of its internal consistency with the over-all set of values and evaluated as a long-term as well as a short-term measure.

Among such steps one might list the development as rapidly as possible of ways in which world-wide organizations can be made individually meaningful to every person in the world—to the school child as he enters a schoolroom or puts a date on his theme, to the citizen as he posts a letter, pays his taxes, reads a book, or picks up a newspaper. There are innumerable devices, well known to historians and political scientists, which have aided in creating a sense of common membership in societies which have been assembled from adjacent, relatively hostile, or unrelated bits into a whole.[9] Types of organization which include whole occupations or interest groups throughout the world, but which have a symmetrical relationship with other such world-wide organizations, should be encouraged. Varieties of overlapping regional organizations different for each function can be very valuable if they are seen as growths toward a world culture and not as mere administrative subdivisions, dependent in their varying size on the varying budget of different governmental agencies. Elections for world organizational functions, through which the peoples of the world learn that the issues involved are important, should be encouraged, and devices by which individuals can be nominated in one country, but might run for election in a second country,[10] could be experimented with. The functions of large-scale business enterprises which cross existing national borders should be articulately explored rather than relegated to arguments between opposing political ideologies alone. Religious groups which provide a great source of moral force but often conflicting and discrepant operations in this field should be encouraged to reassess their peculiar strengths and weaknesses in promoting a sense of world community. Unless there is a definite attempt to introduce such measures, *pari passu* with the development of an over-all sense of direction, and to encourage the necessary basic research, the urgency of the actual world situation may be such that the best efforts of the social scientists may fail.

In summary it may be said that world community seems most likely to be attained by working toward certain over-all abstract and inclusive values, within which the different peoples of the world, who now see one another as separate, competitive, or unrelated, will be able to feel themselves a part, the cultures of each regularly related to the whole to which all give allegiance in different ways congruent with their own cultural values. Thus we would be working toward the type of multidimensional world culture, within which there would be interdependence of diverse values rather than a world in which any one interest or function so dominated the others that single value scales, competition, and destruction were the concomitants.

The World Community, 1948, pp. 47-55.

REFERENCES

1. Wright, L. Q. (ed.), 1948, p. vi.
2. Mead, M., 1942c.
3. Bateson, G., 1946b.

4. Bateson, G., 1942b.
5. Frank, L. K., 1942.
6. Mead, M. (ed.), 1937.
7. Benedict, R., 1946a.
8. Ashby, W. R., 1947.
9. Tannenbaum, F., 1946.
10. Suggested by Gregory Bateson; personal communication.

Part III

12

Anthropologist and Historian: Their Common Problems*

The idea that periods of contact between hitherto isolated human societies have been periods of fruitful development is so old, so well accepted, that it is astonishing how often we have failed to use it as an analogy in discussing cooperation among different fields of human endeavor. Whether the advocates of "interdisciplinary" research have felt it necessary to cast their arguments into a sterner pattern to match the self-conscious "purity" of those who wish to keep each discipline pure and uncorrupted by intellectual contact, only a specific inquiry could tell us. But it is evident, even to the casual ear, that "breaking down the barriers between disciplines" has usually been presented as a very arduous and, consequently, moral and exacting form of intellectual activity.

---

* In this paper, which first was presented in part at the "Conference on American Civilization" held at Brown University, November 1950, I took as a kind of bench mark *The Cultural Approach to History*, edited by Caroline Ware.[1] The volume, which was an outgrowth of a consideration of the subject at several sessions of the American Historical Association, in 1939, included an excellent summary by Geoffrey Gorer of existing theory in cultural anthropology. Taking its suggestions into account, I attempted to add to it in the light of the growth in anthropological theory and my experience in working in interdisciplinary teams, both those which did not include historians and those in which I could work closely with historians and with members of the culture being studied, who had been well grounded in the history of some aspect of their own culture. These last two experiences are distinct and differently rewarding—at least for an anthropologist.

From those who have attempted interdisciplinary research, we hear report after report of hard going—how each group has held on to their own concepts and resisted the concepts of the others.

Even a summer holiday in Italy might be described in such unrewarding terms by a traveler who spoke only English—who, eyes to the ground, refused to eat fresh almonds unless they were pronounced in English, and by the Italian vendor who insisted that he would eat his own almonds himself unless they were designated in the exact lilt of the local dialect. But this is not the way lovers of foreign travel speak in describing how every cell in one's body feels different when one wakes in a strange land and eats a new kind of breakfast served with the accompanying excitement of a strange tongue in which the word for almond blends with the taste of almonds and with the quality of the sunlight on the Mediterranean.

Perhaps in a cooperative venture in which both "social sciences"—history and anthropology—are also often grouped together as "humanities," it may be possible to preserve enough of the concrete pleasures of the new and strange, that some of the grimmer aspects of interdisciplinary cooperation—including the training table overtones of the phrase "team work"—may be avoided in favor of the adventure of exploring each other's methods and delighting in each other's insights.

Historians and anthropologists—in contrast to social scientists in other fields—have a special relationship to their concrete materials, to the particular document or to the sequence of rites performed at a particular ceremony. For these concrete materials—whether they be the single copy of an obscure document from a remote historical period or the single record of the only initiation ceremony ever witnessed and recorded in a tribe which has since given up initiation, or whether they be one of a set of documents which differ among themselves or one of twenty records of initiation from the same tribe—are nevertheless irreplaceable, unique events from the details of which new insights may be drawn by succeeding, more sophisticated generations. Both historians and anthropologists are dependent upon that which occurs *in the natural course of human social life* for their materials, every facet of which becomes precious. This loving preservation of the actual detail contrasts with the single-minded emphasis upon abstractions and generalizations of the scientist who works with experiments that can be repeated and from whom it is required not that he "surrender to the material," but that he set up his hypotheses and so construct his experiments that they will provide him with data to prove or disprove them. The little phrase "the data show" suggests a proper humility in the historian and anthropologist—and a state of incompetence in the experimenter.

From the necessities of their methods, both historians and anthropologists place a special value on the unique event in all its uniqueness. They know that it is the fine web of specific relationships, when something was done in relation to the occurrence of some other small act—a conversation, a letter, a resignation, a quarrel—which makes it possible for later historians, for other anthropologists, to ask, and to get answers to, new questions from old materials. The footnotes and interpolations and misspellings, which would be lost in re-editing and rearranging materials, become invaluable sources. Similarly, the anthropologist may find that faces in the background of a photograph or moving picture provide a way of testing a hypothesis not fully developed in the field. So in the Balinese material,[2] psychiatrists who looked at the pictures were inclined to question the difference in the tone of voice of the mother who—lightheartedly—teased her child, and of the child who—heavyhearted—reacted against the same teasing by sulky withdrawal. A re-examination of films of the crowd scenes of two rituals—one of which embodied the parents' attitudes toward children (the *Sangijang Dance*) and the other the children's attitudes toward parents (the *Tjalonarang*)—showed a marked contrast in the faces of the children in the two crowds: relaxed, gay, and unanxious in the former; anxious and tense in the latter. If the abstractions had been drawn from the material and the "data" had then been thrown away, no such further exploration would have been possible.

This preoccupation with the actual data, which serves to unite historians and anthropologists, is less intelligible to those scientists who create their data by experiments as they need it; as critics they always seem to be asking why one didn't go somewhere else or study a different period, insensitive to the importance of learning what a particular culture or a particular period can provide—better than any other. It is only when historians and anthropologists become interested not only in what did happen and what does exist but also in the nature of social processes and in the regularities which may be found in them, that this gap between historical fidelity and experimental freedom can be bridged.

Traditionally, historians and anthropologists have been distinguished from one another by the materials which they have studied: the historian dealing with past periods and the anthropologist with primitive peoples. This distinction is fast becoming obsolete as both are turning their attention to contemporary problems of the great civilizations of the world—including our own. There has also been a difference in the degree to which members of each discipline have been able to take the *whole* of a society into account. The early anthropologist dealt with part of the culture of a society, usually with a society which was already in process of rapid change; he attempted to reconstruct from the accounts of elderly informants such parts of the formal pattern as could be worked out without a detailed study of any living interacting group of human beings. The historian was limited by the nature of the documents which were available and by the current conventions of historiography which dictated the kind of constructs one could make from such documents. The units of both these traditional types of research were *items of behavior*, performed at an identified time and in an identified place by identified individuals; from them, patterns of "feudalism" or of "age societies" could be derived. In neither procedure was it possible to study living societies in which the units for analysis are not items of behavior, but instead *individuals* and *groups of individuals*.[3] The study of whole societies waited for field work in which the anthropologist would stop digging into the memories of old men and women and instead learn to speak the native language and record the living, changing, particular primitive community of his own time,* and research in which the historian would regard as part of his task the study of living institutions against the time depth provided both by the memory of older men and by available documentation.†

The discussions at the 1939 meetings of the American Historical Association suggested the growing preoccupation with groups which had been neglected by historians —the illiterate, the socially obscure, the peasant, the worker, the immigrant, and with sources, such as oral tradition, which had been overlooked in the past. The anthropologist was paralleling this new inclusiveness by adding observations of actual behavior to his former principal reliance on descriptive words. At the same time, both historian and anthropologist were looking for new types of connections which could be recognized when old sources were examined from a new point of view.‡

So, both in anthropology and in history, we have been working steadily from a consideration of those parts of the society or those aspects of the culture, which our traditional methods made accessible, toward methods through which more of the whole could be included. For both disciplines this search has led to unorthodox uses of sources. The search has led also into the areas of the inarticulate, the unrecognized, the unformulated. Penetration of these new areas has been very much facilitated in anthropological studies, less so in historical studies proper, by the inclusion of findings from studies of human

* The work of Bronislaw Malinowski in the Trobriands, my work in Samoa, Ruth Bunzel's work in Zuni, and the series of studies carried on under Radcliffe-Brown at the University of Sydney, are early examples of this shift in emphasis from attempts to reconstruct the culture of a bygone period to work with whole communities as they do exist.

† Philip Mosely's studies of the Zadruga are pioneer studies in this combination of the historical approach with the case studies of actual joint families.[4]

‡ For example, Ruth Benedict's treatment of the material on the Kwakiutl Indians in *Patterns of Culture*[5] and R. K. Lamb's work in which hitherto unemphasized connections through family and clique membership among statesmen and landed and merchant families provided a new basis for the analysis of early American entrepreneural history.[6]

growth and learning and from clinical explorations of the unconscious.[7]

Anthropologists have begun to work toward theories of social change and so to compensate for their previous concentration on synchronic studies of single societies at one moment of time, and historians have begun to lay more emphasis upon the total social complex at a given period. In the past, anthropologists have compensated for the lack of a time dimension in their studies by spatial studies of the distribution of traits. The definition of the place of a given culture in a known "culture area"—the traits of which were also described—was, in effect, a way of holding "history constant,"[8] a way of saying that, as a member of a given culture area, the particular society may be assumed to have had access at some unspecified period to such a trait as the dog sled or pottery making. The enforced necessity of working without documents on the primitive level was carried over to some extent into early applications of anthropological methods to our society, notably in the Yankee City Series.[9]

Criticism of the lack of a complete time perspective in these earlier studies has sometimes been carried over into uncritical attacks on studies of contemporary American life which are not also historical treatises. It would be useful for anthropologists and historians together to clarify how cross-sectional studies, on the one hand, and studies of single developments through time, on the other, can be made so as not to violate their combined standards for the proper allowance for time-space dimensions. The present level of criticism both within and between the two disciplines tends to be either pejorative or meaningless, as studies are pronounced "too narrow" or "too broad," "too limited" or "too ambitious" without reference to criteria that have been agreed upon or are even identifiable. The more we try to work with *wholes*—with whole societies, with members of those societies seen as whole persons, and with whole periods—the more important it will be to find some way of deciding what whole should be taken into account in considering a given problem.

Within both disciplines, attempts to handle wholes—synchronically by historians and diachronically by anthropologists—and to relate structure, function and change, have been given impetus by concepts of equilibrium and balance: in anthropology by the new approach of cybernetics; in economic history by Schumpeter's theory of "moving equilibrium." [10] This is perhaps the area where the use of models drawn from the natural sciences may be expected to provide the basis for cooperation among anthropologists and historians who are interested in systematizing problems of social change.

Another area where anthropologists' and historians' problems meet is that area, generally known as "personality and culture," and in certain contexts more specifically referred to as "national character," because of the emphasis in such studies upon the contemporary cultures of great nation states. These present studies have little in common with earlier methods for the delineation of national character by reference to race or climate; instead they are ways of relating anthropological studies of culture, historical studies of consistencies within the same group of people over time, Freud's work on the formation of the individual character, and modern studies of child development and learning. In the Romanes lecture which he gave fifty years after Thomas H. Huxley's famous lecture on "Science and Ethics," Julian Huxley has pointed out that recent studies of the way learning takes place in childhood have provided us with the necessary links between man's biological nature and social ethics, so that man's highest aspirations as well as his most undisciplined and antisocial impulses can now be included within the natural order—rooted in the way human beings learn the patterns of their cultures.[11]

Briefly, these modern studies of national character are concomitant analyses of the character structure of individuals of different ages who embody a culture and of the child rearing, educational, and initiatory practices of the culture within which these individuals have been reared. By cross-checking these observations, we arrive at a diagrammatic statement of the particular process of character formation by which human beings—at birth capable of learning any human language and the rest of any human culture—come to learn a particular language and to embody their particular culture. In such a study, areas of experience are explored which are unverbalized or which are publicly disallowed, as well as those areas which are made explicit. We are thus carried one step further toward considering the whole, toward placing man-in-society with a long social history and man-as-a-mammal with a long biological history in one frame of reference.

National character studies, as these were developed during World War II, were wartime efforts to obtain rapid information about the expected behavior of enemies and allies. They were partial studies in that only a few adult informants were available, so that the behavior of a few adults, in interview situations, had to be analyzed in the light of reported, rather than observed, methods of infant care and education. This emergency method has now been developed, under the continued stress of need to understand peoples whose societies are inaccessible to direct observation, into a method that can be used to bridge the gap between the procedures of the historian and the cultural anthropologist. By working together on the understanding of the culture of societies which have greatly changed, so that there are only individual survivors and the culture can no longer be perpetuated (for example, the culture of Great Russia previous to the 1917 Revolution[12]), or the members of which have dispersed into new environments in groups which still can be studied (for example, the culture of the Eastern European Jewish *shtetl* or small town[13]), the special contribution of each discipline can actually become apparent to the other.

The crux of the methodological differences between historians and anthropologists can be summed up in the two words "document" and "informant." The historian uses written materials which have been created within the ordinary ongoing social process without reference to his inquiring intent, and he distrusts material as probably biased, when it has been written for the purpose for which he, himself uses it. In contrast, the anthropologist finds informants, whose place in their society he learns very carefully so that from these living human beings he can elicit materials on the culture, which traditionally he writes down, on the spot.

This contrast in method was summed up vividly by an experience in Bali with a visiting Dutch student of native law who had expressed an interest in the recent spread of a new dance form, called the *djanger*, which had recognizable European elements. We asked him whether he would like to see some *djanger texts*—meaning running observations in Balinese and in English and verbatim reports of conversations which had taken place at the meetings of the local *djanger* club. He was eager to do so, but then exclaimed in dismay: "These aren't texts! These are something that just happened."

Further light is thrown on the problem by the ill fate which met my attempt to regularize group research in contemporary cultures by having all the interviews with informants processed for group use, numbered and filed. When one of the group wrote an article in which he referred to this unpublished material by number, it was turned down by an anthropological editor on the ground that the article was based "only on unpublished material" —although it is acceptable anthropological practice to base published work on a statement of the order: "This material was collected during ten months' field work on the island of Borabora in 1910." Conversely, an historical editor asked me very severely on how many interviews with informants a certain statement was based. When I asked how many published documents would have been needed to authenticate it, he agreed that he would accept a minimum of one, providing there were no contradictory evidence. Finally, a young historian recently advised us to call our recorded interviews with carefully identified informants "unpublished memoirs."

In the course of cooperative work such as I shall suggest, most of these misunderstandings will disappear, if it is possible to push behind these disciplinary blind spots, so that an anthropologist can watch an historian criticize the usefulness of a *document*, weigh it, test it, compare it with "other evidence," and if an historian can watch an anthropologist record a series of interviews with an informant and weigh them, test them, and compare them with "other evidence." And they will disappear, I believe, in the exploration of what is meant by the term "other evidence"—which, aside from other documents, has re-

mained largely inexplicit among historians as each one
trusted to his growing "feeling for the period." This is
an area in which anthropologists have become steadily
more self-conscious; in their case, the "other evidence"
can be handled systematically by reference to successive
steps in the learning process or to the formal characteristics of some other facet of the culture.

For example, during the early days of our Balinese field
work, we continually received accounts of "marriage by
capture." This was definitely not in accord with such
"other evidence" in Balinese culture as the almost complete absence of any physical fighting among children,
the handling of quarrels by silence, and a break in all
communication between the disputants, etc. Here historians, distrusting a document, and anthropologists, distrusting informants' reports, are still on the same ground
—the item of information does not fit. We were able to
solve this apparent incongruity when we found that "marriage by capture" was a carefully planned elopement in
which it was necessary to simulate capture as a gesture
of courtesy to the culturally preferred marriage which was
being evaded, and that this was done with conscious
theatricality. The theatricality of the Balinese could further be referred to in the way in which the climatic
expression of emotional sequences was broken in childhood by a mother whose only fully enacted sequences are
of theatrical or simulated emotion.[14]

I would suggest that the most practical way for historians and anthropologists to learn from each other is in
a situation in which they can really experience each
other's methods. Such a situation would be provided by
work on a common problem located in a period for which
both living persons—as informants—and well-ordered
documents were available, a problem so conceived that
each facet would be systematically referable to larger
structural wholes.

Such a group working together might, for example,
investigate a small New England city between 1900-1914,
studying its economic and social development with particular reference to changes in job opportunity, shifts in
ownership and decision-making, and in the way in which
the small city was integrated with the social and economic

life of the region, the nation, and the world. Older men and women could be used as informants, actual changes in residence and communication within the community could be mapped, the history of economic and social change could be followed through local records. The pictures of the past obtained by the different methods could be systematically compared, and materials obtained by members of both disciplines could be referred to the series of widening circles or wholes within which the study was made.

In such a joint venture, historians would be responsible for maintaining the sense of trend, of movement over time, and for making it clear to the anthropologists why they regarded it necessary to go back to the Civil War in examining one sequence, back only to 1890 in examining another, and why they were willing to label a sequence as new, or beginning in a certain year. At present it is exceedingly difficult for anthropologists to discover how the historian makes such selections, what in fact are the criteria by which the historian decides that certain periods provide the most relevant sequential or diachronic setting for his investigations. Instead of the young historian learning from his seniors until he got a "feel" for the necessary data, he would be challenged by a "why" from his contemporaries trained in a different discipline.

Meanwhile, the anthropologist, who would be responsible for the adequacy and inclusiveness of the working model of the "whole community" and the "whole culture," would be equally and relevantly pressed. Instead of carrying over in bits and pieces his knowledge that kinship or ceremonials of crisis are something one ought to investigate, he would have to show the relationship between the biological requirements of a human society (in which men and women with defined biological needs and potentialities must reproduce and nourish and train the young) and the culture and specific social structure of that society.

Working together, historians and anthropologists would also become more sharply aware of the problems involved in surrendering their traditional devices for maintaining detachment—the historian by working with periods which are in the past,* the anthropologist by working with primitive peoples whose value systems are far removed from his own. Neither type of detachment is feasible for those working on contemporary societies.

Historians, after trying to obtain perspective on their material by permitting a sufficient amount of time to elapse, have often been much franker than other social scientists in recognizing that they belong to their own period and are writing for it. The interpretation itself has been treated as normative with a hope that it is tempered by a longer time perspective and the seasoned wisdom which comes from the knowledge of the follies men have committed, the depths to which men have fallen, and the heights to which they have risen again.

Anthropologists have taken a somewhat different course. We have explicitly demarcated an area of "applied anthropology" in which we are using our disciplined knowledge to affect the lives of identified people or groups. (A comparable area in the discipline of history would be the role of historians in policy formation, in international organizations, in the revision of textbooks for occupied countries, etc.) For this particular area we have adopted a code of professional ethics,[16] in which we assume responsibility for the foreseeable effects of our acts.

Studying and publishing upon our own civilization falls inevitably under the heading of applied science, because each pronouncement upon contemporary culture by historian, anthropologist, or any other student of society, will change that culture. One way of meeting this challenge is purposely to include the cultural membership of research workers in the research, orchestrating the research team by the inclusion of members of the culture being studied and members of at least two other cultures. It should be anticipated that in cooperative research on

* How dangerous it can be to surrender the detachment provided by a lapse of time without replacing it by some new ethic, is only too vividly demonstrated in *The Spoilage*, by Dorothy Thomas and Richard Nishimoto,[15] a book which was published immediately after World War II. Overtly the study lacks value judgments, but a covert bias is displayed in the choice—as subject matter—of the 10 per cent of the interned Japanese for whom the experience was disastrous.

recently past periods, in which historians and anthropologists might work together for the express purpose of exploring each other's methods, this same procedure might be followed. In a study of American civilization of a given region between 1900-1914, a working team would include individuals who had matured in that city and at that period, younger students, and, in addition to American anthropologists and American historians, social scientists from at least one European society.

I myself have found the mere attempt to outline some of the possibilities of such collaboration so stimulating that it would seem reasonable that the experience of working on a common problem might prove rewarding to members of both disciplines.

The American Quarterly, Vol. 3, No. 1 (1951), 3-13.

REFERENCES

1. Ware, C. F. (ed.), 1940; Gorer, G., 1940.
2. Bateson, G., and M. Mead, 1942.
3. Bateson, G., 1936; Linton, R., 1936; Mead, M. (ed.), 1937; Radcliffe-Brown, A. R., 1940.
4. Mosely, P., 1940.
5. Benedict, R., 1934.
6. Lamb, R. K., 1950.
7. Bateson, G., 1942c; Dollard, J., 1935; Erikson, E. H., 1950; Gesell, A. L., and F. L. Ilg, 1943; Mead, M., 1947d; Riesman, D., 1950.
8. Bateson, G., 1944.
9. Warner, W. L., 1959; Warner, W. L., and J. O. Low, 1947; Warner, W. L., and P. S. Lunt, 1941 and 1942; Warner, W. L., and L. Srole, 1945.
10. Bateson, G., 1949; Chapple, E. D., and C. S. Coon, 1942; Richardson, L. F., 1939; Ruesch, J., and G. Bateson, 1949; Schumpeter, J. A., 1934; Tannenbaum, F., 1946.
11. Huxley, T. H., and J. S. Huxley, 1947.
12. Gorer, G., and J. Rickman, 1950.
13. Zborowski, M., and E. Herzog, 1952.
14. Bateson, G., and M. Mead, 1942.
15. Thomas, D. S., and R. S. Nishimoto, 1946.
16. Mead, M., 1942c, 1950; Mead, M., E. D. Chapple, and G. G. Brown, 1949.

13

Our Educational Emphases
in Primitive Perspective

In its broadest sense, education is the cultural process,
the way in which each newborn human infant, born with
a potentiality for learning greater than that of any other
mammal, is transformed into a full member of a specific
human society, sharing with the other members a specific
human culture. From this point of view we can place
side by side the newborn child in a modern city and the
savage infant born into some primitive South Sea tribe.
Both have everything to learn. Both depend for that
learning upon the help and example, the care and tute-
lage, of the elders of their societies. Neither child has
any guaranty of growing up to be a full human being
should some accident interfere with its human education.
Despite the tremendous difference in what the New York
infant and the New Guinea infant will learn, there is a
striking similarity in the whole complicated process by
which the child takes on and into itself the culture of
those around it. And much profit can be gained by concentrating on these similarities and by setting the procedure of the South Sea mother side by side with the
procedure of the New York mother, attempting to understand the common elements in cultural transmission. In
such comparisons we can identify the tremendous potentialities of human beings, who are able to learn not only
to speak any one of a thousand languages but to adjust
to as many different rhythms of maturation, ways of
learning, methods of organizing their emotions and of
managing their relationships to other human beings.

In this paper, however, I propose to turn away from
this order of comparison—which notes the differences

between human cultures, primitive and civilized, only as means of exploring the processes which occur in both types of culture—and to stress instead the ways in which our present behavior, which we bracket under the abstraction "education," differs from the procedures characteristic of primitive homogeneous communities. I propose to ask, not what there is in common between contemporary America and South Sea societies with a Stone Age level of culture, but to ask instead: What are some of the conspicuous differences, and what light do these differences throw upon our understanding of our own conception of education? And, because this is too large and wide a subject, I want to limit myself still further and to ask: What effects has the mingling of peoples—of different races, different religions, and different levels of cultural complexity—had upon our concept of education? When we place our present-day concept against a backdrop of primitive educational procedures and see it as influenced by the intermingling of peoples, what do we find?

I once lectured to a group of women—all of them college graduates—alert enough to be taking a fairly advanced adult-education course on "Primitive Education" delivered from the first point of view. I described in detail the lagoon village of the Manus tribe, the ways in which the parents taught the children to master their environment, to swim, to climb, to handle fire, to paddle a canoe, to judge distances and calculate the strength of materials. I described the tiny canoes which were given to the three-year-olds, the miniature fish spears with which they learned to spear minnows, the way in which small boys learned to calk their canoes with gum, and how small girls learned to thread shell money into aprons. Interwoven with a discussion of the more fundamental issues, such as the relationship between children and parents and the relationships between younger children and older children, I gave a fairly complete account of the type of adaptive craft behavior which was characteristic of the Manus and the way in which this was learned by each generation of children. At the end of the lecture one woman stood up and asked the first question: "Didn't they have any vocational training?" Many of the others

laughed at the question, and I have often told it myself
as a way of getting my audience into a mood which was
less rigidly limited by our own phrasing of "education."
But that woman's question, naïve and crude as it was,
epitomized a long series of changes which stand between
our idea of education and the processes by which members of a homogeneous and relatively static primitive
society transmit their standardized habit patterns to their
children.

There are several striking differences between our concept of education today and that of any contemporary
primitive society; but perhaps the most important one
is the shift from the need for an individual to learn
something which everyone agrees he would wish to know,
to the will of some individual to teach something which
it is not agreed that anyone has any desire to know. Such
a shift in emphasis could come only with the breakdown
of self-contained and self-respecting cultural homogeneity.
The Manus or the Arapesh or the Iatmul adults taught
their children all that they knew themselves. Sometimes,
it is true, there were rifts in the process. A man might
die without having communicated some particular piece
of ritual knowledge; a good hunter might find no suitable
apprentice among his available near kin, so that his skill
perished with him. A girl might be so clumsy and stupid
that she never learned to weave a mosquito basket that
was fit to sell. Miscarriages in the smooth working of the
transmission of available skills and knowledge did occur,
but they were not sufficient to focus the attention of the
group upon the desirability of *teaching* as against the
desirability of *learning*. Even with considerable division
of labor and with a custom by which young men learned
a special skill not from a father or other specified relative
but instead from a master of the art, the master did not
go seeking pupils; the pupils and their parents went to
seek the master and with proper gifts of fish or octopus
or dogs' teeth persuaded him to teach the neophyte. And
at this level of human culture even close contact with
members of other cultures did not alter the emphasis.
Women who spoke another language married into the
tribe; it was, of course, very important that they should
learn to speak the language of their husbands' people,

and so they learned that language as best they could—or failed to learn it. People might compliment them on their facility or laugh at them for their lack of it, but the idea of *assimilating* them was absent.

Similarly, in the spread of special cults or sects among South Sea peoples, the desire to *join* the sect rather than the need to make converts was emphasized. New ceremonies did develop. It was necessary that those who had formerly been ignorant of them should learn new songs or new dance steps, but the onus was again upon the learner. The greater self-centeredness of primitive homogeneous groups (often so self-centered that they divided mankind into two groups—the human beings, i.e., themselves, and the nonhuman beings, other people) preserved them also from the emphasis upon the greater value of one truth over another which is the condition of proselytizing. "*We* (human beings) do it this way and *they* (other people) do it that way." A lack of a desire to teach *them* our ways guaranteed also that the *we* group had no fear of any proselytizing from the *they* groups. A custom might be imported, bought, obtained by killing the owner, or taken as part of a marriage payment. A custom might be exported for a price or a consideration. But the emphasis lay upon the desire of the importing group to obtain the new skill or song and upon the desire of the exporting group for profit in material terms by the transaction. The idea of conversion, of purposely attempting to alter the ideas and attitudes of other persons, did not occur. One might try to persuade one's brother-in-law to abandon his own group and come and hunt permanently with the tribe into which his sister had married; physical proselytizing there was, just as there was actual import and export of items of culture. But, once the brother-in-law had been persuaded to join a different cultural group, it was his job to learn how to live there; and you might, if you were still afraid he would go back or if you wanted his cooperation in working a two-man fish net, take considerable pains to teach him this or that skill as a bribe. But to bribe another by teaching him one's own skill is a long way from any practice of conversion, although it may be made subsidiary to it.

We have no way of knowing how often in the course

of human history the idea of Truth, as a revelation to or possession of some one group (which thereby gained the right to consider itself superior to all those who lacked this revelation), may have appeared. But certain it is that, wherever this notion of hierarchical arrangements of cultural views of experience appears, it has profound effects upon education—and it has enormously influenced our own attitudes toward education. As soon as there is any idea that one set of cultural beliefs is definitely superior to another, the framework is present for active proselytizing, unless the idea of cultural superiority is joined with some idea of hereditary membership, as it is among the Hindus. (It would indeed be interesting to investigate whether any group which considered itself in possession of the most superior brand of religious or economic truth, but which did not regard its possession to be limited by heredity, could preserve the belief in that superiority without proselytizing. It might be found that active proselytizing was the necessary condition for the preservation of the essential belief in one's own revelation.) Thus, with the appearance of religions which held this belief in their own infallible superiority, education becomes a concern of those who teach rather than of those who learn. Attention is directed toward finding neophytes rather than toward finding masters, and adults and children become bracketed together as recipients of conscious missionary effort. This bracketing-together is of great importance; it increases the self-consciousness of the whole educational procedure, and it is quite possible that the whole question of methods and techniques of education is brought most sharply to the fore when it is a completely socialized adult who must be influenced instead of a plastic and receptive child.

With social stratification the possibility of using education as a way of changing status is introduced, and another new component of the educational idea develops. Here the emphasis is still upon the need to learn—on the one hand, in order to alter status and, on the other, to prevent the loss of status by failure to learn. But wherever this possibility enters in there is also a possibility of a new concept of education developing from the relationship between fixed caste and class lines and education. In a static society members of different caste or class groups may have been teaching their children different standards of behavior for many generations without any essential difference between their attitudes toward education and those of less complex societies. To effect a change it is necessary to focus the attention of the members of the society upon the problem, as conditions of cultural contact do focus it. Thus, in pre-World War II Bali, the high castes sent their daughters to the Dutch schools to be trained as schoolteachers because in their eyes it was pre-eminently important that learning should be kept in the hands of the high castes and profoundly inappropriate that low-caste teachers should teach high-caste children. They felt this strongly enough to overcome their prejudices against a course which took high-caste women out into the market place.

As soon as the possibility of shift of class position by virtue of a different educational experience becomes articulately recognized, so that individuals seek not only to better their children or to guard them against educational defect but also to see the extension of restriction of educational opportunity as relevant to the whole class structure, another element enters in—the relationship of education to social change. Education becomes a mechanism of change. Public attention, once focused upon this possibility, is easily turned to the converse position of emphasizing education as a means toward preserving the status quo. I argue here for no historical priority in the two positions. But I am inclined to believe that we do not have catechumens taught to say "to do my duty in that state of life into which it has pleased God to call me" until we have the beginning of movements of individuals away from their birth positions in society. In fact, the whole use of education to defend vested interests and intrenched privilege goes with the recognition that education can be a way of encroaching upon them. Just as the presence of proselytizing religions focuses attention upon the means of spreading the truth, upon pedagogy, so the educational implications of social stratification focus attention upon the content of education and lay the groundwork for an articulate interest in the curriculum.

Movements of peoples, colonization, and trade also bring education into a different focus. In New Guinea it is not uncommon to "hear" (i.e., understand without speaking) several languages besides one's own, and many peoples not only "hear" but also speak neighboring languages. A head-hunting people like the Mundugumor, who had the custom of giving child hostages to temporary allies among neighboring peoples, articulately recognized that it was an advantage to have members of the group be well acquainted with the roads, the customs, and the language of their neighbors, who would assuredly at some time in any given generation be enemies and objects of attack. Those who took the hostages regarded this increased facility of the Mundugumor as a disadvantage which had to be put up with. But the emphasis remained with the desirability of learning. After European contact, with the growth of pidgin English as a lingua franca, bush natives and young boys became most anxious to learn pidgin. Their neighbors, with whom they could trade and communicate more readily if they knew pidgin, were, however, not interested in teaching them. But the European colonist was interested. He saw his position as an expanding, initiating, changing one; he wanted to trade with the natives, to recruit and indenture them to work on plantations. He needed to have them speak a language that he could understand. Accordingly, we had the shift from the native who needed to learn another language in order to understand to the colonist who needed to have someone else learn a language so that he, the colonist, could be understood. In the course of teaching natives to speak some lingua franca, to handle money, to work copra, etc., the whole focus was on teaching; not, however, on techniques of teaching, in the sense of pedagogy, but upon sanctions for making the native learn. Such usages develop rapidly into compulsory schooling in the language of the colonist or the conqueror, and they result in the school being seen as an adjunct of the group in power rather than as a privilege for those who learn.

Just as conquest or colonization of already inhabited countries brings up the problems of assimilation, so also mass migrations may accentuate the same problem. This has been true particularly in the United States, where education has been enormously influenced by the articulate need to assimilate the masses of European and other immigrants, with the resulting phrasing of the public schools as a means for educating other peoples' children. The school ceased to be chiefly a device by which children were taught accumulated knowledge or skills and became a political device for arousing and maintaining national loyalty through inculcating a language and a system of ideas which the pupils did not share with their parents.

It is noteworthy that, in the whole series of educational emphases which I have discussed here as significant components of our present-day concept of "education," one common element which differentiates the ideas of conversion, assimilation, successful colonization, and the relationship between class-caste lines and education from the attitudes found in primitive homogeneous societies is the acceptance of discontinuity between parents and children. Primitive education was a process by which continuity was maintained between parents and children, even if the actual teacher was not a parent but a maternal uncle or a shaman. Modern education includes a heavy emphasis upon the function of education to create discontinuities—to turn the child of the peasant into a clerk, of the farmer into a lawyer, of the Italian immigrant into an American, of the illiterate into the literate. And parallel with this is the attempt to use education as an extra, special prop for tottering continuities. Parents who are separated from their children by all the gaps in understanding which are a function of our rapidly changing world cling to the expedient of sending their children to the same schools and colleges they attended, counting upon the heavy traditionalism of slow-moving institutions to stem the tide of change. (Thus, while the father builds himself a new house and the mother furnishes it with modern furniture, they both rejoice that back at school, through the happy accident that the school is not well enough endowed, son will sit at the same desk at which his father sat.) The same attitude is reflected by the stock figure of the member of a rural school board who says, "What was good enough for me in school is good enough for my children. The three R's, that's enough."

Another common factor in these modern trends of

education is the increasing emphasis upon change rather than upon growth, upon what is done to people rather than upon what people do. This emphasis comes, I believe, from the inclusion of adults as objects of the educational effort—whether the effort comes from missionaries, colonizers, conquerors, Old Americans, or employers of labor. When a child is learning to talk, the miracle of learning is so pressing and conspicuous that the achievement of the teachers is put in the shade. But the displacement, in an adult's speech habits, of his native tongue by the phonetics of some language which he is being bullied or cajoled into learning is often more a matter of triumph for the teacher than of pride for the learner. Changing people's habits, people's ideas, people's language, people's beliefs, people's emotional allegiances, involves a sort of deliberate violence to other people's developed personalities—a violence not to be found in the whole teacher-child relationship, which finds its prototype in the cherishing parent helping the young child to learn those things which are essential to his humanity.

We have been shocked in recent decades by the outspoken brutality of the totalitarian states, which set out to inculcate into children's minds a series of new ideas which it was considered politically useful for them to learn. Under the conflicting currents of modern ideologies the idea of *indoctrination* has developed as a way of characterizing the conscious educational aims of any group with whom the speaker is out of sympathy. Attempts to teach children any set of ideas in which one believes have in this way become tainted with suspicion of power and self-interest, until almost all education can be branded and dismissed as one sort of indoctrination or another. The attempt to assimilate, convert, or keep in their places other human beings conceived of as inferior to those who are making the plans has been a boomerang which has distorted our whole educational philosophy; it has shifted the emphasis from one of growth and seeking for knowledge to one of dictation and forced acceptance of clichés and points of view. Thus we see that the presence of one element within our culture— a spurious sense of superiority of one group of human beings over another, which gave the group in power the impetus to force their language, their beliefs, and their culture down the throats of the group which was numerically, or economically, or geographically handicapped—has corrupted and distorted the emphases of our free schools.

But there has been another emphasis developing side by side with those which I have been discussing, and that is a belief in the power of education to work miracles—a belief which springs from a sense of the new. As long as the transmission of culture is an orderly and continuous process, in a slowly changing society, the child speaks the language of his parents; and, although one may marvel that this small human being learns at all, one does not marvel that he learns French or English or Samoan, provided that this be the language of the parents. It took the discontinuity of educational systems, purposive shifts of language and beliefs between parents and children, to catch our imagination and to fashion the great American faith in education as creation rather than transmission, conversion, suppression, assimilation, or indoctrination. Perhaps one of the most basic human ways of saying "new" is "something that my parents have never experienced" or, when we speak of our children, "something I have never experienced." The drama of discontinuity, which has been such a startling feature of modern life and for which formal education has been regarded in great measure responsible, suggested to men that perhaps education might be a device for creating a new kind of world by developing a new kind of human being.

Here it is necessary to distinguish sharply between the kind of idea which George Counts expressed in his discussion, *Dare the Schools Build a New Social Order?*[1] and the idea of education as creation of something new. Dr. Counts did not mean a new social order in the sense of an order that no man as yet had dreamed of, so much as he meant a very concrete and definite type of society for which he and many others believed they had a blueprint. He was asking whether the teachers would use the schools to produce a different type of socioeconomic system. His question was still a power question and partook of all the power ideas which have developed in the long period during which men in power, men with dominating ideas, men with missions, have sought to put their ideas over upon other men. His question would have been phrased more accurately as "Dare the schools build a different social order?" The schools of America have these hundred years been training children to give allegiance to a way of life that was new to them, not because they were children to whom all ways were new, not because the way of life was itself one that no man had yet dreamed of, but because they were the children of their parents. Whenever one group succeeds in getting power over the schools and teaches within those schools a doctrine foreign to many of those who enter those doors, they are building up, from the standpoint of those students, a different social order. From the standpoint of those in power, they are defending or extending the old; and, from the moment that the teachers had seriously started to put Dr. Counts's suggestion into practice, they would have been attempting by every method available to them to extend, in the minds of other people's children, their own picture, already an "old" idea, of the sort of world they wanted to live in.

It is not this kind of newness of which I speak. But from those who watched learning, those who humbly observed miracles instead of claiming them as the fruits of their strategy or of their superior teaching techniques, there grew up in America a touching belief that it was possible by education to build a new world—a world that no man had yet dreamed and that no man, bred as we had been bred, could dream. They argued that if we can bring up our children to be freer than we have been— freer from anxiety, freer from guilt and fear, freer from economic constraint and the dictates of expediency—to be equipped as we never were equipped, trained to think and enjoy thinking, trained to feel and enjoy feeling, then we shall produce a new kind of human being, one not known upon the earth before. Instead of the single visionary, the depth of whose vision has kept men's souls alive for centuries, we shall develop a whole people bred to the task of seeing with clear imaginative eyes into a future which is hidden from us behind the smoke screen of our generation's defective and irremediable educational handicaps. This belief has often been branded as naïve and simple-minded. The American faith in education, which has been recognized as one of the dominant American culture traits, has been held up to ridicule many times. In many of its forms it is not only unjustified optimism but arrant nonsense. When small children are sent out by overzealous schoolteachers to engage in active social reforms—believed necessary by their teachers—the whole point of view becomes not only ridiculous but dangerous to the children themselves.

Phrased, however, without any of our blueprints, with an insistence that it is the children themselves who will some day, when they are grown, make their own world on the basis of their better upbringing, the idea is a bold and beautiful one, an essentially democratic and American idea. Instead of attempting to bind and limit the future and to compromise the inhabitants of the next century by a long process of indoctrination which will make them unable to follow any path but that which we have laid down, it suggests that we devise and practice a system of education which sets the future free. We must concentrate upon teaching our children to walk so steadily that we need not hew too straight and narrow paths for them but can trust them to make new paths through difficulties we never encountered to a future of which we have no inkling today.

When we look for the contributions which contacts of peoples, of peoples of different races and different religions, different levels of culture and different degrees of technological development, have made to education, we find two. On the one hand, the emphasis has shifted from learning to teaching, from the doing to the one who causes it to be done, from spontaneity to coercion, from freedom to power. With this shift has come the development of techniques of power, dry pedagogy, regimentation, indoctrination, manipulation, and propaganda. These are but sorry additions to man's armory, and they come from the insult to human life which is perpetuated whenever one human being is regarded as differentially less or more human than another. But, on the other hand, out of the discontinuities and rapid changes which have accompanied these minglings of people has come another invention, one which perhaps would not have been born in any other setting than this one—the belief in education as an instrument for the creation of new human values.

We stand today in a crowded place, where millions of men mill about seeking to go in different directions. It is most uncertain whether the educational invention made by those who emphasized teaching or the educational invention made by those who emphasized learning will survive. But the more rapidly we can erase from our society those discrepancies in position and privilege which tend to perpetuate and strengthen the power and manipulative aspects of education, the more hope we may have that that other invention—the use of education for unknown ends which shall exalt man above his present stature—may survive.

American Journal of Sociology, Vol. 48, No. 6 (1943), 633-39.

REFERENCES

1. Counts, G., 1932.

14

Cultural Contexts of Nutrition Patterns

The inclusion[1] of the sciences of anthropology and psychology in the approach to the problems of nutrition has been historically compromised by the concreteness of the issues and by the precision which has been attained in nutritional research. Where there are no concrete measurable quantities involved, where an issue can be seen as one involving "fear" or prejudice or superstition, the scientist based in the natural sciences is willing to invoke the collaboration of those disciplines which specialize in the study of human tradition and of the human psyche. But in the sciences of food and nutrition, the issues have seemed exceedingly simple, a matter of obtaining large enough quantities of the right foods, distributing them among the people who need them, and teaching people to stop eating the wrong foods and start eating the right ones. To bridge the gap between traditional and unplanned methods by which human societies fed themselves and forms of food production, distribution, and consumption which would reflect the present technical knowledge about food and nutrition has been seen simply as a shift from the "wrong," i.e., prescientific way of doing things, to the "right," or currently accepted scientific way of doing things. The focus was upon the food itself, its quality, the proportions in which it should be produced, processed, distributed, and eaten, with the assumption that those who ate the food would accept a mixed moral-scientific imperative to alter their habits. Thus the question which was asked by those specialists who attempted to alter the consumption habits of an individual or of a group, was: "How can we change their food habits?" The tenacity with which individuals or groups clung to methods of food preparation or a dietary pattern that had been proved to be nutritionally less desirable than other methods and patterns available to them in terms of food supply was branded as stubborn, backward behavior based on wrong habits.

The shift which has taken place in the last ten years, especially under the stimulus of the feeding problems which developed during World War II, has been an increasing attention to the nature of food habits, the role which learning plays in the establishment and maintenance of a viable dietary pattern. We now ask, not how can we change a people's bad habits to good habits, but what are their habits, how are they learned, by what mechanisms are the self-preservative choices of some foods and rejections of others, perpetuated.[2] Just as any changes in agricultural production have to be based not only upon a preliminary assay of the soil, the climatic conditions, and experiments in the introduction of crops not hitherto grown under such conditions, but also upon a study of the traditional agricultural practices, so the scientific approach to any culturally maintained dietary pattern must include not only a description of what that pattern is, but also an analysis of how it is maintained. In such a description, the traditional methods of learning what to eat and what to avoid, with the particularization of time, place, amount, sequence, method of preparation and of serving, are as important as a description of the actual food, its nutritional content, the nutritional implications of the methods of production, preservation, transportation, and preparation. Stated concretely this means that whether children are rewarded and punished with food, in a given society at a given time, is as important as whether the method of cooking the only green vegetable involves an almost complete loss of vitamin C content. To stress one set of data, involving vitamin loss, mineral loss, utilization of the less nutritious part of a food supply and discard of the more nutritious, while ignoring the other set of data on methods of teaching and learning used in the society, the extent to which age, sex, and caste identity is established by rejection of or insistence upon certain foods, gives an incomplete account of a people's dietary pattern.

However, there is still great danger that the two kinds of data, those which come from agricultural, technical, and nutritional researches, and those which come from anthropological and psychological researches, will not be integrated because the concrete nexus between learning and food will be ignored. The same cultural mechanisms may be invoked in two behaviors with very different nutritional consequences. For example, among the Arapesh of New Guinea,[3] food is divided into two categories called *bonah* and *shaloh,* food for those in vulnerable states of reproductive growth and those who are in less vulnerable states. This categorization includes nutritionally relevant and nutritionally irrelevant considerations; for example, meat is forbidden among one section of the Arapesh, to all young people between puberty and the birth of a first child, during what is known to be a period of growth where a nutritious diet is very important. Adolescents are also forbidden to eat oddly shaped fruit, which share with meat a quality antithetical to the maturation of the reproductive functions. Any examination of the cultural sanctions or the psychological attitudes involved will show high similarity, and the disciplines concerned with a description of the behavior of the people, tend to concentrate upon such similarities, to discuss food taboos when attempting to change dietary patterns, but the understanding of the way in which learning underwrites the dietary pattern is obscured. On the other hand, the nutritionist, assessing a set of diets, may find that in diets of three different cultural groups, men—in contrast to women—refuse to eat green vegetables. If the emphasis is placed merely upon the deficiency of nutrients obtained from green vegetables and if an attempt is made either to persuade men to eat green vegetables or to persuade them to alter their diet to include other foods containing many of the nutrients obtained from green vegetables, without taking into account the cultural position of green vegetables, here again only partial understanding will result. For there is a significant difference between the rejection of green vegetables because they are food for ruminant animals, rejection of green vegetables because they do not produce virility, rejection of green vegetables as the low status food of a conquered or servitor people, etc. The very learning which includes the rejection of green vegetables may also underlie the acceptance of the rest of the particular diet upon which the strength of the men of each group depends, and the dilution or destruction of one part of the pattern—regarded as nutritionally weak—may also undermine the parts which are nutritionally needed.

Only by a recognition of the importance of learning, on the part of those sciences which deal with soil, food, and physiology, and of the importance of the particular constitution of actual concrete food by those sciences which deal with social tradition, learning, and individual psychological behaviors can these one-sided emphases be resolved. Such a combination of the approaches and techniques of all the related sciences involved has never been completely worked out on a single group of people. In this discussion, therefore, it is necessary to rely upon partial studies, knowledge of the way in which children learn in one society, of the ceremonial feasting pattern, of its significance for food distribution in another society, and in still other societies, of the sorts of substitution of new foods which occur under new geographical conditions. We have to illustrate the importance of methods of cooking from studies which have been made independently of the way in which those methods of cooking have been learned and transmitted. The integration of those scattered discrete studies and descriptions into an ordered statement of the cultural context of nutritional patterns is possible only because the science of nutrition, on the one hand, and of culture on the other,[4] are sufficiently advanced so that systematic extrapolations from known data are possible. If the nutritionist is presented with a rough statement of the foods used by a people on the other side of the world, whose diet is based on tubers, the nutritional content of which has never been assayed, and with photographs of their children with highly distended abdomens who have never had any sort of medical examination, he may extrapolate from known relationships between diets with too great dependence upon starch and disturbances in growth pattern. He will not, however, have any certainty of obtaining a full understanding, because other factors such as some unknown intestinal parasite may also be involved, but he may have a fair expectation of making relevant hypotheses. In comparable fashion the anthropologist provided the information that a given people are exceedingly talkative, are poor at learning new languages, and are extremely recalcitrant about accepting new foods, will be able, from our knowledge of the way learning occurs, to make certain predictions about the way in which their children are taught to talk and to eat.

A brief description of the required demonstration research which would effectively tie together our differently derived knowledge of human diet seems appropriate before I go on to outline what may be said with fair certainty without such demonstration studies. For a complete study of the cultural context of a dietary pattern, we would need to select a group of people whose food history was known, to the degree that they were known to have belonged for an appreciable length of time (as indicated by the language they spoke, archeological remains, historical records, etc.) to a given region with a known food pattern, e.g., a rice-eating area based on a wet rice economy, and a garnish of pork, fowl, fish, and vegetables. We would need to know when, approximately domestic animals had been introduced, or the religious system had been altered to permit killing and eating animals not previously eaten, or the group had moved to an area with a different source of animal food supply, or new agricultural techniques such as the oxen-drawn plough had become available. In addition to this historical information, we would need situational data for the last quarter century, whether there had been drought, pests, hurricane or earthquake, war, epidemic or migration, involving periods of unusual scarcity or plenty, wiping out particular crops, altering the proportional dependence upon different crops, etc. Then for a representative food cycle, which is usually approximately a calendar year (except in those cases where major ceremonials geared to a longer period than the lunar year are the occasion for special aggregations of food), we would need a record of the entire agricultural, animal husbandry, and fishing and hunting behavior, including the prevalence and proportions of those crops which were slightly eaten, and those animals and fish which were not utilized fully. Thus, for a full understanding of the food culture of any people, it must always be seen within the whole environment, which means that sources of food that are known and rejected and sources of food that are not known must also be recognized. Otherwise, it is not possible to judge accurately the differential ways in which peoples with different traditions will respond to scarcity and malnutrition. Some peoples, with records of successful survival under exceedingly unfavorable environmental circumstances, shift very quickly from a selective habitual diet into a more omnivorous acceptance of the environment.

Such a study of the annual food-gathering and food-producing cycle would include all those culturally patterned triggers of action, the extra field planted for the special ceremony, the crocodile hunt organized especially to provide food for death ceremonies, the extra harvest garnered and stored against a famine year, so that it would be possible to tell to what extent the food behavior was adjusted to conditions in the physical environment as well as the ways in which social arrangements, such as ceremonial for life crises and war behavior, provided a framework within which food was more or less plentiful. At both primitive and more complex social levels, there is a wide variety as between those societies which accept food deprivation as an inevitable condition of life—accompanying war, or cycles of rain and drought—and those which organize their resources in the face of emergencies to bring the food supply to a new level, and those which do neither. "In order to have an initiation ceremony it was necessary to organize hunts for foods"—the approach of the aboriginal Australian living in an exceedingly harsh desert environment—contrasts with the reply of the Apache living in a similar environment who was asked, "When did you have a feast?" and answered, "When someone had found some meat."

Following the detailed study of food production, we would need an equally detailed study of distribution, from the hunt or the harvest through the many steps of gift, sale, resale, storage, treatment, and preparation for the table. Finally we would need to know whether or not the food was actually consumed at the table, and by whom. This would include all the variations from the Japanese wife who ate the rice left to burn from the last meal, while her husband and children ate fresh rice, to the well-to-do householder who shares his large share of meat with his favorite dog, or to the practices where children's uneaten food is put carefully away to reappear, meal after meal, until eaten.

In addition to a study of the calendar, the fasting and feasting and social classification of foods, the actual material paraphernalia for food preparation and consumption, the type of fuel and stove, types of cooking vessels, and methods of disposal of waste must be studied in detail, seen both as devices for the preservation of the customary food pattern and as the technological basis within which particular nutrients are conserved or lost. Migration from a temperate climate to a less temperate climate, for instance, not only involves changes in some of the foods available, but also radical changes in the methods of food preservation—for example, the boiling of milk in the tropics or the introduction of refrigeration into a European food pattern when it was transplanted to the United States. Changes from a slow cooking over charcoal to a rapid cooking over gas, from baking in an earth oven to boiling in a clay pot, from cooking in leaves to roasting on spits—all of these involve very considerable changes in the available nourishment obtained from the same food. Yet at any given moment in history, the interrelations between the food available and the technical and social habits of those who utilize it form an indispensable framework within which that people obtain their nourishment.

A complete study of the dietary practices of any people would also include the way in which infants born into that society learn to eat the appropriate foods, on the appropriate occasions, and to avoid, with fear, disgust, or simply incomprehension of the possibility of eating them, foods which are regarded as inappropriate.

At each stage in such a study, there would be relevant assays of the soil, of the foods as they were harvested, of

losses during storage, drying, smoking, etc., of the foods
as they emerged from the pot or the fire, and of the actual
nutritional status of the members of the society at different stages of development, different times of the year,
and during different types of activity. Students of nutrition will recognize how very far we are from any such
complete study even in societies within which as much
careful work has been done as in the United States and
Western Europe in the last twenty-five years.[5]

With the full understanding that statements about the
cultural contexts of nutritional patterns can be made
only as systematic statements based upon our general
knowledge of culture, illuminated with particular and
partial instances taken from different cultures at different
periods, it is possible to discuss certain particularly significant aspects of dietary patterns.

In all known human societies, dietary patterns are
based on learned behavior in which each detail must be
conveyed, explicitly or inexplicitly, to each new generation of children and to adult immigrants who enter the
society. The combination of foods sufficient to maintain
life at a reproductive level, which is seen by the student
of human nutrition as a set of nutrients occurring in
different proportions, will be perceived by the group of
human beings who eat this combination in a large variety
of ways independent of specific nutritional content. Foods
will be classified in terms of sociological source, as when
a man is forbidden to eat from the harvest of his own
seed; in terms of the manner of killing—as in the pro-
visions for the killing of animals among orthodox Jews—
or among the Jains—a sect which can eat meat but not
take life; in terms of the way in which it is prepared, with
different sets of utensils, varying from taboos on cooking
in vessels in which washing is done, or on boiling eggs in
a tea kettle, to taboos on eating from the same pot in
which game killed by a blood brother has been cooked.
Foods may be classified by caste or class, so that certain
foods will be seen as fit for animals but not for men, fit
for men of one caste but not for higher castes, fit for the
poor but not for the well-to-do, fit for foreigners but not
for natives, fit for children but not for adults. They may

be classified by their place in time, as food for holidays
but not for everyday, food for periods of mourning but
not for feasting, or for mourning and feasting but not for
more neutral periods, suitable for the first meal of the day
but inappropriate for the evening meal, or edible only in
summer or in the dead of winter. Actual place of eating
may be significant, certain foods being suitable for eating in the fields, on the hunt, by the army at war, on ship-
board, on the street, at a picnic. The investigator, start-
ing with a given food, venison, blackberries, shark meat,
potatoes, dragon flies, sago, pork, or mushrooms, will find
that a whole cluster of qualities, each of which refers to
the acceptance or rejection of the particular food source
in a particular cultural pattern, will be evoked.

When the meal pattern of a people is examined, the
principles of classification that bring together foods, prepared in certain ways will again be found to be culturally
systematic, however nutritionally arbitrary. So "dinner"
in the United States, whether eaten at noon, as in certain
regions and classes, or in the evening, is characterized by
a central main dish; the prominence of the oval-shaped
platter or large round casserole as a container overshadows
in importance the nutritional classification of the food, so
that a starch like macaroni can be substituted for the
habitual meat dish, but an attempt to introduce protein
in the form of milk as a beverage would be met with
resistance. For dinner, people eat a "main dish," not
protein. At a somewhat higher level of abstraction, meal
patterns can be analyzed in various patterns such as a
basic carbohydrate with a meat or vegetable garnish, in
which case it will be easier to substitute one carbohydrate
for another—bread for potatoes or potatoes for bread—
than to change the proportions. The pattern may also be
a diet based almost entirely on meat with a few berries
and mosses as seasoning—with the necessary dependence
on eating the whole animal—or a diet in which the proportions are more evenly distributed, etc. These basic
proportions among types of food serve as a framework
within which crops are planted, marketing done, trade
undertaken, provisioning done for city shops, wages spent,
cooking done, and food eaten. It is only necessary to fol-

low food behavior in wartime or in times of scarcity to see
the effort which peoples make to substitute and change
within the framework of the existing pattern.

The sequence of meals in a week, of meals in a day, of
courses within a meal, may be classified as main dishes
and garnish, whether meat or rice, as "meat, fish, eggs,"
or "eggs and cheese," "fruits," or "fruits and vegetables,"
and "potatoes, rice, bread, noodles," or in some other
arrangement, half nutritional, half traditional, or as
"dishes," plain cooked, raw, or as "pudding" or "soup,"
etc. Such an analysis permits us to see how macaroni may
replace meat, or tomato juice become a breakfast drink
in the United States in 1949, with a classification of fruit
juice with fruit, followed by a classification of "juices,"
which included tomato juice, probably reinforced by educational campaigns on sources of vitamin C. It also makes
it possible to trace or to plan the introduction of a new
grain into an old form of food preparation.

An even more abstract statement of dietary pattern
can be made in terms of taste, smell, texture, temperature,
consistency, homogenity. The tie between tomato juice
and orange juice in the modern American breakfast would
then be seen to be related to the American pattern of
selecting a first breakfast course in which tang and acidity
were prominent whereas the fruit as a last course in some
British breakfasts emphasized sweetness and goes over
into jam or marmalade as an alternative.

Thus any new food may be rejected or accepted for
a variety of reasons of quite different levels; it may be
sociologically acceptable but texturally objectionable in
the particular place in the meal pattern or the particular
type of preparation in which it is introduced. It may fit
in taste and texture perfectly but revolt the disciplined
disgust pattern of a people, as in the case of Australian
officials in New Guinea who refused to eat hornbill breast
if they knew what it was, but otherwise accepted it as
rather peculiar beefsteak. It has been shown how migration from one region to another within the United States
may impoverish the diet, as when an individual who has
been accustomed to eating red raspberries moves to a
region where raspberries are black, or where white corn
meal is replaced by yellow. Studies of migration and

change provide us with the best material on the proportionate strength of different elements in a pattern, as we can test whether there is more probability of getting acceptance of a new drink in an old container,[6] of a new container if presented with a familiar drink, or substituting a red vegetable for a red fruit, or one vegetable for another, etc. It is also possible to study experimentally areas of receptivity to a new food. Interviewing may reveal very deeply ingrained attitudes such as the puritanical approach to food of the respondent whose comment on soy was "anything that tastes as bad as that must be good for you." [7]

A dietary pattern may also be analyzed into a network of persons whose division of labor puts them into positions of varying strength in perpetuating the pattern or modulating change. So the grain crops, the stock of domestic animals, the breed of poultry, the make-up of the vegetable garden may be controlled nationally, and thus by officials at a national level. The control may be an aspect of international trade in which decisions are made for purely financial, not nutritional reasons; it may be determined by a series of fairs and prizes, national or local, engineered by mail order houses, influenced by recipes in women's magazines, determined by the vision of a local prophet or the whim of the harvest magician. The way in which such "channels" may be identified and described was shown by Kurt Lewin[8] in the most detailed analysis of housewives in an urban economy. He showed not only how crucial in selection is the role of the housewife whose task it was to spend money on food, but also the way in which the factors of price, which first tended to make her refuse a food, operated, once she had purchased it, because of her determination that her family eat something which had cost so much. Studies in rural regions have demonstrated the great importance of the general food store in stocking seed or a certain kind of food. So it is possible to look at the dietary behavior of a people in terms of those social roles through which the major decisions are made which conserve it or change it, rather than describing it flatly in terms of type of food produced or eaten by whom, when, under what circumstances. In either type of analysis the unit of observation, however, must include the food itself, as seed, in the ground, standing harvest, stored, ready for sale, purchased, eaten.[9]

This requirement of specificity of observation by which the particular seed selected, bought for sale, recommended in a catalogue, or chosen by a prestige person must always be specified, or the particular food purchased by husband or wife indicated, is due to the extreme interdependence and complexity of human dietary patterns in which the supply of essential nutrients may be carried by single foods or may be endangered by the alteration in one particular area, such as method of food preparation or collection of food for feasting, or organization of work shifts in factories.

One of the most dramatic demonstrations of the importance of the particular detailed behavior is the material on sources of calcium in certain Mexican diets. Here the major source of calcium is the lime water in which the maize used in making *tortillas* is soaked. Substitution of finely milled white flour, highly acceptable on a variety of counts ranging from the saving of labor to prestige, nevertheless means a great although inexplicit deficit in Mexican diet. Similarly, in the Orient the introduction of the Christian Sabbath into an economy with a three- or four-day market may radically upset the purchase of some essential fresh food. Studies made during World War II demonstrated how those workers in Seattle, Washington,[10] who worked at hours which necessitated their eating two "lunches" and one dinner were less well nourished than those workers one of whose three meals could be socially defined as "breakfast," with a different nutritional content. As soon as it was realized that a diet could not be evaluated in calories alone, but that the exact combination of foods, with specified nutritional content at the time they were eaten, was essential, the methodological imperative to discuss the cultural context of dietary patterns, *specifically*, became evident. Studies of food distribution within the family have demonstrated that uneven distribution as among husband and wife and children, such as occurs in parts of Britain, or uneven distribution of work among individuals fed on the same marginal diet, as has been reported for urban China, may be nutritionally crucial. The recognition that all human dietary patterns are learned and depend, not upon man's capacity as an animal to select appropriate foods, but upon his capacity as a social animal to develop and transmit an artificial pattern of behavior within which his nutrition can be assayed raises other problems. Man is a domestic animal, but self-domesticated with an even greater dependence upon the traditional behaviors of domestication which he has developed than have those animal breeds which he has claimed from a wild state. There are some indications—very slight in the case of human beings—that man is not completely devoid of the capacity to select a nutritionally balanced diet,[11] of that capacity indeed which has been demonstrated experimentally in the choices of rats among vitamins and minerals made available to them by the recent chemical ingenuity of man. But in the ages during which men have been dependent upon a system of food provision in which there was division of labor, and men—and/or women —collected or produced food, which was then prepared for the family by the wife, or the husband—so that the child had no experience of foraging for itself, and half or more of the adults of one sex usually ate food prepared by someone else, the viability of any food pattern has come to rest upon an intricate pattern of traditional behavior, rather than upon the instinctual choices of each individual. Whereas Richter's experiments[12] on rats demonstrated a possible unexploited potentiality of human beings nutritionally, especially under modern possibilities of isolation of nutrients, the experiments of Young,[13] in which he showed how a learned preference for a palatable food could dominate in a close range choice over a physiological need for water which operated if the palatable food was out of sight, illustrate equally sharply the actual mechanisms which have been invoked historically to keep peoples eating and surviving. As Kurt Lewin has phrased it, people do not eat what they like, they like what they eat (traditionally), and each group has to teach its children, in detail, how to like the particular combination of food upon which their nutrition depends.

This dependence upon learned preferences and repugnances is particularly recognizable in the dietary habits of those groups whose diets are not the result of long trial and error adjustment to the environment, but which have been imposed in terms of some economic pattern, such as in a plantation system, in mining towns, or in single industry towns. In such a situation as in Puerto Rico, or among the sharecroppers of the Southeast of the United States,[14] we find the combination of a nutritionally inadequate diet and a high degree of rigidity of food habits. Studies of the way in which infants learn in the Southeast suggest that they are taught against considerable resistance, to prefer fat to lean meat, the effort with which the original learning is accomplished being reflected in the tenacity with which they adhere to the pattern even when other foods become available to them. Thus the rigidity of food habits which seem actually contrary to the physiological needs of the organism, and which often puzzled physiologists whose data suggest the self-regulative capacities in lower organisms, becomes explicable when seen as a by-product of the enforced adjustment of a human group to a diet with which it has no opportunity to experiment. The extraordinary variety of dietary patterns, each one only one of a series of patterns possible within a given physical environment, is a comment upon the flexibility of the human organism and the extent to which most nutrients occur in a variety of food sources. It also suggests that any traditional food pattern is able to embody a certain number of significant selections that keep the diet in balance, if only to the extent that those groups which fail to establish—possibly only by trial and error—such a balance, would perish in competition with others. Under modern world conditions, however, the composition of the diet of large groups of people may pass out of this sort of traditional control into the hands of those who have a vested interest not only in the products of their labor—in which case they make efforts to provide a nourishing diet—but also in the sale of certain articles of food, as in plantation feeding or tenantry accompanied with credit at a food store. Most situations in which beneficent authoritative organizations attempt to alter the nutrition of groups of individuals—urban workers, populations in wartime, members of armed forces, depressed peasantries whose nutrition is impaired by draining nutritional necessities away as cash crops—involve the attempt to persuade individuals with rigidities of diet based on a narrow subsistence margin to change their habits. Thus there comes to be a frequent concomitance of efforts of nutritional reform and individual resistance to change. The recognition of the relationship between rigidity of learned behavior and diets in which there is very little margin makes these apparently contradictory situations intelligible.

An examination of the way in which children are inducted into the dietary patterns of their groups provides us with another dimension within which to view food patterns. This is so whether emphasis is placed upon the series of cognitive learnings through which the child comes to perceive certain objectives as "food" and others as just "plants," as part of a mass of materials to which the category edible would never apply, or as labeled "inedible," or "poison," or whether emphasis is placed on the affective character of the learning, as certain objects are categorized as "dirty," "disgusting," "revolting." We may proceed from the study of the way in which food sources are perceived to the whole process of being fed, to the mother's use of food as comfort, as reward, of withholding food as punishment, of food as a substitute for love, or her insistence that the child eat against its will, with eating becoming an unpleasant duty. Interwoven with such culturally regular procedures lie the potentialities for various pathologies later, with a pattern of maternal overstuffing of children, combined with an adult tendency toward the use of obesity to symbolize certain sorts of psychological conflict,[15] or with such manifestations as anorexia nervosa.[16] Cultures differ enormously in the extent to which food is treated symbolically in the course of parent-child relationships. In the present age with the attempt to rationalize food patterns in line with the development of the science of nutrition, there would seem to be every reason to seek to decrease the symbolic importance of food and shift the areas of interpersonal conflict in childhood to points of less physiological urgency. A child who refuses to eat and a child who refuses to talk may each be demonstrating a certain type of rebellion, but the immediate consequences for bodily health and growth will be very different. It may well be that the way in which a dietary pattern is learned may be one of those areas in which a qualitative discontinuity may be expected in the future, especially if our food production turns to totally different types of sources of food such as wood waste. The symbolic importance of food during early childhood and the advisability of looking forward to a rationalization of consumption as well as production, to the substitution of a routine number of pellets rather than a synthetic beefsteak, are inextricably connected. The contrast between those individuals who may be said to merely eat to live and those who live to eat is found also in some degree between cultures and suggests that there is a very wide possible range in the kind of learning which can underwrite a viable diet.

As we come to view the problem of food and nutrition on a world scale, the cultural considerations suggest the desirability of distinguishing between several types of dietary adjustment, with differential need for and vulnerability to change, whether the change is planned or not. At one end we have primitive peoples, such as those found in the interior of New Guinea, each with its separate dietary pattern, intimately related to the physical environment, dependent upon a traditional technology and an intricate pattern of social usage and custom. Patterns such as these are vulnerable to drought, epidemic, and war. Also as these peoples come more and more within the purview of modern nations the patterns are vulnerable to relief feeding, to the disturbances introduced by taking individuals away as plantation labor and by the introduction of new technologies which may decimate the food supply—ammunition, better fishing apparatus, dynamite for fishing—or to different foods which may alter the proportional relationships to the diet, as in the introduction of maize with attendant hazards. The introduction of planned public health measures and new methods of maternal and child care also hold particular hazards for such peoples, as for instance in the elimination of supplementary feeding of infants when the health authorities began to war upon the practice of pre-chewing infant food as unhygienic.[17]

The dietary adjustment of such originally self-sufficient and relatively socially undifferentiated population shades over into the conditions of life of the rural peasantries of more complex societies as, for example, India and China. In such populations, the dietary pattern is compromised not only by the state of knowledge and technology, by the existence of patterns which while underwriting a measure of subsistence, limit the use of the available resources, but also by the wider conditions of distribution as between rural and urban regions and different economic classes. Although there is great need for the improvement of the quantity and quality of foods available to such populations, mainly through economic and agricultural measures, there is also need for some care to ensure them against the hazards that accompany the introduction of highly milled grains. Rigidity of food habit still remains a safeguard in communities of this type and one which makes them especially vulnerable to the introduction of certain types of commercial food. The condition of these populations within the instability of changing dietary patterns is accentuated when they migrate and attempt to adopt all or part of the food pattern of an urban area or of another culture. The impoverishment of the diet of the first generation European peasant immigrant to the United States is a case in point, where white bread was substituted for dark bread and the use of sugar increased very disproportionately. Changes of this sort may be seen as the inappropriate carrying over of the old type of learning—white bread was feast bread and the bread of the castle—into a new situation. Finally we have the food conditions in a few areas of the world in which food supply and distribution is more than adequate so that rigid dependence upon a narrow set of habits is no longer either necessary or desirable. These conditions obtain in most parts of the United States and parts of Scandinavia today. Where for most parts of the world, minimal nutrition can still only be assured if there is very slow change in pattern and children are reared to follow the pattern with great fidelity, in areas of maximum food supply the best nutrition is dependent upon rearing individuals with a flexible acceptance of many kinds of food. Within such flexibility changes in supply, either seasonal or annual, and advances in the science of nutrition can be most readily embodied.[18]

The intrinsic incompatibility of rigidity of food habits, whether good or bad, and a culture which must absorb and adapt to both changing supply and changing science is demonstrated by the tale of the public health nurse who exclaimed, "After all those years of climbing stairs to tell Italian mothers not to feed tomatoes to their babies, I now have to climb them all over again, to tell them tomato juice is good for them." It was even more sharply demonstrated during the war when the meager and rigid nutritional knowledge of mothers was exploited by companies which sold a sweetened, synthetic, nutritionally useless orange drink in carefully sanitized milk bottles. Mothers bought it at a high price, having learned, not that Vitamin C was important, but that oranges were vital, and having learned, not the particular reasons for pasteurizing and bottling milk, but that bottled milk was necessary for infants. A recognition of the way in which dietary patterns are part of the total cultural pattern means assuming responsibility for cultural change to parallel our growing scientific capacity to augment our food supply and assess and control its nutritional content.

Centennial, 1950.

REFERENCES

1. The field of food habits was systematically developed during World War II by the Committee on Food Habits of the National Research Council, set up at the request of Dr. M. L. Wilson in 1940. This Committee published two reports, "The Problem of Changing Food Habits" (1943) and "Manual for the Study of Food Habits" (1945). Material in this paper not specifically attributed in the following set of references comes from the unpublished conferences, memoranda, reports, and staff researches of this Committee.
2. Report of the Committee on Food Habits, 1945.
3. Mead, M., 1940c.

 4. Cummings, R. O., 1941; Drummond, J. C., and A. Wilbraham, 1939; Richards, A. I., 1932.
 5. Report of the Committee on Food Habits, 1945.
 6. Festinger, L., 1944.
 7. Woodward, P., 1943a, 1943b.
 8. Lewin, K., 1943.
 9. Report of the Committee on Food Habits, 1945.
10. Engel-Frisch, G., 1943.
11. Davis, C. M., 1928, 1935a, 1935b.
12. Richter, C. P., 1943; Richter, C. P., and B. B. Barelare, 1938.
13. Young, P. T., 1948.
14. Cussler, M., and M. L. de Give, unpublished field researches.
15. Bruch, H., and G. Touraine, 1940.
16. Mead, M., 1943c, 1943d.
17. Pijoan, M., 1943.
18. Pijoan, M., and C. A. Elkin, 1944.

Anthropological Data on the Problem of Instinct

The social anthropologists' contribution to our knowledge of original nature, of which the instinct problem is one formulation, is based upon the utilization of existing cultures as our experimental material for the plasticity of original endowment. In the face of the extreme difficulty of experimenting with human beings in organized social settings, the accidents of history, especially where cultures have been preserved from contact with the main stream of history, are used as data on the possible variations in human behavior. In such an approach, we are working with two sets of variables, the biological equipment of human beings and the historical forms within which this equipment has been patterned. We, therefore, "hold human nature constant" and assume, for the present, that human nature may be regarded as similar for Bushmen, Hottentots, Americans, and so on. Were we not to do so, it would be impossible to conduct such a series of experiments.

We can then collect data on the plasticity of human beings under different cultural conditions, data ranging all the way from slight details, such as gestures of assent and dissent, parts of the body associated with introspective reports of emotion, phonetic systems used in the language, variations in the perception of intraorganic and extra-organic data, through patternings of interpersonal relations and systems of social organization governing the relationships of social groups to each other and to the physical environment. On the basis of such data, we can do two things: (1) criticize existing hypotheses concerning the plasticity of man's original nature, because they fail to provide an adequate base for an explanation of some type of recorded behavior in other cultures, and (2) develop hypotheses which will broaden present theories.

It is important to note that it is not suggested that anthropological data are advanced as *proof* of the final validity of any theory. It is assumed that hypotheses about the instinctive nature of man will ultimately become so refined that they can be put to experimental tests of a quite different order from the tests provided by "experiments in nature." Our data are hypothesis-forming, not theory-validating.

In "holding nature constant" the anthropologist is faced with certain problems: Should he assume a *tabula rasa*? Should he assume some contemporary theory of human nature, such as the series of Freudian assumptions on instinct or the Hullian approach to the problems of drives? Should he make explicit provision for the possibility of hereditary constitutional types with systematic differences in innate equipment, stated perhaps as systematically different patterns of maturation or relative strength of a number of constant drives? What weight should be given to the possible complications introduced by differences between homogeneous and heterogeneous physical stocks, with the possibility that, if there are important individual differences in instinctive equipment, these differences may have become systematically characteristic of groups with a high proportion of common ancestry? What distinction should he make between the usefulness of existing formulations on the instinct problem as "tools of observation" and as "basic assumptions in the interpretation of data"?

So we have here two main questions: (1) What sort of contribution can the anthropologist make to the theory of instincts? (2) What procedures involving instinct hypotheses does he find most helpful in making these contributions? It will readily be seen that these two problems are interdependent. If an existing hypothesis about the number, relative strength, and degree of opposition of mutual reinforcement of different drives be used to define and organize the observations in the field, are the results as valuable, in terms of a contribution to the instinct theory, as if no such special assumptions are made? To this question, I think the answer is an unequivocal negative, on two counts. Accepting any current instinct hypothesis narrows and limits the lines of research in such a way as to obscure data on plasticity—which is all that we can be expected to supply—and, furthermore, material collected from a limiting point of view can not be used for a series of rechecks on developing hypotheses. Conditions of anthropological field work are such that it is usually impossible to make a series of field studies of a primitive people to correspond with a series of shifts in psychological theory. Our greater contribution lies in collecting materials in such a way as to provide useful cross-checks on instinct hypotheses.

This does not mean, however, that the assumption of a *tabula rasa* type of human nature provides anthropologists with a background from which the most relevant types of data on plasticity can be collected. If the *tabula rasa* hypothesis is used, all similarities in behavior found in different and apparently historically discontinuous areas of the world have to be explained in terms of diffusion and borrowing. Unless we assume some series of regular cultural evolution, a series of superorganic evolutionary laws, which there are at present no valid grounds for assuming, anthropological data on widespread similarities become relatively valueless, psychologically. No matter how widely separated in space and time, the historical explanation becomes the only acceptable one in the discussion, for instance, of similar initiatory practices in New Guinea, Africa, Tierra del Fuego, and Australia. Each piece of cultural behavior must be referred to some historically antecedent piece of behavior, the origins of which we can never hope to examine, or test, or even profitably speculate about. The examination of primitive cultures in these terms would leave us psychologically exactly where we started.

The most useful assumption seems to be that we may expect ultimately to identify in human beings an original nature which has very definite form or structure, and possibly systematic individual differences which may be referred to constitutional type within that original nature, but we must make our investigations without particularization in regard to that original nature. By following this course, we can bring under consideration those widespread similarities in cultural behavior which occur in different parts of the world, at different levels of cultural development. Similarities in the personalities of natives of the Manus tribe of the Admiralty Islands and the inhabitants of rural New England can be used as data on the degree of structuralization which original drives contribute to the formation of similar personalities under widely divergent historical circumstances, and furthermore can be used to focus attention upon those aspects of the cultural system which make the most significant contribution to the modification of the original human nature along these parallel lines.

I should like to discriminate between the value of using specific instinct hypotheses *in the field*, as a theoretical frame for the *collection* of data, and the value of testing out existing hypotheses in subsequent *analysis* of the data. Such distinctions as Anna Freud draws in her study, *The Ego and the Mechanisms of Defense*,[1] can most illuminatingly be applied to anthropological data, and it is most probable that, in the course of application, new insights may be developed which will contribute to the development of psychological theories of instinct.

Psychosomatic Medicine, Vol. 4, No. 4, 1942.

REFERENCES

1. Freud, A., 1946.

16

Some Anthropological Considerations Concerning Guilt

The contributions which anthropological research has made to theories of guilt are of several sorts. Most of them, however, stem directly from the attempts to relate the findings of psychoanalysis to the findings of anthropologists working on primitive, exotic, or contemporary modern societies. I shall attempt to intimate briefly the nature and variety of these approaches, and then devote the bulk of the paper to the question of guilt as a sanction for positive constructive behavior as it has been developed in societies in which parents assume the responsibility of rewarding and punishing their children for labeled and discriminated types of good and bad behavior.

There are, first, theories which relate ritual and ritual idiom of definite cultural groups to psychological findings upon expiatory and appeasing rituals found in individuals, using a knowledge of mechanisms involved in individual rituals of the neurotic to interpret both the history and the function of rituals shared by whole groups. These interpretations may take the form of relating a present ritual (such as the totem meal, in which all members of the group, all initiated males, etc., ceremonially eat an animal normally regarded as sacred and taboo and the mythical ancestor or supernatural relative of the group) to some event in the far-distant past (such as the original killing of the old man of the horde by a group of brothers). This type of interpretation, of which the classical example is Freud's *Totem and Taboo*,[1] is more concerned with origin than with function. The ceremony itself is regarded as the datum which is to be explained, and the explanation is found, not in the present behavior of the individuals involved in the ceremony, but in a set of connections which may be traced between the various elements in the ritual. The interpretative statement may then take the form: this ceremony is a ritual expression of killing the father, and the ritual taboos observed the rest of the year, which include respect for and abstention from the totem animal, are a ritual defense against the same act of patricide. Such an analysis may take the further form of being regarded as proof of some earlier social habit, such as deposition and killing of an aging father, very much as a recurrent dream in an adult may be used as evidence of a childhood trauma. The actual historical value of such interpretations is of course low, for just as a fantasied event in the life history of an individual may function in the same way as an event in which other human beings have participated, so ceremonials of this type may be seen also as constructs, as reactive formations to fears or wishes which have at no time in the history of the group ever been acted out. So a ceremony and set of taboos which, when their constituent elements are carefully analyzed, appear to be intelligible as an expression of guilt for which no present antecedents are found in the life of the contemporary members of the group which practice it, may be taken as data on the constructs of some other people who developed the ceremony, but not as data upon any social events which occurred in their historical past, such as patricide, regicide, practice of incest, etc.

When speculation about the content of rituals of sacrifice, scapegoating, extravagant group mourning, etc., was succeeded by field work in which the experience of individuals, both as children and as adults, could be placed side by side with the ceremonies in which those individuals participated, it became possible to point out immediate relationships between the child's experience of closeness to the mother, of castration fears, of frustration of a type which led to strong hatreds and hostilities, and ceremonies designed to make amends for the various types of guilt associated with aroused incestuous or murderous wishes. The most conspicuous explorations of such relationships, particularly emphasizing the genetic connec-

tions between the experiences of infancy and early childhood and later ceremonials, have been made by Géza
Róheim,[2] who has followed up the earlier interpretations
of Australian ceremonials with analysis of children's
games, methods of child rearing, and dreams of individuals and has demonstrated striking correspondences between the inferred affects of the child and the pattern of
the ceremonial.

It is possible to emphasize the function that ritual
activities have in solving conflicts which are culturally
created, either for the whole group or for some members
of the group whose individual experience has developed
a higher degree of self-accusation, feelings of unworthi-
ness, or sense of deeply disapproved wishes, such as
cannibalistic fantasies directed toward parents or siblings.
An example of the former type, the solution of an individual conflict assumed to be engendered in the entire
group, may be found in those mourning ceremonies in
which two souls are distinguished, so that ambivalence
toward the dead may take the form of appeasing and
warding off the bad soul and tenderly cherishing and
providing a comfortable afterlife for the good soul.[3]
Where emphasis is placed upon the contemporary meaning of a ritual observance for those who actually practice
it, it is possible to add to the genetic explanation of the
classical psychoanalytic type such further considerations
as the effect upon the young child of simultaneously
undergoing the interpersonal experiences which appear
to arouse the feelings which will need ritual solution.
Such occurs, for example, when the young child in Bali
simultaneously undergoes the type of teasing from his
mother which appears to induce deep hostility and reactive withdrawal, and an oft-enacted ceremonial in which
the witch surrogate of the mother is actively attacked by
young males who fall down in trance before the magic
power of the witch (an assumed surrogate of the mother),
and are revived by the magic power of the dragon (an
assumed surrogate of the father).[4]

Examples of the relationship between traditional rituals and the experience of selected individuals in a society
may be found in witch societies, types of possession and
shamanism, the peculiar suicide-vow patterns of certain

warrior societies among the North American Plains Indians, the custom of hara-kiri among the Japanese, monastic vows and retreats, etc., in which the society keeps alive patterns of behavior, available to those on whom there have been differential pressures, which develop a capacity to make use of the ritual pattern. Any full understanding of the use of such patterns will include a detailed analysis of the way in which the existence of the ritual pattern of atonement or appeasement is communicated to and gives shape to the psychological behavior of the individuals who make use of it, showing to what extent the expressed need of the individual is itself a function of the presence of the ritual. So the practice of ritual confession can be seen as one element in the development of an individual reliance upon confession, whether that confession be of the habitual type practiced in Roman Catholicism, the type of single confession found in ancient Mexico,[5] or the confession during sickness of a Manus native.[6]

When this type of material is examined from the standpoint of planning for mental health, attention is focused upon the question of the extent to which it is necessary to develop ritual solutions of types of guilt which are engendered by various recurrent social practices, such as the extreme individualism of the economic arrangements of each household in modern North America and ritual giving to the Community Chest, the Red Cross, the Hundred Neediest Cases, etc., and the extent to which it may be advisable to modify the patterns of interpersonal relationships which give rise to types of guilt which need to be ritually assuaged.

Emphasis upon one type of planned social change or the other will vary as to whether the interest is greater in seeing that the individual pays in psycho-physical strain as few prices as possible during childhood and maturity (in which case the recommendation will be to develop a society in which the interpersonal relationships are such that no guilt is aroused to be ceremonially assuaged in social rituals); or, on the other hand, whether attention is directed to the values of a complex culture in which the individual is exposed to a variety of situations arousing profound inadmissible emotions and consequent anxiety and later is given a variety of social forms within which to satisfy his complex emotions. But it is important to realize that most of the material on the destructive aspects of exposure to situations arousing strong and forbidden affects comes from the clinical study of the neurotic and psychotic in societies which are changing so rapidly that socially patterned ceremonial solutions for their complex emotional conflicts are not available, except in the work of the individual who is artistically gifted enough to provide his own. This contemporary situation obscures the relationships which may be found in less rapidly changing societies between the arousal of a welter of incestuous and murderous wishes in children and intricate and esthetically satisfying social rituals and artistic forms.

When contemporary forms of social disorganization are observed against a background of the analysis of the imputed psychological content and social function of primitive and exotic ceremonial, it is possible to put new interpretations upon such social phenomena as occur among peoples whose cultures are disintegrating—nativistic cults,[7] outbursts of chauvinism, scapegoating, pogroms, lynchings, mass suicides, and mass murders, in which disallowed feelings, which are dealt with either imperfectly or not at all by existing social rituals, reach the level of actual, rather than symbolic acting out.[8] From this point of view it is not necessary to assume that the participant in a lynching or a pogrom has more murderous impulses than members of religious groups have whose closest approach to ritual killing is participation in a ceremonial blood meal in which the blood is not blood but some surrogate. The only difference may be that in one society the rituals for symbolic expression of the regularly engendered conflicts are present, and in the other they are not.

Most of the types of analysis of social expressions of guilt referred to above are based upon theories concerning very early childhood and upon the way in which the very young child, helpless, dependent, and phrasing his response to others in all-or-none terms, develops fears of his own impulses, fears of the retaliative behavior of others—both impulses and retaliations often being projected into supernatural beings—or other social groups.[9]

Another type of fear has been phrased[10] as the fear of the superego, that is, the internalized representative of the parent who metes out love and punishment to the developing child. This refers to a type of development which occurs in great part after the child has learned to talk and in which the unconscious elements are the result of repression of what has been conscious and verbalized, rather than due to experiences before the mastery of language made it possible for the child to meet interpersonal situations in terms of the processes characteristic of consciousness. The different quality of the unconscious content of guilt based on preverbal experiences and guilt which may be attributed to the incorporation of parental instruction subsequent to the attainment of language has its counterpart in the levels of social behavior which can profitably be analyzed in terms of these sequential learnings. Ritual, art, myth, are illumined both in interpretation of content and study of their function by reference to these very early infantile situations, while the functioning of moral codes and types of political and social control are illumined by an analysis of type of superego formation and the corresponding moral sanctions in a society.*

When psychoanalytic theory began to develop descriptions of the way in whcih the child incorporated the image of the rewarding and punishing parent, and so learned to behave *as if* that parent were present in the parent's absence and after the parent's death, contemporaneous examination of primitive cultures revealed the necessity for expanding this description to include a wide variety of methods of moral training and corresponding character structure. These expansions have taken the form of challenging the classical picture of the significance of the strong father and the role of the Oedipus situation in the formation of the superego,[12] of comparative studies

* While this seems to be a useful generalization at the present stage of our thinking, recent work on the character structure of prerevolutionary Great Russians suggests that, in certain instances, experiences during the first year of life may provide a definitive basis for attitudes toward authority, without the invocation of regularities of the interpersonal relationships of later childhood.[11]

of the relationships between types of moral sanction and types of social structure,[13] of surveys of types of sanction characteristic of an area,[14] of attempts in the classification of sanctions as guilt, shame, fear, anger, pride, etc.[15] Each step in this procedure, which has gone on for 25 years, has been tentative, and the need for continuous reformulation has increased rather than abated.

In the present state of the data it appears useful to distinguish between internalized and noninternalized sanctions, whether personal or impersonal, and those systems in which the parents are the surrogates which result in a sharply focused point of reference. It is necessary to distinguish the degree of focus as a condition leading to internalization between those systems in which the parents are the executors and interpreters of the sanction, those systems in which the referent is the parents themselves as the approving and disapproving figures, and those in which behavior is enjoined in the name of some wider group, the age group, members of one's own or another caste, "the people," "people," "your possible future mother-in-law." * Where the parents are both the interpreters and the executors of the system and use as a sanction, "I, your father, or your mother, will punish and reward you in terms of your behavior," we have the classical superego formation with the characteristic features of oedipal solutions incident to contrast or similarity in sex and to the relative weakness or strength of male and female parents. Such an upbringing develops in the child the capacity to feel guilt, to award to the self, either in anticipation of an act not yet performed or retrospectively, in terms of a past act, the type of suffering or reward once given by the parent. Before discussing the cultural setting of this type of character structure further, I wish to sketch in briefly the other types of sanction with which it may usefully be contrasted.

Where, instead of the parents or parent surrogates as the referents of approval and disapproval, a larger and less individualized group is invoked, it is useful to dis-

* The clarification of the role of the parent or parent surrogate in focusing and so internalizing guilt, shame, or pride I owe to discussions with Geoffrey Gorer, while working on problems of Russian character structure.

tinguish a continuum between pride and shame. Shame, for purposes of this classification, may be described as that sanction under which the individual's attention is focused upon possible disapproval from a group, in which the whole quality of the behavior is negative and one acts in fear of a negatively valued response. Here again it is useful to distinguish between those settings in which the negatively valued response is anticipated as coming from a positively valued group, i.e., fear of the immigrant child of the treatment he will receive from American classmates, fear of the disapproval of the gang to which one passionately wishes to belong, fear of the disapproval of the appropriate members of the opposite sex to whose favors one aspires, etc., and those settings in which the negative response is anticipated from a negatively valued group, neighbors who are also spoken of disparagingly, classmates in a school to which one does not wish to go, servants who are seen as prying into the weaknesses of their employers, etc. Where the emphasis is upon the feared negative response, whether from valued or devalued groups, it may still be described as shame, but there will be a great difference in the whole quality of the individual response.

American Indians were predominantly characterized by the use of shame as sanction, with a high incidence of negative valuation of the group to whose judgments behavior was referred. The child was told, "If you do that people won't like you," and in the same breath heard the "people" whose disapproval had been evoked described in carping, depreciating terms. Among American Indians it is possible to find the whole gamut of degrees of internalization, from the high internalization among the Objibwa, who may commit suicide from the shame engendered by an unwitnessed event, where despite the verbal reference to the whole group, the child spends a great deal of time in the small family, and the much lower degree of internalization in the Zuñi, where children live a crowded multifamilial existence, in which the "people" referred to are actually present and parents invoke masked supernaturals to punish their children while they themselves mime the position of being the children's defenders.

Pride may be placed at the other end of the shame-pride continuum, and here the emphasis is upon expected approval from groups who are either negatively or positively valued. Just as the maximally strong and emotionally toned shame position may be defined as a fear of disapproval from a negatively valued group instilled in the child by the parent (and accordingly internalized), so the maximum pride position may be defined as an expectation of the approval of a positively valued group of elders or superiors, similarly inculcated. Somewhere along this continuum we may locate those intermediate situations in which a group of equals, who are neither more nor less positively valued than the self, mete out approval and disapproval, according to the particular situation. This is a situation congruent with an age-mate group, just as the typical guilt-producing setting is the relationship between parent and child and the typical shame and pride settings are the relationship between the self and a society in which such considerations as superiority, inferiority, superordination and subordination, caste, class, etc., are operative. The expressed sanction "No woman will seek you as daughter-in-law" may be qualified as "Even a poor no-count woman won't have you as daughter-in-law" or "If you embroider as well as that, the queen herself will be proud to have you as a daughter-in-law."

We thus have four different situations to take into account: (*a*) the extent to which the parents or other emotionally close, highly identified individuals interpret a sanction to the child, whether that be the guilt-producing sanction of "I, the parent will punish you, or reward you," or the interpretative "people will gossip about you" of shame, or "people will applaud and admire you" of pride, and this participation of parents and parent surrogates seems to determine the degree of internalization which occurs, a limited number of figures with whom one has close ties appearing to provide the conditions for incorporation; (*b*) the type of behavior expected, e.g., whether it is predominantly approval, praise, and reward or disapproval, blame, and punishment; (*c*) the individual or group to whom principal reference is made, parents, age mates, specific levels, or the whole of society, or their various supernatural and symbolic surrogates, God, angels, the spirits, the village; and (d) the type of valuation placed on the individual or group to whom behavior is referred, as superior, inferior, loved, feared, etc.

Such a systematic statement immediately reveals the dilemma created by our present terminology, based as it is on the one-sided evidence of the clinical consulting room, and on a theory more concerned with sinners than with saints. While we may speak of "a decent sense of shame," thus referring to fear of the disapproval of a group whose standards are respected, and a "proper pride," referring to an appropriate concern with the impact of one's behavior on a respected audience, we have no terminology for "good guilt," for the internalized sanctions in the individual who has been praised and loved for good behavior, rather than blamed and punished for bad. Just as we have a word for *trauma*, or an injury to the organism, and no word for a *blessing*, when some strength or sensitivity is added, so we have only a word which emphasizes the fear of punishment or withdrawal of love if and when something wrong is done, and no antonym.

The fourfold classification of contributing social settings above might suggest that all cultures could be placed within it, in the degrees and ways in which "guilt," good and bad, pride, and shame are used as sanctions. But this schematization does not yet represent a closed system on which we may expect to classify all cultures; before elaborating further on the question of guilt, I wish to describe briefly two other types of sanction system, the Balinese and the Iatmul.[16] In Bali, the parent or child nurse invokes desired behavior in the child by mimicking fear of some repellent, frightening, or supernatural object, communicating to the child a sense of shared fear, which remains throughout life in an undifferentiated state for which such terms as internalized or externalized, positive and negative, are almost meaningless. The Balinese remains within the pattern of his highly complex culture and responds to suggestions of deviating from the pattern with withdrawal and to disturbances in the pattern with withdrawal, sometimes even to the point of benign stupor. A withdrawal response to disapproved, out-of-pattern behavior has been communicated to him, at somewhat the same level that British mothers who were frightened during air raids communicated their fear to very young infants whom they held in their arms.[17] A fear which is neither verbalized nor rationalized, indiscriminately communicated by all with whom the Balinese child comes in contact, accompanied by no specific punishments or rewards, seems to remain at the same level.

Among the Iatmul we find another type of child rearing, in which the individual learns to control his behavior in lively expectation of openly expressed anger and physical reprisal from others. There is no wide gap in moral or social status between child and parents or between children and other members of the community, no chiefs, no priesthood, no group to whom behavior can be referred, except—after initiation—the opinion of the opposite sex, who are variously invoked on the shame-pride continuum. But the small child is treated, practically from birth, as if he or she were as strong and independent and willful as the adult and as if the only means of control which the adult could exercise was not praise or blame, love or punishment, or the invocation of the opinion or possible reward or punishment of outside groups, but only actual physical force, exercised in false pantomime by a grown man or woman vis-à-vis the child. Children live in a continuous state of alertness, poised to flee blows which must be given with lightning speed ever to fall on a recipient's skin, and in adult life the whole society is organized about the threat and actual event of wrangle and riot between groups conceived of as equally strong. The lack of any system of hierarchical moral control within the individual mirrors and is repeated in the lack of any political control except that exercised by other equally strong groups upon one's own group in the social organization.

I should now like to return to the subject of "guilt, good and bad," in more detail. This type of character structure is characteristic of the English and North American middle class, in which parents differentiate themselves from their children by assuming the moral responsibility of punishing disapproved acts and rewarding approved acts, in such a way as to encourage the child to take final responsibility for the content of its acts. In Germany,[18] on the other hand, there seems strong evidence that the child is rewarded and punished for obedience to authority, rather than encouraged to take personal responsibility for content. Historically this type of character structure which relies on guilt has been identified with the rise of the commercial classes and invoked as a condition of the industrial revolution and the development of modern science and the machine age.[19] It has been reviled as the "Puritan" character with an overpreoccupation with conformity and negative good behavior, a concomitant underdevelopment of the impulse life, a tendency to rigidity, intolerance, etc.

It seems worth while to look for a moment at one small primitive community, the pile-dwelling, seafaring Manus people of the Admiralty Islands,[20] where the same type of character has been developed among a Stone Age people whose religious system consists of guardian ghosts of the last dead male of each household, far from the intricate complexities of the rise of Protestantism and the rise of capitalism.* Yet we find a people with a highly internalized guilt structure devoting their whole energies to the pursuit of a moral way of life which will preserve them from ghostly punishment. They are rigidly puritanical, with strong sex taboos, prudish, anxious, driven, with little place for art or impulse expression. Furthermore these people are competent and efficient, learn to handle machines with ease, have well-developed concepts of number, time, and space relationships. They think in terms of the "how" instead of the "why" or "what" and participate responsibly and with ease in the machine civilization of Europeans. They share with Western European and American Protestant middle-class society a preoccupation with the gastrointestinal tract, with taking in and giving out objects, with reciprocal relations between persons, which is congruent with a tendency to treat persons as things and to emphasize the circulation of goods, trade, turnover, activity.[21] Their capacity to deal with engines, with machines in general, and with

---

* This description refers, of course, to the Manus as they were studied in 1928.

the type of "rational" thinking characteristic of the thought of the late nineteenth and early twentieth centuries in the West may be related to parental insistence upon early moral responsibility in the child and the focusing of the child's attention upon cause-and-effect relationships between his acts and omissions and their consequences. The principal sanction in the society is good and bad guilt, as the child is rewarded and praised for constructive behavior as well as being punished for behavior regarded as wrong.

An examination in detail of the correspondence between the Manus type of character formation and the "Puritan" character of recent centuries in the West suggests that we are dealing with a cultural constellation which involves not only parental upbringing of the child with a strong assumption of moral responsibility, but also the preoccupation with intake and output of food, which is related to a concentration on person-thing rather than person-person relationships, the two together providing an ideal setting for the nineteenth-century view of men and machines. Analysis of the components of this complex, so similar and yet in such contrasting settings, should provide clues as to how to construct a society which retains the positive aspects of this "guilt character" without the emphasis on the gastrointestinal tract which tends to overvalue person-thing relationships and undervalue the individual's relationship to other persons and to his own, reflexly realized inner impulses. It should then be possible to recognize the very great strengths inherent in the character structure which has been developed within our particular historical tradition and to which neither the special preoccupation on the gastrointestinal tract, with its emphasis on objects, nor the negative emphasis on reward for not sinning rather than reward for positive constructive acts is integral or essential.

It may be appropriate to add a few remarks about the possible biological bases for guilt, in the widest sense in which it has been used throughout this paper, which includes the constructs based on infantile experience and also the introjection of the parental command to feel pride or shame, as well as the particular detailed parental command subsumed under the more special use of the word "guilt" for this type of sanction. Julian Huxley[22] concludes his *Touchstone for Ethics* by invoking the natural dependency situation of the human infant as providing a natural setting for the development of love, and consequently of fear of loss of love, and all its later ramifications, which give a basis for the development of conscience. The formulation follows the psychoanalytic formulation which localizes the genesis of guilt in the nature of the parent-child situation, rather than within the organism viewed alone. Historically, the perpetuation, even in those societies in which artificial feeding is superseding breast-feeding, of the old biologically given mother-child nurturing tie has given this development of guilt special, sex-specialized forms, because the female was the original nurturing parent for children of both sexes. This historical form of character formation would be radically altered if society should take the step, made possible by the abandonment of breast-feeding, of a pattern of child rearing in which both sexes participated equally. This would introduce such a radical change in character formation that a basic change in the way in which biological potentialities were involved in the genesis of guilt might also be expected.

But we may also consider whether, in addition to the specific nurturing situation, there may not be a biological basis for guilt of another order covered by the conception of the "metaphysical guilt of creatureliness,"[23] guilt which arises inevitably from the nature of life and death itself, guilt over the domestication which men endure who become responsible fathers and the pain which women take on who become mothers, guilt over all who have suffered and died as the human race struggled to its present position in the world—a deep guilt which is reactivated by any failure in the individual organism to grow, to attain full sex membership, to use its particular gifts and capacities. Such guilt, such consciousness of a debt to life which can only be paid by living, may be so inherent in the nature of human beings, who live in a culture, that it is ineradicable and will always be both the mainspring of man's spiritual strivings and the guarantee of his humanity.

Feelings and Emotions, 1950.

REFERENCES

1. Freud, S., 1918.
2. Róheim, G., 1934; Mead, M., 1935a, 1939b.
3. Mead, M., 1930a.
4. Bateson, G., and M. Mead, 1942; Mead, M., 1940a.
5. Joyce, T. A., 1914.
6. Fortune, R. F., 1935.
7. Mooney, J., 1896; Williams, F. E., 1928.
8. Mead, M., 1947c, 1948, 1949a.
9. Kubie, L. S., and R. H. Kubie, 1948; Rickman, J., 1948.
10. Freud, A., 1946.
11. Gorer, G., 1949; Gorer, G., and J. Rickman, 1950.
12. Malinowski, B., 1927.
13. Mead, M. (ed.), 1937.
14. Pettitt, G. A., 1946.
15. Mead, M., 1940d.
16. Mead, M., 1941.
17. Freud, A., and D. T. Burlingham, 1943.
18. Schaffner, B., 1948.
19. Weber, M., 1930.
20. Mead, M., 1930b, 1932.
21. Mead, M., 1949b.
22. Huxley, T. H., and J. S. Huxley, 1947.
23. Gilbey, T., 1948.

17

Cultural Bases for Understanding Literature*

Among the variety of contributions which modern anthropological research might be able to offer to members of this Association, I plan to stress only one, that which anthropological studies of whole cultures can make to those whose task it is to cherish and cultivate the arts, and especially literature, in the contemporary world. Just because we, the anthropologists, specialize in primitive, usually quite small, societies and take as our focus communities of a few hundred people with an oral tradition which can be no more elaborate than the memories of those few, we are able to include within our study many aspects of human experience which the scholar dealing with a period or trend within a complex high civilization accepts on authority or takes for granted. Yet, to the extent that the scholar who works with the eighteenth century in England must so take for granted the economic arrangements of agriculture or the methods of child care in the nursery, he or she is cut off from watching the intimate interplay between the way a farm laborer is paid or a child rebuked and the images of sophisticated literature, within which these experiences of the poor or immature may be represented by a chain of transmuted images or an explicit counterpoint which cuts them off from the developed consciousness of the small literate elite who inherited and cultivated the literary tradition of the past. Short of time, and very often short of materials, historians have only recently thought it worth while

* An address delivered at a General Meeting of the Modern Language Association of America, in Boston, 28 December 1952.

to consider the "short and simple annals of the poor" or the life of children who were neither the subjects of later literary elaboration by a Samuel Butler or a Proust, nor had even the dubious claims of a Daisy Ashford.

It is not, however, the relationship between the literature of a period—especially the fresh and original literature of a period, in which new emphases are manifested—and the myriad unrecorded acts of everyday life which I wish to stress here, for it has been done abundantly by others. Literary history suffers today not so much from any unwillingness to take these matters into account as from a paucity of materials, from the circumstance that enormous labor is required to establish the simplest facts about the daily life of earlier ages. I wish, rather, to turn to a specific problem: the extent to which the capacity to appreciate a literary medium and to create within it is rooted in the culture as the child experiences it in infancy and early childhood.

Culture may be seen as a system of tradition within which the crude sensations originating within the body—the quickened pulse beat, the tautened throat muscles, the clammy hand—and those originating outside the body—the slowly rising moon or the sudden flash of an electric light bulb, the line of a tree or a lamp post against a wintry sky, the cry of a bird or the grinding machinery of a garbage truck—are given meaning. So, light—in the experience of the infant merely a series of unexpected and unpredictable impacts on the retina—comes to mean safety, to herald the arrival of a succoring human being, to signal the difference between the unbroken dullness or blinding terror of the night and the welcome day, to stand for awareness, for enlightenment, for the Light of Asia and the Light of the World. "First," say the Samoans, "there was darkness, and then came the Light"; and the words for light and for understanding—that which a child develops as it lives among human beings—are the same word, *malamalama*. When we look at the great variety of ways in which human beings through the long eons of human history have ordered such primary experiences, locating grief in the eyes or in the liver or in the heart, finding the human soul lightly nested beneath the breast bone or envisioning separate souls in every joint of the body which are ready to be lured away by the sorcerer's merest whisper, we find not only variety, but also striking differences in the degree and type of complexity. Some languages are rich in imagery and symbolism; others are as bare and clear as a grammarian's daydream. Nor are these differences a matter of level of culture. The richest and most complex imagery may be found associated with low levels of political organization, with the simplest tools. Peoples of the same stock, living side by side in adjacent valleys, may contrast sharply in their approach to the same situation. For one people, warfare over a woman may be heralded by weeks of sophisticated evoking of an elaborated and mythical past; for an adjacent tribe, it may be only a matter of hoisting on a newly cut sapling the multicolored grass skirt of the very woman about whom they are fighting. Relationships between men and women, between parents and children, between the artist and his material or the magician and his spell, may all be simple, direct, and uncomplicated, or they may be woven in wonder. For one people, sexual compatibility between men and women may seem so natural that it is felt to be necessary to erect a series of barriers between them, and for another people, so unlikely that it is felt to be necessary to throw a boy and girl locked in embrace into an open pit and kill them in order to ensure that the other members of the tribe will care to mate.

Such comparisons suggest that human cultures, like the individual personalities whose capacities they both express and underwrite, may be stabilized at very different levels of symbolic expression—may vary from the type of culture in which *"essen trinken schlafen Schluss"* consumes men's efforts and all that is left of their imaginations, to cultures as neatly calibrated to the physical environment as a perfectly designed tool, where men catch the most fish possible in the best way their technological level permits, to cultures in which nine-tenths of men's time is devoted to elaborations of art and ritual, pursued with delight and creativity. Against such variety, the oft-repeated warnings of the humanists—even though these depend, as they so often do, on nostalgic, inaccurate recollections of a past that never was, com-

pared with inaccurate data on the present—do not seem
to the student of human cultures to be ill taken. Because
men have loved to elaborate life, to cast it in nobler and
more universal and enduring forms, does not mean that
there is an innate and inalienable urge to do so which
is strong enough to survive, unnourished, in any sort of
human society. Instead, we may think of human societies
as existing in various degrees of balance between the
needs and capacities of their individual members and the
elaborated imaginative material on which these members
are fed. In some societies, the child may experience the
world in such a way as to develop an insatiable desire for
violence. This desire may be satisfied in different ways—
by head-hunting raids, by spectacles of torture, or by
reading Norse epics or the poems of Robinson Jeffers.
Where there are neither enough head-hunting opportunities nor satisfactory ritual or artistic elaborations, we
may expect such individualistic sporadic outbreaks as we
have today, in which driven human beings, lacking any
socially sanctioned forms to take their agony before God
or their fellow men, react blindly, shooting the first people
they meet. Armed with the full paraphernalia of our
technical civilization, they are more innocent of the resources of the human spirit than a Stone Age savage,
surrounded by spiritual forces strong enough to hold his
impulses in check or to direct their course into socially
approved channels of war or song.

It is true that over and over again in history civilization
has sunk into a dark age in which creativity was banked
beneath the ashes of unpatterned social disorder, temples
were despoiled and laid in ruins, unread books were left
to molder and disappear. And over and over again, enough
sparks have been preserved so that the beauty of a broken
frieze or an armless goddess, discovered in a garden plot,
has rekindled the flame in some ardent mind. In the long,
long run, if we use centuries as units, civilization survives
in the hands of different peoples, while those who were
once its proudest carriers again become peasants, rioting
on marriage nights and bickering in meager and arid
bitterness over half-acres of exhausted soil. If one thinks
only of "the humanities," and not of human beings, this

may be enough—that somewhere, sometime, someone will again read Plato and Shakespeare.

But if within the term *humanities*, in the name of which so much is claimed, we include the rights of every human being to achieve the full stature that the creativity of all past centuries has prepared for him, then there is great cause to worry. Concentration on the survival value of the banked fire can easily blind us to what is happening in the present age, in the United States. This is, it seems to me, particularly likely to happen to teachers as they face groups of high school and college students, scanning the rows of unwilling faces for the single one or two whose attention is caught and held. For although the single young enthusiast may indeed be a future Ph.D. in English, this is a field in which one acolyte no more makes a full-bodied ritual than one young swallow makes a summer, however respectable and plump an elderly swallow he may ultimately become. Finding in high school or college the few who by peculiarities of temperament and gift, by accidents of environment, are still able to feel excitement may, instead, primarily be doing a disservice to those few; to the extent that their minds re-echo Keats and Shelley, they may be permanently alienated from their fellows, not bound to them in a richer communication. From such a tenuous custodianship come our typical young American poets—born in Kansas, searching until they die for a spiritual home, apt to rationalize their isolation by turning against the landscape in which the rich fare their minds have fed upon is strictly unrepresented.

From those who have found, and usually belatedly, significance and meaning in the literature of other lands, we get the sort of repudiation which James, writing in 1870, expressed in *The Madonna of the Future:*[1]

> We are the disinherited of art! We are excluded from the magic circle. The soil of American perception is a poor, little, barren, artificial deposit. Yes! We are wedded to imperfection. An American, to excel, has just ten times as much to learn as a European. We lack the deeper sense; we have neither taste, nor tact, nor force. How should we have them? Our rude and garish climate, our silent past, our deafening pres-

ent, the constant pressure upon us of unlovely circumstances
are as void of all that nourishes and prompts and inspires the
artist as my sad heart is void of bitterness in saying so; we
poor aspirants must live in perpetual exile.

But what makes a climate "crude"? The word *crude*
applies not to nature, but to the works of man. A climate
is crude if no man has sung it beautifully, not of itself.
And why was the past "silent"? The men who founded
America and the men who followed them here came from
Europe, bringing with them the languages in which the
European was believed to work ten times as easily. And
why did the present deafen? Because the voices raised
within it echoed notes designed to pierce through the
roars of a bear-baiting crowd or one assembled to watch
a hanging, but not those of the spectators of a ball game?

If we turn from the American scene—where many of
the issues were confused by the precaution the early
settlers took to apply English words to the strange birds
and beasts they met, to call unfamiliar trees and flowers
by loved English names—to Australia and New Zealand,
we find even more vivid demonstration of the choice that
faces the custodians of the humanities between alienating
from their native heaths those who love literature and
providing them with a medium within which the differently colored birds and flowers become meaningful. Compared with the transition from Old England to New
England, the transition from England to the unfamiliar
landscape of the Southern Hemisphere is much sharper.
The seasons are reversed; at Christmas one first eats roast
pig in traditional piety and then goes swimming. The
very stars are strange. To reach a colder climate, one goes
south. The birds are more silent and less distrustful, and
the English-speaking child is given a choice between finding a way to fit the names of birds like the kookaburra
into the cadences of English verse or rhyming the name
of the Australian cuckoo which, although it lays its eggs
in other birds' nests, neither looks like a cuckoo nor says
"cuckoo." If one learns to respond to the word *June* with
the word *summer* when all the Junes one has known have
been wintry, one is forever lonely both in the wintriness
of an Australian June and among the burgeoning flowers

of June in England, as Katherine Mansfield so poignantly demonstrated.

Sharing as they do all these contrasts of landscape and climate, the responses of English-speaking people in Australia and New Zealand have been strikingly different. The English who went to New Zealand found a country which, although strange, was nevertheless—in its fiords and waterfalls, its high mountains capped with snow, its deeply cut ravines—regarded as beautiful in European romantic terms, and a native people—the Polynesian Maoris—whose epic poetry was reminiscent of the Greeks. Maori words were liquid and lovely and easy to pronounce, and it was not difficult to transmute the English love of landscape and the remembered English cadences into the new names for the new beauties they found. There is still nostalgia, but the almost fierce participation of the New Zealander in the tradition of English poetry is reflected in the incredibly well-stocked shelves of New Zealand bookshops, as well as in the poetry of Eileen Duggan when she writes of a New Zealand Christmas:[2]

> For my heart goes crying through these days of summer,
> Through the sleepy summer, slow with streams and bees,
> Had my land been old then, there He might have lighted
> Here have seen His first moon in the ngaio trees.
>
> . . . .
>
> The sky would be a tumble of summer constellations,
> Our own, alas, hidden, that cluster of loss,
> Exiled from sight by some great thoughtful angel,
> Lest He too soon should look upon a cross.
>
> Oh my heart goes crying through these days of waiting
> We too have oxen and our straw is sweet,
> We too have oxen and stables and a manger.
> Oh for one clear footprint of His little feet.

But in Australia it was different. There was nothing in English experience to make the climate seem other than "crude and garish." The flowers were either so minute in their delicate patterns that no one saw them, or grew so large and gaudy that they offended the taste; English roses transplanted to Tasmania grew as large as cabbages.

The endless dry landscape, which stretched farther
than a man could walk in several days, seemed monotonous and was made the more monotonous when the
twelve hundred varieties of eucalyptus were all given one
name, "gums," thus cutting down further the ability of
the newcomers to see and revel in unfamiliar variety.
The leaves on the "gums" do not behave like the leaves
of European trees. They are sparse and tilted to catch the
small amount of rain; there are special kinds of emergency
leaves which spring out to etch the outline of an old gum
which has been burnt but has not died, and these resur-
rected trees take strange shapes, frightening at night, in
the silent land. It took D. H. Lawrence's eye to begin
to catch the special quality of wonder in Australia, but
he was frightened and repelled, and he opposed to his
descriptions of the landscape the power-driven men,
modeled on a leader whom he nicknamed Kangaroo.[3]
Today there are few copies of *Kangaroo* to be found in
Australia. Where the English who went to New Zealand
found a people who traced their arrival genealogically,
who related their own time and space to that of the gods,
those who colonized Australia found a native people who
lived in a timeless world in which men and animals were
caught in such close communion that words were hardly
necessary, and in which the landscape was so integral to
the myth that to get a myth told properly it was necessary
to follow, on foot, the path of the characters in the story
from rock to waterhole. The Australian native hardly saw
his world, so closely did he live in it, expressing it in ritual
dance and stylized drawing. To the children of aborigines, the idea of European perspective is a revelation,
and a whole school of youthful painting was started off
by the recognition of a gifted aboriginal child who suddenly shouted, "Oh, now I see, you don't paint it the
way you *know* it is, you paint it the way you *see* it." But
this close, timeless communion with a country that
seemed harsh, arid, unfriendly, and monotonous to European eyes had little to offer the colonist, nostalgic for
the green fields of England and a landscape shaped for
centuries by human hands. The Australian native did
nothing with his environment—in European eyes—except to live within it, surviving with the most primitive

tools, carrying a burning brand to warm his naked body, coating his hair with grease to protect his eyes, fastening up his small, ritual, stone objects in his knotted hair. His language was difficult, his appearance uninviting; after the first encounters when he took the Europeans for the ghosts of his own dead, he began to "share" their sheep as they "shared" his game—equally without a by-your-leave. The early hostilities in which Tasmanian aborigines were rounded up and shot, or whole groups of Australian aborigines were given poison flour for a feast, later gave place to interdependence between newcomers and natives on the great sheep stations, and a growing responsibility for black Australians by white Australians. The early romantic attitude of the white New Zealander toward the noble Maori has deteriorated as the former proud and poetic native has become proletarianized, a slightly un-reliable unskilled worker in dairy or lumber mill. But the marks of the early contact remain; the Maori's treatment of the environment—verbal, romantic, communicable to those bred in a Greco-Roman tradition—provided a bridge over which the English colonist passed to integrate imaginatively a landscape which also was beautiful in European terms. The unintelligible names the Australian natives used, the strange rituals, patterns wrought in blood and feathers, dances by naked men around a fire, provided no such comprehensible entry for the colonist—and that in a land where an entry was more urgently needed. The tradition of English poetry has barely held its own in Australia in the balladry of the frontier, in such lines as the closing verses of A. B. Paterson's *Song of the Artesian Waters*:[4]

And it's clear away the timber, and it's let the water run,
How it glimmers in the shadow, how it flashes in the sun.
By the silent belts of timber, by the miles of blazing plain
It is bringing hope and comfort to the thirsty land again.
    Flowing down, further down,
      It is flowing further down
To the tortured thirsty cattle, bringing gladness in its going
Through the droughty days of summer, it is flowing, ever flowing
It is flowing, ever flowing further down.

It is rather in painting, in learning to make a direct visual response to the strange environment for which their language had only harsh words and angry images, that the Australians have expressed themselves. And along the railway tracks which stretch across the desert where the aboriginal child once lived, there are small settlements where children of English stock stand squinting at the sun, holding a hand up to protect their eyes, while their fair hair is coarsened and dried without benefit of kangaroo fat, this in an environment where the aboriginal child was once protected by a culture rich in meaning. The Australian novelist, Eleanor Dark, working with the notes of anthropologists, has recreated the sensuous experience of such a child:[5]

> He was conscious of the world, and conscious of himself as part of it, fitting into it, belonging to it, drawing strength and joy and existence from it, like a bee in the frothing yellow opulence of the wattle. He was conscious of an order which had never failed him, of noises such as the chorus of cicadas, less a sound than a vibration in his ear drums, of scents which he had drawn into his nostrils with his first breath, and of the familiar scratchy touch against his bare skin of sand and twig, pebble and armoured leaf. So that his sulkiness remained isolated in a mind abandoned to sensation—something which, for the present, would go no further than the outthrust lip and the liquid darkness of the eye, while he absorbed, in absent minded voluptuousness, his secure and all-sufficient world.

I have dwelt on this experience of English-speaking people in two different countries on the other side of the world as a prelude to my real theme, the concern of teachers of English—and of the language and literature of other civilizations—with the basic imagery which children encounter long before they go to school. It is in these early years that children will either learn to think in images, to endow their outer experiences with inner meaning and their inner feelings with forms derived from the outer world, or will learn to live, efficiently and quite contented, in a world of very low symbolization, or to feel that life is unbearable because there are no symbols to express what is intensely felt or that life is so overwhelmingly oversymbolized that there is no place for their own imagination to work at all. All of these are possible kinds of learning, and each represents a type of culture: the periods we think of as the great creative ages, when the balance between inner and outer perception gave the gifted a chance to write in a world of those who had learned to listen or to read; the periods of cultures in which people neither had nor seemed to need more than the arid symbolism of the birthday cake and the standard Christmas card, the pile of coconut or the beaded human bone; the periods or cultures like modern Australia or the America of Henry James in which those who want to write feel starved and alienated; or the last days of civilizations so overelaborated that the mind is finally emptied and flaccid in spite of the strength of the original artistic impulse which produced Gothic towers, the Bronze Age, or the thrice-pictured, picturing walls of Venice.

Any civilization may move in any of these directions; most civilizations for which we have long records have exemplified at different periods several of these potentialities. Historians have tended to treat the changes as mysteries, at best to be explained by plagues or by periods of political unrest or technological change. But such explanations say nothing about how a people whose literary inheritance is rich become poor. This process occurs within individual human beings, not on some national arena where words like *war* and *depression* are used to sum up the recurrent events in many individual lives. We may find the roots of continuing imagination or of loss of imagination in the experiences of small children, who learn—either through the speech of their elders, when that speech is richly laden with imagery as is the speech of the peasants of so many parts of the world, or through literature—that words and phrases are a way of relating themselves to the world about them. The closer the words to the child's immediate experience, the better the chance of such learning. Poems about snow read in the hot desert or about the desert read among the snowy mountains may quicken the imagination of those who have never heard a lovely line about their own natural environment—but only at the risk of alienation. If the vivid experience of the moon, seen through the window, or the snow on the ledge can be caught and kept in words, then a genuine groundwork for poetic understanding can be laid. For the child experiencing snow, it matters little whether an unlettered grandmother exclaims, "Oh, lovey, isn't it lovely, like white feathers," or a literate grandmother exclaims, " 'The stiff rail was softened to swan's down, and still fluttered down the snow'." If the words *swan's down* have shifted from an image of the swan's soft breast to an image of expensive white fluff sewn on the edge of an evening coat, something will be lost. But, provided the grandmother's voice keeps the sense of metaphor and the comment is accompanied by an image in the grandmother's eyes of *some* swan's down, the real or the man-made ornament, the child will learn that there are words which other people, whom one loves and trusts, use to make snow not just something dazzlingly white, incredibly soft and crisp or wet, but also something that may be related to the rest of experience. From "cold as ice" to "eyes of icy blue" to the splinter of ice in little Kay's heart is then an easy path, and later in life to say that someone is "cold" will not be an empty description of the formality of a bread-and-butter letter but will contain possibilities of passion as well as of its lack:[6]

> Queens, their eyes blue like the ice,
> Are dancing in the crowd.

And they will be prepared to understand:[7]

> In coldest crucibles of pain
> Her shrinking flesh was fired.

But the phrases that fall from the grandmother's lips may no longer have the tried imagery of the unlettered, but may be instead the empty words of the poorly educated. Then, in the course of an unaccustomed reading of an English book, if the word *downs* appears, it may no longer be read with a sense of meaning. The child asks, as the adult's voice falters: "What is a *downs?*" And the adult, who no longer has a clear picture of the soft contours of the English countryside, answers, "I think it's a funny English word that means a hill or something," and the child murmurs sadly, "Oh, I thought it had something to do with the down in the quilt"—a fragile link has been broken, perhaps irrevocably. There is still a chance to mend such a broken mesh of meaning if, in kindergarten and elementary school, the poetry the child hears is closely related to its immediate world, the sights and sounds and smells of its own landscape and milieu. "The Moon's the North Wind's cooky" [8] still has a chance with a child who has never heard of the "silver" moon, who has never sung:

> Sippity sup, sippity sup,
> Nice bread and milk in a china cup.
> China cup with a silver spoon,
> Made from a piece of the silver moon,

but who can thrill with mixed horror and delight when "greedy North Wind" eats "the bright New Moon" again. If the familiar image is carefully invoked, without the strange and unfamiliar words the child has been taught to distrust as "funny English" or "funny foreign" or "queer old-fashioned," then the child who learns to respond to: [9]

> Asters by the brookside
> Make asters in the brook

may later regain its historical birthright in a swan it has never seen and learn to see—in the mind's eye: [10]

> The swan on still St. Mary's Lake
> Float double, swan and shadow.

We have been living, in the United States, on the residue of another age, when a combination of circumstances—an elder generation who could still read English (as distinguished from American) and hardly knew they were doing so, and a great population of immigrant and native country folk whose speech cherished in phrases like "blackberry winter" and "coffee cow" ("a cow that gives just enough milk for a cup of coffee")—preserved the capacity to read and perhaps write within the literary tradition for which this speech had been a base. But in the last quarter of a century many things have happened. We have become an urban people, and the limited literacy of the city streets is harder put to underwrite the imagination than is that of the countryside where the child is closer to primary experience cast in other than human terms. We have a decreasing number of peasant grandmothers to croon age-old lullabies, while images of the old world dance through their minds and gleam through their words to catch the inner eye of their drowsy charges. American as a language has separated us more and more from English, so that the stamp of foreignness is likely to be placed on the everyday English words which crop up in rhyme and story and song, as well as upon the Polish or Italian words which the little child learned for *cracker* or *cooky*.

And meanwhile, out of the fragmentation of verbal experience, in a new landscape for the English-speaking, in a whole new world for the non-English-speaking, there has come a weakening of visual imagery, of the tie between the experience, the image, and the word. Only a people who have not only not had a cultural fostering of imagery, but who also have been submitted to processes which destroy it, could develop and continue to use such phrases as "He sits around and gets in your hair," with its wearying invocation of complicated metaphor and inappropriate handling of scale, or could suggest shutting someone up with "Oh, put a lid on the drip," or say of a lover whom they hope to win before summer, "I'll have to cut him down to size."

Beneath these confusing, muddled clichés which depend on shock for their first effect and on unimaginative slavishness to the contemporary for their survival, there is a motor imagery so vigorous, so free, so undisciplined that it scarcely contributes at all to the materials of literature—the imagery of a Walt Disney, in which anything can change into anything else and back again at any speed. It is upon this type of imagery that the timing of the radio, the humor of the animated cartoon, the bare cognitive economy of the comics where no one wears a gun that will not be needed to shoot with, all depend. Somehow we need to find a way to reintegrate it with our whole literary tradition.

The ways that are being taken at present are secondary and unsatisfactory. There is the ten-year-old boy who willingly reads "good books" like *Treasure Island* and

Huckleberry Finn, provided, and firmly provided, that he has first encountered them either in a comic or a movie. Only given this guarantee that these "good books" were really part of a world he understood, was he willing to approach them. But so approached they are thoroughly enjoyed, and similarly vouched for "good books" are eagerly awaited. In the tremendous task that lies ahead of us in our culture, where semiliteracy is stamping out oral tradition but providing no genuine literacy to take its place, it is necessary to experiment with and explore every possible avenue—nursery rhymes, radio, television, toys—through which the child may learn how to knit image and word together.

The proposed experiment of the Modern Language Association with teaching languages in elementary schools is a case in point. American indifference to and contempt for foreign languages are learned before a child enters school, learned when it is taught that a particular four-legged animal is a *dog*, but that foreigners have other words—not for the animal, but for the word *d o g*—which are not so good, in languages that keep them from speaking English properly and their mothers from being fit to belong to the PTA. Not until we devise some culture-wide way to convey to children that English is just one language among the many by which people deal with the world, and that each word for the animal we call *dog* is as valid as d-o-g, can we expect to make a success of any foreign language program, no matter where it is begun or by what methods it is pursued. The striking contrast between the success of the Dutch in teaching native peoples to speak not only Dutch but other languages as well, and the difficulties English-speaking peoples have even in teaching English, attests vividly (and in many separate historical contexts) to the importance of the cultural attitude toward foreign languages—as something that can and should be learned, or as something that really shouldn't exist.

What happens in the nursery and kindergarten and in the thousand popular media to which our children are exposed should be of immediate concern to custodians of our rich literary tradition. It is there rather than in high school English classes that the capacity to appreciate can be most actively fostered or most seriously marred.

PMLA, Vol. 68, No. 2, 1953.

REFERENCES

1. James, H., 1922.
2. Duggan, E., 1939.
3. Lawrence, D. H., 1950.
4. Paterson, A. B., 1954.
5. Dark, E., 1941.
6. Yeats, W. B., 1906.
7. Wylie, E., 1932.
8. Thompson, B. J., 1932.
9. Jackson, H., 1892.
10. Wordsworth, W., 1923.

18

Toward More Vivid Utopias*

When one is asked to speak to a group primarily interested in the sciences from a platform defined by the humanities, it seems important to state more specifically where one's own discipline lies within the academic fields and what contribution one may expect to make from its specific interests. Anthropology holds a unique position, formally recognized in its inclusion in the National Research Council, where it belongs as a biological science; the Social Science Research Council, among those sciences which take man's biological nature as given; and the American Council of Learned Societies, because of its concern with language, so often defined as a pure humanity, without reference to the larynx or the delicate mechanism of the human ear.

This triple membership springs partly from the tradition of anthropological field work, in which single workers, with small funds and a narrow margin of time, visited, in what was conceived as probably the only careful study which would ever be made, small primitive societies whose ancient and distinctive ways of life were disintegrating even as we tried to set them down. Not only did we work with urgency, as might a student of literature, trying to take down from dictation a new poem from the lips of a dying poet, or a student of painting, who found a painter of great gift drawing in an impermanent ink on the exposed, whitewashed walls of a public square—where the rain would wash it all away tomorrow or the next day—but we also, both by the nature of the situation in which

* This article is based on the Phi Beta Kappa lecture delivered before the American Association for the Advancement of Science at the New York meeting, December 1956.

we found ourselves and by the canons of our craft, looked at the whole people, at their bodies as well as at the social arrangements of their lives; at the music they made, or at least at the musical instruments with which they made it; at the dances, which might be seen as art to be appreciated as well as analyzed; at their rituals, which might be catalogued as *rites de passage* or regarded as an artistic product of generations of imaginative creativity, anonymous, time binding, with its own esthetic.

The anthropologist who works in this way comes to have an equal interest and respect for those aspects of human life which are concerned with the perception and ordering of observed regularities in nature and for those aspects of human life in which the "seeing eye" turns as much inward as outward, as the mind matches proprioception with perception in an outer world which already contains—in the shape of a roof, the line of a dance, the flick of a wrist at a sacrifice—the patterned perpetuation of earlier imaginative and creative acts.

Because we are also always committed to a scientific ordering of our material, these products of human imagination can not only be subjected to analysis of their function in a given society but can also be related to certain capacities of the human mind—themselves becoming better known through the imaginative scientific inquiries of investigators like Piaget and Inhelder, Gesell and Ilg, Erikson, and Margaret Lowenfeld. Delight in the imaginative creation of individuals or in the intuitive— that is, simultaneous and so unanalyzed—grasp of these as wholes by whole societies, does not prevent analytic work, also. The two methods of approach—that of the humanities, which focuses upon a recognition of the unique character of a work of the imagination, and that of the sciences, which attempt by careful observation, analysis, and finally experiment to understand the lawfulness of the behavior involved—can be used.

It is from this particular background of research that I wish to describe the role which men's visions of a possible and more desirable future play in the development of a culture. Utopias may be seen from many points of view—as projections from individual experience; as projections from individual experiences stamped by the point of view of a particular period; as sterile blueprints, too narrow to confine the natural varieties of the human mind for very long, as when they are lived out by small cult groups who pare and mould the individuals born within them to a confining and crippling mode. Or they may be seen as those visions of future possibilities which lead the minds of men forward into the future, giving life a meaning beyond the grave or beyond the simple domestic perpetuation of one's own life in the lives of one's children, with an interest in the trees planted in one's own garden but no interest in the trees in one's neighbors' garden. The Golden Age, a retrospective utopia of the days when all men lived like gods, and walked and talked with gods—the days before death or work or separation came into the world—may also, of course, play a significant role in keeping a whole people caught in a dream unrelated to the requirements of the contemporary world.

Using models from primitive cultures, we may, from this point of view, look at those cultures in which life is held steady by a view of the past, of which the present is a poor copy, a vale of tears where once there was Olympian laughter, at those cultures which live a hand-to-mouth existence, wrapt in the small urgencies of the present, and at those which move, generation after generation, toward Heaven—which may be the heavenly Jerusalem "with milk and honey blest," the Jerusalem to be rebuilt and reinhabited, which informed the imagination of Jews throughout the Diaspora, or the Jerusalem to be built "in England's green and pleasant land." Against these may be placed Nirvana, with its insistent comment on the lack of value in all earthly and individualized life.

Within a culture as complex as our own, which draws on the inheritance of so many earlier and partly recorded pasts and which now has available an even larger number of incomparable and imaginatively stimulating "presents," from accounts of the peoples whose lives were part of a different stream—in Africa, in the Orient, and in the New World—it is obvious that we may live not only on different visions at different periods but also on different and incompatible visions at the same time. Part of the excitement and the difficulty of the modern world, which makes the artist feel that he has no whole context within which to create his personal, special new vision and which makes the scientist turn to the anonymous writing of science fiction nightmares, is just the way in which different sorts of utopias—one man's dream and another man's nightmare—jostle each other even within the confines of one political speech or one brief editorial, as we yearn for a past, rage at or delight in the present, or promise or threaten a future. While it always has been and will probably always be the mark of the more educated man that he lives in a longer time perspective, both into the past and into the future, than his less well-educated contemporaries, where this education is underwritten by no habitual pattern of thought and speech within which such time perspectives are implicitly expressed, the presence of so many and such contrasting world views may seem fragmenting and mechanical rather than living.

Yet, from comparative materials, it seems quite clear that the utopias men live by are of vital importance in such mundane matters as whether they will struggle to preserve the identity of their society, their class, their religion, or their vocation; whether they will plant trees which take two lifetimes to mature; whether they will take thought to stop the forests from being depleted, the good soil from being washed into the sea, or the gene pool from becoming exposed to too much radiation. Men who believe that the ultimate good state will mean the abolition of identity are hardly likely to take an active interest in public health, and those who believe that the Day of Judgment is near, when the sheep will be separated from the goats and the whole world will go up in a holocaust directed by a punishing Deity, see the atom bomb as an addition to the Lord's armory of destruction.

Within any determinedly other-worldly religion, there is a perpetual conflict between the active acceptance of early death (so the little, innocent souls may go up to God at once, unstained by sin) and the need for public health measures and preventive medicine as well as for the compassionate dole to the beggar or care for the dying. The Catholic Church has fought a long battle against an otherworldliness which would have as its logic an overvaluation of death—which has occasionally been the response of literal-minded savages to enthusiastic Christian preaching about heaven. On the other hand, the modern public health movement has its problems in an overvaluation of the importance of individual life, which leads to a lowering of death rates before there is a compensating rise in the standard of living and a fall in the birth rate, with the result that famine and misery are the portion of the very individuals whose lives were to be bettered.

At the same time, all visions of heaven, in this world and in the next, have a curiously tasteless, pale blue and pink quality, whether the image is one of cherubim and seraphim "casting down their golden crowns around the glassy sea" or of a time when "ploughs in peaceful industry shall supersede the sword," when "the dictatorship of the proletariat shall be realized in ideological completeness," or when lions shall lie down with lambs, or of a world in which women shall have been freed from all the incidental consequences of their reproductivity and will spend long vacations with their lovers of the moment, flying Chinese kites.

Beside any picture of heaven above or heaven on earth, the pictures of hell and destruction stand out in vivid and compelling intensity, each detail strong enough to grip the imagination as the horrid creations of a Wells, an Orwell, or an Aldous Huxley unroll before our horrified eyes. Where positive utopias are insipid and a detailed heaven is unbearable to think of as a permanent abode, the creators of terror, the repudiators of man's future, have no such problem. So, if utopian visions are the stuff by which men live, it would seem a legitimate subject of inquiry to ask what is the matter with them? Why is Hell always so much more vivid than Heaven? Why, as I heard a young priest say recently, are all images of heaven "while not exactly not true, not as true as they might be"?

There have been attempts to give scientific answers to this question: that the prefiguration of bliss lies in the womb, where the child has no chance to use its distance receptors, and so the feeling remains one of undifferentiated and unspecified ecstasy; that analysis destroys a vision by introducing an element of self-consciousness and detachment of part of the self. These may be adequate explanations of the way in which the individual, in terms of his life experience, seeks for or experiences visionary ecstasy, but they seem insufficient answers to the problem of why the imagination of the human race, which has produced its long procession of great creations, has never yet succeeded in building a picture of a future really unlike the present, either in this world or in the next, where anyone passionately wished to live except when it was counterpointed against a Hell, delineated with the greatest precision. Heaven and all the pallid utopias are, in fact, even like Nirvana, blank white spaces —or spaces a little tinted with pastel and furnished with plastic gadgets—and are given reality only by contrast with the fear, pain, and agony of some other state.

Yet it is by visions of a better world or place or state that men make positive efforts—in contrast to fiddling while Rome burns or refraining from evil all their days in fear of hell-fire. So it would seem legitimate to ask why human imaginations are, apparently, so handicapped in the creation of such essential visions and whether there is any way in which our present scientific knowledge of human behavior and of the way in which societies function can be used to create conditions within which utopias might be created whose positive hold on men's minds would be stronger than the negative hold of the Infernos and Lost Paradises. For the last 50 years we have experimented with the compelling character of negative images, as the prophecies of the dangers of modern warfare have grown ever sharper. When warfare is upon them, men will struggle; but they sink into a kind of paralysis when there is need to fight even harder—in peacetime—to prevent a recurrence of war. We need more vivid utopias.

One answer to the question comes from an examination of the struggle that institutionalized religions, which present the other world as desirable, must go through to deal with suicide, either condemning it as a dereliction in stewardship, as Christianity does, and treating the living out of life on earth as a trust, or hedging it around with terribly difficult steps, as in parts of India, where, in order to die a holy and self-elected death, a man must give up caste and family and must become purified until, at last,

dressed for the next world and in a trance, he is lowered
into the earth "alive." The next world must not be so
desirable that it completely competes with this one and
leads a majority of believers to suicide or toward a too-
willing death in war, with the promise of a warriors'
heaven. A long life of preparation—as a shaven and dedi-
cated celibate, completely cloistered or moving through
the streets with a begging bowl and making a contribution to the ongoing life of the world as teacher, nurse, or
supplicant—this is feasible.

Similarly, Communism has always had difficulties with
those who, regarding the Soviet Union as heaven on earth,
have wished to go and live there instead of remaining in
their own unregenerate countries, working at dull organizational jobs in the hope of a World Revolution which
they themselves might not live to see. Sometimes short
trips to the Soviet Union, as circumscribed as visions of
the next world to a cloistered religious, were permitted.
But the tension between the vision and the present must
not include any way of immediately slackening it by a
self-elected entry into heaven.

In fact, through the emphasis on dedication, attention
is shifted from the self to the fate of others; through
prayer for the souls in purgatory, teaching the young, or
preparing for the revolution from which others will benefit, the necessary distance seems to be created so that a
vision can be compelling, drawing one on like a magnet,
but not too fast or too far. So perhaps it may be said
that it is only when the visionary or the prophet, the poet
or the painter wants to involve the individual directly in
the future vision that the danger of immediate response
is allowed for in the interpreters and spectators by a dilution of its intensity. Then Heaven or the Perfect Socialist
State may be seen as being too insipid and as tasting like
sawdust. A feeling of less involvement may be achieved
by concentrating the individual's effort on the relation
between someone else and the desired state—where the
nexus can have both the intensity of devotion to the
other and devotion to the dream without the temptation
to relax and try to get there oneself.

Even here the other temptation—to force history at
once to disgorge a visionary paradise at no matter what

cost of suffering and death—is present as soon as Heaven is too vividly conceived even for the other, who must then be saved, by the rack or by brain washing, to become a denizen of someone else's too compelling dream. The ability of any people to cultivate protective devices against other people's compelling visions—against which the best defenses seem to be either laughter or else revolt against any individual being in thrall to the will of another —must also be considered as one component in their ability to create utopian dreams which inspire but do not limit them.

But there seems also to be another explanation of the relative lack of vividness of the good vision as compared with the nightmare. In pictures of Hell, of dictatorships armed with concentration camps and thought control, the appeal is made to human beings' most shared and least differentiated responses; pain, hunger, thirst, being bound, tortured, cut off from other human beings, and battered day and night by intolerable stimuli—these are experiences which repel every human being and under which the savage and the civilized, the illiterate and the scholar ultimately break down.

Men of different temperaments will break in different ways and at different points, but the effect of Medieval images of the tortures of Hell, when conjured up by a gifted preacher, or of the tortures actually administered in Nazi and Communist prisons is, in the end, to break all but the exceptional martyr sustained by a vision (which, only in this exceptional situation, cannot be called too vivid) of another world to which he is personally totally committed. (So Jehovah's Witnesses are said to stand up well to Communist pressures, and Orthodox Jews went chanting to the gas chambers as the early Christians, in the days when the Second Coming was felt to be very near, faced the lions.)

But the utopian vision, which is vivid enough to compel men's imagination and yet not so compelling that men must resort to rack and torture to bring others into it—the vision which men want to share with others and entrust to their expanding imagination rather than the vision in which they wish to entrap and imprison others —is built not upon the universals of fear and pain, hunger and thirst, ultimate fatigue and weakness, but upon the great diversity of human propensities and gifts. It must be, in terms of modern information theory, redundant enough to catch the developed imagination of each so-different member of any society.

Reduction to fear and pain gives men a common basis of the unbearable which can be elaborated—a nightmare peopled with Sisyphus endlessly rolling his stone and Tityus in agony. But reduction to our common good human experience leaves us with images of milk and honey, which stand very little elaboration before they are disintegrated by the involvement of our specific imaginations, by the differences in our childhood images of love and trust and bliss: it was not honey but strawberry jam, not the hum of bees but the flash of dragonfly wings, not a pointed breast but a round one which gave one suck. The recitation of such particular delights of food and drink as goat's milk or palm wine, durian, or witchetty grubs only resonates in the minds of those who once drank or ate them and falls dead upon the ears of those who never knew these pleasures. A whole society can be drawn on only by a utopian vision which contains the separate experiences of different regions, different classes, and different vocations, combined with the varied notes on each theme played by men of different temperament, disciplined and shaped by the prevailing forms of the culture. So it is no wonder that utopias are hard to come by.

Yet the world today is sorely in need of a vision which will endow our lives with meaning and responsibility and will make safe the terrible powers of destruction and the almost limitless powers of construction which scientific research has put into our hands. We can specify some of the characteristics this vision must have: it must be vivid enough to compel the heart, but not so vivid that one moves too quickly, by death or emigration or the coercion of others, to attain it; it must be so conceived that it is sought for the sake of others rather than solely for the self—for other men, for the whole next generation, or for men eons ahead—with nice adjustments which make it not too immediate (just the next generation) and not too distant, lest one become lost in a world without imaginable relation to the present; and it must be complex, redundant enough to catch and hold the imaginations of men and women of many different types of temperament and experience, and stylized enough, in terms of culture and period, to carry the weight of past ages of formal esthetic moulding and polishing and to speak with cadences and lines grown powerful by long usage.

These prescriptions I am giving are of the sort which can be derived from the scientific comparison of cultures; they are prescriptions for conditions. So one may compare ages and countries in which a particular art or science has flourished with those in which they have not so flourished, dissect out what appear to be the facilitating conditions, list and describe them.

Possibly all these may be necessary but not sufficient causes. Yet it is by the specification and attempted realization of conditions within which events desired and deemed necessary may occur that the sciences that deal with man can work in the world, stating conditions within which a child can grow, an idea can take root, an institution can flourish, and a man's hand and eye can grow cunning, his mind sharp, and his imagination wide. Though we remain dependent upon the caliber of individuals for our great achievements, the contrasts between one culture and another—between peoples whose every movement is a work of art and peoples, of the same human species, who limit their artistry to a few scratches on the edge of a pot—leave little doubt that the cultural conditions for any kind of creativity are very important. And as, by the scientific comparative study of cultures, we learn more about them, we can turn from hand-wringing, viewing with alarm, and the role of Cassandra to build the world closer to our heart's desire.

What, then, may the conditions be within which we may foster more vivid utopias? Three resources which seem accessible to us with our present knowledge are these: the imagination of little children, where each new-born child brings a unique and new potential to our perception and ordering of the world; the provision of materials from other cultures, so that in the interplay between the great achievements of the human race in the many separate, unique, but comparable cultures men have built, new combinations and forms may occur; and the creation of conditions within which those who know the possibilities for the future, which are emerging from scientific discoveries, can combine their insights with the insights of those who know the full and astounding range of what man has achieved in the past, without mutations or the hypertrophies of extrasensory perception currently invoked by the creators of our folklore of the future, the writers of science fiction.

The imaginative capacities of young children, initially part of the processes of growth and evolution, as Edith Cobb has phrased it, are then one source to which we must turn. Within the growing child, the capacity to bring order out of the perception of the outside world and the capacity to create something unique and new out of his perception of himself in the world are, initially, two parts of one process. Concentration on one at the expense of the other robs the child, and so the world, of what could have come from both.

The current experiments of Jean Piaget and Bärbel Inhelder, in Geneva, provide a vivid illustration of these two approaches. Piaget and Inhelder have developed a set of experiments to test the child's growing capacity to recognize some of the principles essential to scientific thought. One of these, which Piaget calls "reversibility," is exemplified in the child's recognition that when a large, round lump of clay is thinned out to a narrow cylinder, it will still have the same weight and be the same amount of clay. When these experiments are reported only in words, with the emphasis placed upon growth, with chronological age and school training, of the ability to recognize such points, the *other* things the child does are catalogued simply as failure. But when a method of reporting is used which records the entire behavior of children at different ages—through sound film, film and tape, or the verbatim recording of words—then the whole child comes into the picture and we see something else.

Thus, in the test situation (Fig. 1), the child is presented with a laboratory apparatus by which a colored fluid can be released gradually from the upper glass chamber, through a cock, into a glass below. The child is shown how this works and is allowed to try it. Then he is given series of cards picturing the state of the apparatus before any fluid enters the glass, at various stages, and, finally, when all of it has entered the glass. The card

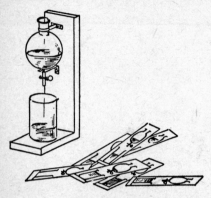

Fig. 1. Demonstration apparatus and scrambled cards for part I of Flowing Liquid Test in which a simple sequence of cards showing correct relationships is presented. [From the experimental work of Bärbel Inhelder, in the Laboratory of Jean Piaget, Institut des Sciences de L'Éducation, University of Geneva.]

series are presented to the child in a scrambled state, and the child is asked to arrange them. One little boy, whose achievement on the test—like that of many children of his age—would have been reported as "failure," made a response which can be described as poetic (Fig. 2) as he "rhymed" the cards instead of arranging them to represent the reality of colored water passing into a glass in an orderly way (Fig. 3). Using the same materials, he drew on another capacity of his mind. Had this been a class in "design" or in "making pleasing patterns," his answer would have been the "right" answer, whereas when he was being tested for ability to use a kind of thinking basic to modern science, it was a "wrong" answer.

In the kind of training given in European schools of the Swiss type, the child has to learn to handle this kind of reversibility after first encountering a world in which rigid one-way sequences in behavior and among material things have been heavily emphasized. By contrast, it is the problem of how to handle rigid sequences —which cannot be reversed in fact, however they may

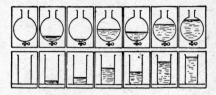

Fig. 2. A "poetic" answer to part II of the test, when the child is presented with a double set of cards. This answer, made by a boy of 5 years and 8 months of age, is described by the experimenter as containing "some mistakes characteristic of children of this age." Note the complexity of the rhyming, like a Bach two-part invention.

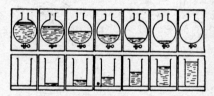

Fig. 3. The correct answer to part II of the test.

be reversed in thought—that must be learned by the first generation of a people who encounter factory methods, people who have arranged life in their heads in poetic patterns and who have not been told that this is the "wrong" answer. Recently I saw a group of educated men and women who had been presented with some simple problems in building manifolds by means of brightly colored units; the men classified the exercise as "art" and, although they were much better in mathematics and science in college than the women, failed, while the women, who also classified the exercise as "art," at which they thought themselves good, succeeded easily. By failing to cultivate both sides of the child's ability, by opposing them and negating one or the other, we are losing not only artists but also scientists, and we are splitting our society, as well as our individual children, into incompatible parts, destructively at war with each other. A different type of education, which recognizes the early stage in which children can apprehend form through color and kinesthetic feel and the recognition of sets, is a precondition for preserving the creativity with which each generation of newborn children enters the world.

The second necessary condition, a knowledge of what men have done before, again involves the presentation of wholes—not the current split between the history of science and technology, on the one hand, and art museums and literature courses, on the other. In real life the imagination of the painter and the poet are essential to the conditions within which the scientist works, for the fearful presage of the poet reaches ahead of invention. A few years ago an attempt was made to design an exhibition which would show the effect upon painting of modern scientific invention in building design; but in looking at the materials it was discovered that in every case the painter's vision had preceded the necessary technological invention, as the myth of Icarus preceded the Wright brothers. So we need arrangements which will bring together, for the experience of the student and the adult, whole historic periods—their buildings and their ideas, their books and their economics, their painting and their technology, their mathematics and their poetry—so that out of the perceived relationships and comparisons among them new ideas may be born and the present ignorance among scientists of man's past and present greatness, surpassed only by the ignorance among most humanists and many artists of man's future, made possible by science, may be overcome.

Finally, it seems to me, in this age when the very survival of the human race and possibly of all living creatures depends upon our having a vision of the future for others which will command our deepest commitment, we need in our universities, which must change and grow with the world, not only chairs of history and comparative linguistics, of literature and art—which deal with the past and sometimes with the present—but we need also Chairs of the Future, chairs for those who will devote themselves, with all the necessary scholarship and attention, to developing science to the full extent of its possibilities for the future, and who will devote themselves—in the light of all our knowledge—as faithfully to the fine detail of what man might very well be as any classicist or medievalist devotes himself to the texts of Pindar and Horace or to the thought of St. Thomas Aquinas.

Science, Vol. 126, November 8, 1957.

BIBLIOGRAPHY

Carstairs, G. M., 1957
Cobb, E., 1959
Erikson, E. H., 1950
Frank, L. K., 1956
Gesell, A. L., and F. L. Ilg, 1943
Harrison, G. R., 1956
Hendrix, G., 1950
Lowenfeld, M., 1939, 1954
Mead, M., 1940a, 1947d, 1953, 1954
Morris, C. W., 1956
Piaget, J., 1946, pp. 5-36
Sewell, E., 1952
Tanner, J. M., and B. Inhelder, 1956-1960
Walter, W. G., 1956

**Consolidated
Bibliography**

Bibliography

ABEL, THEODORA M.
  1938. "Free Designs of Limited Scope as a Personality Index," *Character and Personality*, VII, No. 1, 50-62.
ADORNO, T. W., *et al.*
  1950. *The Authoritarian Personality*. New York, Harper.
ASHBY, W. R.
  1947. "The Nervous System as Physical Machine," *Mind*, new ser., LVI, No. 221, 44-59.
BATESON, GREGORY
  1932. "Social Structure of the Iatmul People of the Sepik River, Part 3," *Oceania*, II, No. 4, 401-53.
  1935. "Culture Contact and Schismogenesis," *Man*, XXXV, Article No. 199, 178-83.
  1936. *Naven*. Cambridge, Cambridge University Press. 2nd ed. 1958, Stanford University Press.
  1941a. "Experiments in Thinking about Observed Ethnological Material," *Philosophy of Science*, VIII, No. 1, 53-68.
  1941b. "The Frustration-Aggression Hypothesis and Culture," *Psychological Review*, XLVIII, No. 4, 350-55.
  1942a. "Morale and National Character." In *Civilian Morale*, ed. Goodwin Watson. Boston, Houghton Mifflin, pp. 71-91.
  1942b. "Social Planning and the Concept of Deutero Learning." In *Science, Philosophy, and Religion, Second Symposium*, Lyman Bryson and Louis Finkelstein, eds. New York, Conference on Science, Philosophy, and Religion, pp. 81-97.
  1942c. "Some Systematic Approaches to the Study of Culture and Personality," *Character and Personality*, XI, No. 1, 76-84.
  1943a. "Cultural and Thematic Analysis of Fictional Films," *Transactions of The New York Academy of Sciences*, Ser. 2, V, No. 4, 72-78.
  1943b. "The Science of Decency," *Philosophy of Science*, X, No. 2, 140-42.
  1944. "Cultural Determinants of Personality." In *Personality and the Behavior Disorders*, II, ed. J. McV. Hunt. New York, Ronald, pp. 714-35.
  1946a. "From One Social Scientist to Another," *American Scientist*, XXXIV, No. 4, 648, 536-46.

1946b. "The Pattern of an Armaments Race," Parts I and II, *Bulletin of the Atomic Scientists*, II, Nos. 5 and 6, 10-11; Nos. 7 and 8, 26-28.

1949. "Bali: The Value System of a Steady State." In *Social Structure*, ed. Meyer Fortes. Oxford, Clarendon Press, pp. 35-53.

BATESON, GREGORY, AND MARGARET MEAD

1941. "Principles of Morale Building," *Journal of Educational Sociology*, XV, No. 4, 206-20.

1942. *Balinese Character: A Photographic Analysis.* Special Publications of The New York Academy of Sciences, II. The New York Academy of Sciences. Reprinted 1962.

1951. *First Days in the Life of a New Guinea Baby.* New York University Film Library, 16 mm., sound, 19 min.

BEAGLEHOLE, ERNEST, AND PEARL BEAGLEHOLE

1946. *Some Modern Maoris.* Wellington, N. Z., Council for Educational Research.

BENEDICT, RUTH

1934. *Patterns of Culture.* Boston, Houghton Mifflin.

1946a. *The Chrysanthemum and the Sword.* Boston, Houghton Mifflin.

1946b. "The Study of Cultural Patterns in European Nations," *Transactions of The New York Academy of Sciences*, Ser. 2, VIII, No. 8, 274-79.

BIRDWHISTELL, RAY L.

1963. "The Use of Audio-visual Teaching Aids." In *Resources for the Teaching of Anthropology*, David G. Mandelbaum, Gabriel W. Lasker, and Ethel M. Albert, eds. Berkeley and Los Angeles, University of California Press, pp. 49-61.

BREWSTER, OWEN

1945. "Let's Not Be Suckers Again," *American Magazine*, CXXXIX (January), 24-26.

BRUCH, HILDE, AND GRACE TOURAINE

1940. "Obesity in Childhood: V. The Family Frame of Obese Children," *Psychosomatic Medicine*, II, No. 2, 141-206.

BRYSON, LYMAN, AND LOUIS FINKELSTEIN (EDS.)

1942. *Science, Philosophy, and Religion, Second Symposium.* New York, Conference on Science, Philosophy, and Religion.

BRYSON, LYMAN, LOUIS FINKELSTEIN, AND R. M. MACIVER (EDS.)

1950. *Perspectives on a Troubled Decade: Science, Philosophy, and Religion 1939-1949, Tenth Symposium.* New York, Harper.

CARSTAIRS, G. MORRIS
  1957. *The Twice-Born*. London, Hogarth.
CHAPPLE, ELIOT D.
  1949. "The Interaction Chronograph: Its Evaluation and Present Application," *Personnel*, XXV, No. 4, 295-307.
CHAPPLE, ELIOT D., AND CONRAD M. ARENSBERG
  1940. "Measuring Human Reactions: An Introduction to the Study of the Interaction of Individuals," *Genetic Psychology Monographs*, XXII, No. 1, 3-147.
CHAPPLE, ELIOT D., AND CARLETON S. COON
  1942. *Principles of Anthropology*. New York, Holt.
CHAPPLE, ELIOT D., AND LEONARD R. SAYLES
  1961. *The Measure of Management*. New York, Macmillan.
COBB, EDITH
  1959. "The Ecology of Imagination in Childhood," *Daedalus* (Summer), 537-48.
COMMITTEE ON FOOD HABITS
  see Report of the Committee on Food Habits.
COUNTS, GEORGE
  1932. *Dare the Schools Build a New Social Order?* New York, John Day Pamphlets, No. 11.
CUMMINGS, R. O.
  1941. *The American and His Food*. University of Chicago Press.
DARK, ELEANOR
  1941. *The Timeless Land*. New York, Macmillan.
DAVIS, CLARA M.
  1928. "Self-selection of Diet by Newly Weaned Infants," *American Journal of Diseases of Children*, XXXVI, No. 4, 651-79.
  1935a. "Choice of Formulas Made by Three Infants throughout the Nursing Period," *American Journal of Diseases of Children*, L, No. 2, 385-94.
  1935b. "Self-selection of Food by Children," *American Journal of Nursing*, XXXV, No. 5, 403-10.
DENNIS, WAYNE
  1940. *The Hopi Child*. New York, Appleton-Century.
DOLLARD, JOHN
  1935. *Criteria for the Life History*. New Haven, Yale University Press. Reprinted 1949, New York, Peter Smith.
DRUMMOND, JACK C., AND ANNE WILBRAHAM
  1939. *The Englishman's Food*. London, Cape.
DUBOIS, CORA
  1944. *The People of Alor*. Minneapolis, University of Minnesota Press.

DUGGAN, EILEEN
   1939. "A New Zealand Christmas." In *Poems*. New York, Macmillan, p. 37.

DYER, A. M., AND MARGARET MEAD
   1944. "It's Human Nature," *Education* (CBS Broadcast), LXV, No. 4, 228-39.

ENGEL-FRISCH, G.
   1943. "A Study of the Effect of Odd-shifts upon the Food Habits of War Workers." In "The Problem of Changing Food Habits," Report of the Committee on Food Habits, 1941-1943. *National Research Council Bulletin*, No. 108, 82-84.

ERIKSON, ERIK H.
   1939. "Observations on Sioux Education," *Journal of Psychology*, VII, First Half, 101-56.
   1943. "Observations on the Yurok: Childhood and World Image," *University of California Publications in American Archaeology and Ethnology*, XXXV, No. 10, 257-302.
   1945. "Childhood and Tradition in Two American Indian Tribes." In *The Psychoanalytic Study of the Child*, I. New York, International Universities Press, pp. 319-50.
   1946. "Ego Development and Historical Change." In *The Psychoanalytic Study of the Child*, II. New York, International Universities Press, pp. 359-96.
   1950. *Childhood and Society*. New York, Norton.

FESTINGER, L.
   1944. "Effect of Container on Food Preference." Committee on Food Habits, National Research Council. (March.) Mimeographed.

FORTUNE, R. F.
   1935. *Manus Religion*. Philadelphia, American Philosophical Society.

FRANK, LAWRENCE K.
   1940. "The Cost of Competition," *Plan Age*, VI, Nos. 9 and 10, 314-24.
   1942. "World Order and Cultural Diversity," *Free World*, III, No. 1, 389-95.
   1956. "Imagination in Education." In *Imagination in Education*. New York, Bank Street College of Education, pp. 64-72.

FRENKEL-BRUNSWIK, ELSE, AND R. NEVITT SANFORD
   1945. "Some Personality Factors in Anti-Semitism," *Journal of Psychology*, XX, Second Half, 271-91.

FREUD, ANNA
   1946. *The Ego and the Mechanisms of Defense*, trans. Cecil Baines. New York, International Universities Press.

FREUD, ANNA, AND DOROTHY T. BURLINGHAM
    1943. *War and Children*. New York, Medical War Books.
FREUD, SIGMUND
    1918. *Totem and Taboo*, trans. A. A. Brill, New York, Moffat, Yard.
FROMM, ERICH
    1941. *Escape from Freedom*. New York, Farrar and Rinehart.
GAJDUSEK, D. CARLETON
    1962. "Kuru: An Appraisal of Five Years of Investigation," *Eugenics Quarterly*, IX, No. 1, 69-74. (See especially the bibliography.)
"GERMANY AFTER THE WAR, ROUND TABLE—1945."
    1945. *American Journal of Orthopsychiatry*, XV, No. 3, 381-441.
GESELL, ARNOLD L., AND FRANCES L. ILG
    1943. *Infant and Child in the Culture of Today*. New York and London, Harper.
GILBY, T.
    1948. "The Genesis of Guilt," *Proceedings of the International Conference on Medical Psychotherapy*, III, 10-19.
GLADWIN, THOMAS
    1961. "Oceania." In *Psychological Anthropology*, ed. Francis L. K. Hsu. Homewood, Ill., Dorsey Press, pp. 135-71.
GORER, GEOFFREY
    1938. *Himalayan Village*. London, Michael Joseph.
    1940. "Society as Viewed by the Anthropologist." In *The Cultural Approach to History*, ed. Caroline F. Ware. New York, Columbia University Press, pp. 20-30.
    1943. "Themes in Japanese Culture," *Transactions of The New York Academy of Sciences*, Ser. 2, V, No. 5, 106-24.
    1949. "Some Aspects of the Psychology of the People of Great Russia," *American Slavic and East European Review*, VIII, No. 3, 155-66.
GORER, GEOFFREY, AND JOHN RICKMAN
    1950. *The People of Great Russia*. New York, Chanticleer Press.
HALLOWELL, ALFRED I.
    1955. *Culture and Experience*. Philadelphia, University of Pennsylvania Press.
HARRISON, GEORGE R.
    1956. *What Man May Be: The Human Side of Science*. New York, Morrow.
HENDRIX, GERTRUDE
    1950. "Prerequisite to Meaning," *Mathematics Teacher*, XLIII, No. 7, 334-39.

HENRY, JULES, AND MELFORD E. SPIRO
  1953. "Psychological Techniques: Projective Tests in Field
     Work." In *Anthropology Today*, ed. A. L. Kroeber. Uni-
     versity of Chicago Press, pp. 417-29.
HICKS, GRANVILLE
  1946. *Small Town*. New York, Macmillan.
HOAGLAND, HUDSON, AND RALPH W. BURHOE (ISSUE EDS.)
  1961. "Evolution and Man's Progress," *Daedalus* (Sum-
     mer), 411-610.
HUXLEY, THOMAS H., AND JULIAN S. HUXLEY
  1947. *Touchstone for Ethics*. New York, Harper.
JACKSON, HELEN
  1892. *Poems*. Boston, Robert Brothers.
JAMES, HENRY
  1922. "The Madonna of the Future." In *The Novels and
     Tales of Henry James*, XIII. New York, Scribner, pp. 435-
     92.
JOYCE, THOMAS A.
  1914. *Mexican Archaeology*. London, Warner.
KLUCKHOHN, CLYDE, AND DOROTHEA LEIGHTON
  1946. *The Navaho*. Cambridge, Harvard University Press.
KRIS, ERNST
  1944. "Art and Regression," *Transactions of The New York
     Academy of Sciences*, Ser. 2, VI, No. 7, 236-50.
KUBIE, LAWRENCE, S., AND ROBERT H. KUBIE
  1948. "Destructive Personalities," *Human Organization*, VII,
     No. 4, 36-40.
LABARRE, WESTON
  1948. "Columbia University Research in Contemporary Cul-
     tures," *Scientific Monthly*, LXVII, No. 3, 239-40.
LAMB, ROBERT K.
  1950. "Entrepreneurship in the Community," *Explorations
     in Entrepreneurial History*, II, No. 3, 114-27.
LAWRENCE, D. H.
  1950. *Kangaroo*. London, Heinemann.
LEWIN, K.
  1943. "Forces behind Food Habits and Methods of Change."
     In "The Problem of Changing Food Habits," Report of
     the Committee on Food Habits, 1941-1943. *National
     Research Council Bulletin*, No. 108, pp. 35-65.
LINTON, RALPH
  1936. *The Study of Man*. New York, Appleton-Century.
LOWENFELD, MARGARET
  1939. "The World Pictures of Children," *British Journal of
     Medical Psychology*, XVIII, Pt. 1, 65-101.

1954. *The Lowenfeld Mosaic Test*. London, Newman Neame.

LOWREY, LAWSON G., AND VICTORIA SLOANE (EDS.)
1948. *Orthopsychiatry 1923-1948: Retrospect and Prospect*. New York, American Orthopsychiatric Association.

MCGRAW, MYRTLE B.
1935. *Growth*. New York, Appleton-Century.

MACGREGOR, GORDON
1946. *Warriors without Weapons*. University of Chicago Press.

MALINOWSKI, BRONISLAW
1922. *Argonauts of the Western Pacific*. New York, Dutton.
1927. *Sex and Repression in Savage Society*. New York, Harcourt Brace.

MATARAZZO, JOSEPH, D., GEORGE SASLOW, AND RUTH G. MATARAZZO
1956. "The Interaction Chronograph as an Instrument for Objective Measurement of Interaction Patterns during Interviews," *Journal of Psychology*, XLI, Second Half, 347-67.

MEAD, MARGARET
1928a. *Coming of Age in Samoa*. New York, Morrow. Reprinted 1949, Mentor Book MP 418, New York, New American Library.
1928b. "A Lapse of Animism among a Primitive People," *Psyche*, IX, No. 1, 72-77.
1928c. "The Role of the Individual in Samoan Culture," *Journal of the Royal Anthropological Institute*, LVIII, Pt. 2, 481-95.
1930a. "An Ethnologist's Footnote to *Totem and Taboo*," *Psychoanalytic Review*, XVII, No. 3, 297-304.
1930b. *Growing up in New Guinea*. New York, Morrow. Reprinted 1953, Mentor Book MD 255. New York, New American Library.
1930c. "Social Organization of Manua," *Bernice P. Bishop Museum Bulletin*, LXXVI, 1-218.
1931. "Two South Sea Educational Experiments and Their American Implications." In "Eighteenth Annual Schoolmen's Week Proceedings, March 8-21, 1931." *University of Pennsylvania School of Education Bulletin*, XXXI, No. 36 (June 20), 493-97.
1932. "An Investigation of the Thought of Primitive Children, with Special Reference to Animism," *Journal of the Royal Anthropological Institute*, LXII, Pt. 1, 173-90.
1934. "Kinship in the Admiralty Islands," *Anthropological Papers of The American Museum of Natural History*, XXXIV, Pt. 2, 181-358.

1935a. "Review: *The Riddle of the Sphinx* by Géza Róheim," *Character and Personality*, IV, No. 1, 85-90.

1935b. *Sex and Temperament in Three Primitive Societies*. New York, Morrow. Reprinted 1950, Mentor Book MP 370. New York, New American Library.

1938. "The Mountain Arapesh. I. An Importing Culture," *Anthropological Papers of The American Museum of Natural History*, XXXVI, Pt. 3, 139-349.

1939a. *From the South Seas*. New York, Morrow.

1939b. "Researches in Bali, 1936-1939. I. On the Concept of Plot in Culture," *Transactions of The New York Academy of Sciences*, Ser. 2, II, No. 1, 24-27.

1940a. "The Arts in Bali," *Yale Review*, new ser., XXX, No. 2, 335-347.

1940b. "Character Formation in Two South Sea Societies —Iatmul Tribe of New Guinea and the Balinese of Bali," *Transactions of the American Neurological Association*, 66th Annual Meeting, 99-103.

1940c. "The Mountain Arapesh. II. Supernaturalism," *Anthropological Papers of The American Museum of Natural History*, XXXVII, Pt. 3, 317-451.

1940d. "Social Change and Cultural Surrogates," *Journal of Educational Sociology*, XIV, No. 2, 92-109.

1941. "Administrative Contributions to Democratic Character Formation at the Adolescent Level," *Journal of the National Association of Deans of Women*, IV, No. 2, 51-57.

1942a. *And Keep Your Powder Dry*. New York, Morrow.

1942b. "Anthropological Data on the Problem of Instinct," *Psychosomatic Medicine*, IV, No. 4, 396-97.

1942c. "The Comparative Study of Culture and the Purposive Cultivation of Democratic Values." In *Science, Philosophy, and Religion, Second Symposium*, Lyman Bryson and Louis Finkelstein, eds. New York, Conference on Science, Philosophy, and Religion, pp. 56-69.

1942d. "Educative Effects of Social Environment as Disclosed by Studies of Primitive Societies." In *Environment and Education*. Human Development Series, I. Supplementary Educational Monographs No. 54. University of Chicago, pp. 48-61.

1942e. Preface: *The American Character*. Harmondsworth, England, Penguin Books.

1943a. "Anthropological Techniques in War Psychology," *Bulletin of the Menninger Clinic*, VII, No. 4, 137-140.

1943b. "Can You Tell One American from Another," *The Listener* (BBC, London), XXX, No. 777, 640.

1943c. "Dietary Patterns and Food Habits," *Journal of the American Dietetic Association*, XIX, No. 1, 1-5.

1943d. "The Problem of Changing Food Habits: With Suggestions for Psychoanalytic Contributions," *Bulletin of the Menninger Clinic*, VII, No. 2, 57-61.

1943e. "The Problem of Changing Food Habits." In "The Problem of Changing Food Habits," Report of the Committee on Food Habits, 1941-1943. *National Research Council Bulletin*, No. 108, pp. 20-31.

1943f. "Why We Americans Talk Big," *The Listener* (BBC, London), XXX, No. 772.

1944a. *The American Troops and the British Community.* London, Hutchinson. (Pamphlet.)

1944b. *A Bread and Butter Letter from a Lecturer.* Los Angeles, Occidental College. (Pamphlet.)

1944c. "Cultural Approach to Personality," *Transactions of The New York Academy of Sciences.* Ser. 2, VI, No. 3, 93-101.

1944d. "Ferment in British Education," *Journal of the American Association of University Women*, XXXVII, No. 3, 131-33.

1944e. "A GI View of Britain," *New York Times Magazine* (March 19), 18-19, 34.

1944f. "What is a Date?" *Transatlantic*, No. 10 (June), 54, 57-60.

1945a. "How Religion Has Fared in the Melting Pot." In *Religion in the Post-War World*, III: *Religion and Our Racial Tensions*, ed. Willard L. Sperry. Cambridge, Harvard University Press, pp. 61-81.

1945b. "Human Differences and World Order." In *World Order: Its Intellectual and Cultural Foundations*, ed. F. Ernest Johnson. New York, Harper, pp. 40-51.

1945c. "Research on Primitive Children." In *Manual of Child Psychology*, 2nd ed., ed. L. Carmichael. New York, Wiley, pp. 735-80.

1946. "Trends in Personal Life," *New Republic*, CXV, No. 12/1660 (September 23), 346-48.

1947a. "Age Patterning in Personality Development," *American Journal of Orthopsychiatry*, XVII, No. 2, 231-40.

1947b. "The Concept of Culture and the Psychosomatic Approach," *Psychiatry*, X, No. 1, 57-76.

1947c. "The Implications of Culture Change for Personality Development," *American Journal of Orthopsychiatry*, XVII, No. 4, 633-46.

1947d. "On the Implications for Anthropology of the Gesell-Ilg Approach to Maturation," *American Anthropologist*, XLIX, No. 1, 69-77.

1947e. "The Mountain Arapesh. III. Socio-Economic Life. IV. Diary of Events in Alitoa," *Anthropological Papers of The American Museum of Natural History*, XL, Pt. 3, 163-419.

1948. "Collective Guilt." In *International Congress on Mental Health London 1948*, III. Proceedings of the International Conference on Medical Psychotherapy. New York, Columbia University Press, pp. 57-66.

1949a. "Character Formation and Diachronic Theory." In *Social Structure*, ed. Meyer Fortes. Oxford, Clarendon Press, pp. 18-34.

1949b. *Male and Female*. New York, Morrow. Reprinted 1955, Mentor Book MP 369. New York, New American Library.

1949c. "The Mountain Arapesh. V. The Record of Unabelin with Rorschach Analyses," *Anthropological Papers of The American Museum of Natural History*, XLI, Pt. 3, 289-390.

1950. "The Comparative Study of Culture and the Purposive Cultivation of Democratic Values, 1941-1949." In *Perspectives on a Troubled Decade: Science, Philosophy, and Religion 1939-1949, Tenth Symposium*, Lyman Bryson, Louis Finkelstein, and R. A. MacIver, eds. New York, Harper, pp. 87-108.

1953. "Some Relationships between Social Anthropology and Psychiatry." In *Dynamic Psychiatry*, Franz Alexander and Helen Ross, eds. University of Chicago Press, pp. 401-48.

1954. "Cultural Discontinuities and Personality Transformation," *Journal of Social Issues*, Suppl. Ser., No. 8, 3-16.

MEAD, MARGARET (ED.)

1937. *Cooperation and Competition among Primitive Peoples*. New York, McGraw-Hill. Reprinted 1961, Beacon BP 123, Boston, Beacon.

MEAD, MARGARET, ELIOT D. CHAPPLE, AND G. GORDON BROWN (EDS.)

1949. "Report of the Committee on Ethics," *Human Organization*, VIII, No. 2, 20-21.

MOONEY, J.

1896. "The Ghost-dance Religion and the Sioux Outbreak of 1890," *United States Bureau of American Ethnology, 14th Annual Report 1892-1893*, Pt. 2, 641-1136.

MORRIS, CHARLES W.

1956. *Varieties of Human Values*. University of Chicago Press.

MOSELY, PHILIP
  1940. "The Peasant Family: The Zadruga." In *The Cultural Approach to History*, ed. Caroline F. Ware. New York, Columbia University Press, pp. 95-108.

NADEL, S. F.
  1937a. "Experiments on Culture Psychology," *Africa*, X, No. 4, 421-35.
  1937b. "A Field Experiment in Racial Psychology," *British Journal of Psychology* (general section), XXVIII, Pt. 2, 195-211.

PALTHE, G. VAN WULFFTEN
  1933. "Psychiatry and Neurology in the Tropics," *Malayan Medical Journal*, VIII, No. 3, 133-45.

PARSONS, TALCOTT
  1945. "The Problem of Controlled Institutional Change," *Journal of Psychiatry*, VIII, No. 1, 79-101.

PATERSON, A. B.
  1954. *The Collected Verse of A. B. Paterson*. Sydney and London, Angus and Robertson.

PETTITT, GEORGE A.
  1946. "Primitive Education in North America," *University of California Publications in American Archaeology and Ethnology*, XLIII, No. 1, 1-182.

PIAGET, J.
  1946. *Le développement de la notion de temps chez l'enfant*. Paris, Presses Universitaires de France.

PIJOAN, MICHEL
  1943. "Certain Factors Involved in the Struggle against Malnutrition and Disease." In *Inter-Americana*, Short Papers, V. Proceedings of the Conference on Latin America in Social and Economic Transition, April 14-15, 1943. Albuquerque, University of New Mexico Press, pp. 11-19.

PIJOAN, MICHEL, AND C. A. ELKIN
  1944. "Secondary Anemia Due to Prolonged and Exclusive Milk Feeding among Shoshone Indian Infants," *Journal of Nutrition*, XXVII, No. 1, 67-75.

RADCLIFFE-BROWN, A. R.
  1940. "On Social Structure," *Journal of the Royal Anthropological Institute*, LXX, Pt. 1, 1-12.

REPORT OF THE COMMITTEE ON FOOD HABITS, 1941-1943
  1943. "The Problem of Changing Food Habits," *National Research Council Bulletin*, No. 108, Washington, D.C. Reprinted 1962.

REPORT OF THE COMMITTEE ON FOOD HABITS
  1945. "Manual for the Study of Food Habits," *National Research Council Bulletin*, No. 111. Washington, D.C. Reprinted 1962.

RICHARDS, AUDREY I.
  1932. *Hunger and Work in a Savage Tribe*. London, Routledge.
RICHARDSON, H. B.
  1945. *Patients Have Families*. New York, Commonwealth Fund.
RICHARDSON, LEWIS F.
  1939. "Generalized Foreign Politics," *British Journal of Psychology*, Monograph Suppl., VII, No. 23, 1-91.
RICHTER, CURT P.
  1943. "The Self-selection of Diets." In *Essays in Biology in Honor of Herbert M. Evans*. Berkeley and Los Angeles, University of California Press, pp. 499-506.
RICHTER, CURT P., AND BRUNO B. BARELARE, JR.
  1938. "Nutritional Requirements of Pregnant and Lactating Rats Studied by the Self-selection Method," *Endocrinology*, XXIII, No. 1, 15-24.
RICKMAN, JOHN
  1948. "Guilt and the Dynamics of Psychological Disorder in the Individual." In *International Congress on Mental Health London 1948*, III. Proceedings of the International Conference on Medical Psychotherapy. New York, Columbia University Press, pp. 41-47.
RIESMAN, DAVID
  1950. *The Lonely Crowd*. New Haven, Yale University Press.
RÓHEIM, GÉZA
  1934. *The Riddle of the Sphinx*, trans. R. Money-Kyrle. London, Hogarth.
RUESCH, JURGEN, AND GREGORY BATESON
  1949. "Structure and Process in Social Relations," *Psychiatry*, XII, No. 2, 105-24.
SCHAFFNER, BERTRAM
  1948. *Father Land*. New York, Columbia University Press.
SCHUMPETER, J. A.
  1934. *The Theory of Economic Development*. Cambridge, Harvard University Press.
SEWELL, ELISABETH
  1952. *The Field of Nonsense*. London, Chatto and Windus.
TANNENBAUM, FRANK
  1946. "The Balance of Power in Society," *Political Science Quarterly*, LXI, No. 4, 481-504.
TANNER, JAMES M., AND BÄRBEL INHELDER (EDS.)
  1956-1960. *Discussions on Child Development*, 4 vols. New York, International Universities Press.
TAYLOR, EDMOND
  1947. *Richer by Asia*. Boston, Houghton Mifflin.

THOMAS, DOROTHY S., AND RICHARD S. NISHIMOTO
  1946. *The Spoilage*. Berkeley and Los Angeles, University of California Press.

THOMPSON, BLANCHE J.
  1932. "The Moon's the North Wind's Cooky." In *Silver Pennies*. New York, Macmillan, p. 18.

The Triumph of Will.
  1934-1936. Director: Leni Riefenstahl; Producer: NSDAP. A Record of the Congress of the NSDAP, Nuremberg, September 5-10, 1934. 11 reels, 16 and 35 mm., sound.

VON NEUMANN, JOHN, AND O. MORGENSTERN
  1944. *Theory of Games and Economic Behavior*. Princeton University Press.

WALTER, W. GREY
  1956. *The Curve of the Snowflake*. New York, Norton.

The War for Men's Minds.
  1943. Director: John Grierson; Producer: Stewart Legg. National Film Board of Canada. The World in Action Series. 16 mm., 21 min., sound.

WARE, CAROLINE F. (ED.)
  1940. *The Cultural Approach to History*. New York, Columbia University Press.

WARNER, W. LLOYD, and PAUL S. LUNT
  1941. *The Social Life of a Modern Community*. Yankee City Series, I. New Haven, Yale University Press.
  1942. *The Status System of a Modern Community*. Yankee City Series, II. New Haven, Yale University Press.

WARNER, W. LLOYD, AND LEO SROLE
  1945. *The Social Systems of American Ethnic Groups*. Yankee City Series, III. New Haven, Yale University Press.

WARNER, W. LLOYD, AND J. O. LOW
  1947. *The Social System of the Modern Factory*. Yankee City Series, IV. New Haven, Yale University Press.

WARNER, W. LLOYD
  1959. *The Living and the Dead*. Yankee City Series, V. New Haven, Yale University Press.

WEBER, MAX
  1930. *The Protestant Ethic and the Spirit of Capitalism*, trans. Talcott Parsons. London, Allen and Unwin.

WHEELER, B. K.
  1945. "Critics Air U.S.-British Views," *Washington Star*, January 14.

WHITING, JOHN W. M.
  1941. *Becoming a Kwoma: Teaching and Learning in a New Guinea Tribe*. New Haven, Yale University Press.

WILLIAMS, F. E.
   1928. *Orokaiva Magic*. Anthropology Report, Government of
   Papua, Nos. 6-8. New York, Oxford University Press.

WOODWARD, PATRICIA
   1943a. "Attitudes Towards the Use of Soybeans as Food."
   Committee on Food Habits, National Research Council.
   (October.) Mimeographed.
   1943b. "A Study of the Relative Effectiveness of Different
   Combinations of Appeals Used in Presenting New Foods
   —Soya." Committee on Food Habits, National Research
   Council. (October.) Mimeographed.

WORDSWORTH, WILLIAM
   1923. "Yarrow Revisited." In *The Poetical Works of
   William Wordsworth*. New York, Oxford University Press,
   p. 385.

WRIGHT, L. QUINCY (ED.)
   1948. *The World Community*. University of Chicago Press.

WYLIE, ELINOR
   1932. "Epitaph." In *Collected Poems of Elinor Wylie*. New
   York, Knopf, p. 51.

YEATS, WILLIAM B.
   1906. "The Happy Townland." In *The Poetical Works of
   William B. Yeats*, I. New York, Macmillan, p. 303.

YOUNG, PAUL T.
   1948. "Appetite, Palatability and Feeding Habit: A Critical
   Review," *Psychology Bulletin*, XLV, No. 4, 289-320.

ZBOROWSKI, MARK, AND ELIZABETH HERZOG
   1952. *Life Is With People*. New York, International Universities Press.